Risk and Crisis Managem in the Public Sector

Second edition

Every decision that is made by managers and policy-makers in a public sector organization requires an evaluation and a judgement of the risks involved. This vital requirement has been recognized in the growth of risk management. However, risks can never be fully prevented, which means that public managers also have to be crisis managers.

Today's crises develop in unseen ways; they escalate rapidly and transform through the interdependencies of modern society, and their frequency is growing: the global financial crisis, the European volcanic ash cloud, the Japanese tsunami and subsequent Fukushima nuclear plant meltdown, the Christchurch earthquake and the Queensland floods. All highlight the extreme challenges that public sector organizations across the world have had to face in recent years.

Risk and Crisis Management in the Public Sector Second Edition responds to these challenges by presenting the only guide for public managers and public management students which combines lessons about risk and crisis management together in a single, accessible text. It equips readers and public managers with the knowledge and skills to understand key issues and debates, as well as the capacity to treat risks and better prepare for, respond to and recover from crisis episodes.

This exciting new edition enhances the original text with contemporary cases and a greater focus on the international, transboundary and multi-agency dimensions of risk and crisis management. These enhancements reflect the fact that today's public manager must increasingly operate within a global and interdependent governance context.

Dr Lynn T. Drennan is Education Programme Director at the Institute of Risk Management, UK

Professor Allan McConnell is Professor in Public Policy at the University of Sydney, Australia

Dr Alastair Stark is Lecturer in Public Policy at the University of Queensland, Australia

'The revision of this helpful textbook confirms the validity of the ideas underpinning the first edition: to provide an integrated and sophisticated, yet succinct and highly teachable overview of the theory and practice of contemporary risk management and crisis management. These fields address different sides of the safety, security and business continuity coin. This book does a great job of allowing readers to see the connections between the challenges of identifying risks and preventing them from materializing on the one hand, and dealing with the consequences of risks that materialize and escalate in the form of major disruptions and emergencies on the other. It will be of great value to students, scholars and practitioners alike in both in the corporate and public sectors.'

Paul 't Hart, Utrecht University School of Governance,
the Netherlands

'"Nothing sells risk management like a crisis." Unfortunately, interest after a crisis demonstrates bad timing. Further, passions (and political will) for future preparedness subside over time, and an all too common cycle emerges-Crisis/A Vow to Change/Weakening of the Vow/Next Crisis! This book provides expert guidance both on breaking that cycle and on constructing and implementing effective crisis response strategies and methods. It should be required reading for public leaders and managers.'

Peter C. Young, PhD, 3M Endowed Chair in International
Business, University of St. Thomas-Opus College
of Business Minneapolis, Minnesota, USA

ROUTLEDGE MASTERS IN PUBLIC MANAGEMENT

Edited by Stephen P Osborne

Routledge Masters in Public Management series is an integrated set of texts. It is intended to form the backbone for the holistic study of the theory and practice of public management – as part of

- a taught Masters, MBA or MPA course at an university or college,
- a work based, in-service, programme of education and training, or
- a programme of self guided study.

Each volume stands alone in its treatment of its topic, whether it be strategic management, marketing or procurement and is co-authored by leading specialists in their field. However, all volumes in the series share both a common pedagogy and a common approach to the structure of the text. Key features of all volumes in the series include:

- a critical approach to combining theory with practice which educates its reader, rather than solely teaching him/her a set of skills,
- clear learning objectives for each chapter,
- the use of figures, tables and boxes to highlight key ideas, concepts and skill,
- an annotated bibliography, guiding students in their further reading, and
- a dedicated case study in the topic of each volume, to serve as a focus for discussion and learning.

Managing Change and Innovation in Public Service Organizations
Stephen P. Osborne and Kerry Brown

Risk and Crisis Management in the Public Sector Second Edition
Lynn T Drennan, Allan McConnell and Alistair Stak

Contracting for Public Services
Carsten Greve

Performance Management in the Public Sector Second Edition
Wouter van Dooren, Geert Bouckaert and John Halligan

Financial Management and Accounting in the Public Sector Second Edition
Gary Bandy

Strategic Leadership in the Public Sector
Paul Joyce

Risk and Crisis Management in the Public Sector

Second edition

Lynn T. Drennan,
Allan McConnell
and Alastair Stark

Routledge
Taylor & Francis Group

LONDON AND NEW YORK

First published 2007
Second Edition published 2015

by Routledge
2 Park Square, Milton Park, Abingdon, Oxon OX14 4RN

And by Routledge
711 Third Avenue, New York, NY 10017

Routledge is an imprint of the Taylor & Francis Group, an informa business

British Library Cataloguing in Publication Data
A catalogue record for this book is available from the British Library

Library of Congress Cataloging in Publication Data
Risk and crisis management in the public sector / Lynn T Drennan,
Allan McConnell, Alastair Stark.—2nd Edition.
     pages cm.—(Routledge masters in public management)
   Includes bibliographical references and index.
   1. Risk management.   2. Crisis management.   3. Policy sciences.
   I. McConnell, Allan, 1957–   II. Stark, Alastair.   III. Title.
   HD61.D74 2015
   352.3'79—dc23   2014023148

ISBN: 978-0-415-73968-9 (hbk)
ISBN: 978-0-415-73969-6 (pbk)
ISBN: 978-1-315-81645-6 (ebk)

Typeset in Perpetua and Bell Gothic
by Keystroke, Station Road, Codsall, Wolverhampton

Printed and bound in Great Britain by
TJ International Ltd, Padstow, Cornwall

Lynn T. Drennan
For all the people that manage risk and, occasionally, crises in public service organizations who continue to inspire me

Allan McConnell
For my mother-in-law, the remarkable and resilient Minnie Stevenson

Alastair Stark
To the bumble bee that brightens up our world (and needs our love and our protection)

Contents

X

Figures, tables and boxes

FIGURES

TABLES

FIGURES, TABLES AND BOXES

BOXES

Acknowledgements

ACKNOWLEDGEMENTS FOR THE FIRST EDITION

The authors are grateful for the support of academic and professional colleagues who reviewed chapters of the book as it developed and offered valuable feedback and suggestions for improvement. In particular, Lynn Drennan would like to thank Martin Fone (UK), Kevin Knight (Australia), Professor Brian Toft (UK) and Professor Peter Young (University of St Thomas, USA). Glasgow Caledonian University generously provided the time and resources to allow her to write and colleagues, Jennifer Adams and Dr Bill Stein, gave much-valued friendship and moral support throughout. The risk management case study was provided by the Australian Quarantine and Inspection Service, winners of the 'Innovative Initiative' category of the 2005 Comcover Awards for Excellence in Risk Management 2005. This was adapted by the authors and reproduced with the permission of Peter Yuille, AQIS Executive Director. Involvement with ALARM, over many years, stimulated Lynn's interest in the field of public sector risk management and she is grateful to members of the Board for their confidence in her and for their endorsement of this book.

Allan McConnell is indebted to Arjen Boin (Leiden University) and Paul 't Hart (Australian National University and Utrecht University) for their friendship, encouragement and support – reading drafts of all the 'crisis' sections and making innumerable suggestions which have benefited the book enormously. He is also grateful to them for allowing use of an unused draft which Allan had originally written for a separate edited book with them (*Crisis and After: Case Studies in the Politics of Investigation, Accountability and Learning*) as the basis for Chapter 7 of the present text. Other researchers helped with background research, EndNote databases, copy-editing and organizing the manuscript into submission format. We are grateful in these regards to Kathy Kang, Marika Donkin and Anika Gauja. A case study was also generously written for us by Ed van Thijn, Mayor of Amsterdam at the time of the 1992 Bijlmer plane crash. Colleagues at the Discipline of Government and International Relations at the University of Sydney provided a very stimulating and encouraging environment in which to work – far away from Allan's home country of Scotland! Last but certainly not least is Iris Kirkpatrick, who has provided love, support, patience, inspiration and unwavering encouragement along the way.

ADDITIONAL ACKNOWLEDEGMENTS FOR
THE SECOND EDITION

Lynn T. Drennan is further indebted to former colleagues on the Board of ALARM, the public risk management association, particularly Peter Andrews and Paul Dudley, who helped push the boundaries forward and shared their work on a national framework for, and core competencies in, risk management with the wider public risk management community. Also to colleagues at the Institute of Risk Management, whose efforts to provide thoughtful leadership has resulted in a substantial contribution to the debates on key issues such as risk culture and risk appetite, which affect both the private and public sectors.

Allan McConnell is grateful to colleagues at the University of Sydney in the Department of Government and International Relations, School of Social and Political Sciences and Faculty of Arts and Social Sciences for a diverse, stimulating and supporting working environment. He is also thankful that his family, and in particular his wife Iris Kirkpatrick, keeps him grounded.

Alastair Stark is grateful for the friendship and collegiality of colleagues at Glasgow Caledonian University and the University of Queensland. In particular, Dr Stewart Davidson who remains his biggest critic and most valued friend in the academy.

Both Lynn and Allan would also like express their thanks to Alastair who took on the not inconsiderable task of becoming a third author in the wake of a very successful first edition of the book. He probably got more than he bargained for, but the fully revised and updated version has benefited considerably from his input.

We all wish to thank Nicola Cupit at Routledge for her professionalism and support.

Glasgow, Sydney, Brisbane
June 2014

Abbreviations

AIRMIC	Association of Insurance and Risk Managers
ALARM	National Forum for Risk Management in the Public Sector
ALARP	as low as reasonably practicable
ANZFA	Australia and New Zealand Food Agency
AS/NZS	Standards Australia/ Standards New Zealand
ASX	Australian Stock Exchange
BCI	Business Continuity Institute
BCM	business continuity management
BCP	business continuity planning
BSE	bovine spongiform encephalopathy (mad cow disease)
CAP	Common Agricultural Policy (EU)
CCS	Civil Contingencies Secretariat
CDEM	Civil Defence and Emergency Management
CEO	chief executive officer
CRIP	commonly recognized information picture
DfID	Department for International Development (UK)
DG ECHO	Directorate General Humanitarian Office
DM	discretionary mutual
DRR	disaster risk reduction
EDC	endocrine disrupting chemicals
EDF	Électricité de France
EEA	European Environment Agency
ERM	enterprise risk management
EU	European Union
FEMA	Federal Emergency Management Agency (US)
FERMA	Federation of European Risk Management Associations
FMD	foot and mouth disease
FSA	Financial Services Authority (UK)
GM	genetically modified
HIA	health impact assessment
HIP	home insulation programme

HR	human resources
HRO	high reliability organization
HSE	Health and Safety Executive (UK)
IDETF	Interdepartmental Emergency Taskforce (Australia)
IEM	integrated emergency management
IRGC	International Risk Governance Council
IRM	Institute of Risk Management
ISO	International Organization for Standardization
IT	information technology
LRC	Lampuuk Recovery Center
MAFF	Ministry of Agriculture, Fisheries and Food (UK)
MAOT	maximum acceptable outage time
NAO	National Audit Office (UK)
NCC	National Consumer Council (UK)
NGO	non-governmental organization
OECD	Organization for Economic Cooperation and Development
OGC	Office of Government Commerce (UK)
ORM	organization risk management
PPP	private–public partnerships
PSO	public service organization
RFF	Rapid Reflection Force
SARS	Severe Acute Respiratory Syndrome
SITREP	situation report
TAI	Tasmanians Against Incineration
TQM	total quality management
UMAL	Universities Mutual Association Limited
UN	United Nations
UNISDR	United Nations International Strategy for Disaster Reduction
USAID	United States Agency for International Development
WHO	World Health Organization
WTO	World Trade Organization

Preface

Many things have changed since the original publication of this book, particularly in terms of the nature of globalization and its impact on risk and crisis management. The first edition of *Risk and Crisis Management in the Public Sector* was written under the long shadows cast by 9/11 and Katrina – two domestic crises that made our respective communities ask whether or not our knowledge was up to the task of creating effective policies *within* our own borders. As we write this preface, the world is still reflecting on the fallout from two more significant crises. The first is Fukushima, a truly remarkable 'transboundary' crisis in which a natural catastrophe transformed into a technological nightmare. And the second is the global financial crisis, surely the clearest embodiment of the way in which unpredictable risks can be channelled around the pathways of a global community. This reflection has led crisis management scholars to ask a series of questions: is our current knowledge up to the task of creating effective policies *across* our borders (whether organizational, sectoral or national)? Are we properly evaluating and learning from crises? And what role might communities play in terms of crisis management? The emerging answers to such questions are redrawing the map of crisis management knowledge. As a consequence of these upheavals, we have significantly rewritten most of the crisis-related chapters and sections of this second edition.

The previous book was also written at a point in time when risk management was only just beginning to be seen as an interconnected, global public management concern. In their time, early attempts to create international risk management standards and codes gave us an insight into an exciting new future of global risk management practice, which is now very much the industry norm. However, although the world of risk management continues to expand and interconnect globally, in the risk field the core concepts and fundamental knowledge have for the most part remained stable and in need only of refinement. As a consequence, we have updated and fine-tuned the arguments, examples and readings in the chapters that define risk and its drivers (Chapters 1 and 2), as well as those dealing with assessing and responding to risk (Chapters 3 and 4).

While a great deal has changed in the world, the core challenge for risk and crisis managers remains much the same today as it did seven years ago. Operating in a climate of high uncertainty, with limited resources, public managers must put in place policies that moderate the risks of today, anticipate the risks of tomorrow and somehow respond to the inconceivable risks that breed crises.

As the essence of the challenge remains the same, the second edition's essence remains the same too. This is still a book that explores both the theory and practice of risk and crisis management from an organizational and a public policy/management perspective. It also remains, as before, a guide that is aimed at students of public management, public administration, risk and crisis management as well as professional practitioners in these fields. Fundamentally, this is a book about how to understand the complexities and contradictions of risk and crisis, ranging from disputes about their meaning and causes through to how we can manage them. In the course of doing so we also, on occasion, offer up guidance and aspects of good practice. However, we are perfectly aware that no academic book can teach a skill or an art – these can only materialize when theory meets practice 'out there' in the real world.

Chapter 1 establishes the fundamentals of risk and crisis management, defining the many ways in which risk and crises can be viewed in theoretical and pragmatic terms. This discussion also introduces a number of fundamental concepts and tools that are germane to managerial practices in each field, including the crisis management cycle and ISO31000, which is now *the* global standard for public sector risk management. An important aspect of this chapter (completely rewritten from the first edition) is an understanding of different schools of thought about what constitutes a 'crisis'. We not only offer our own definition, rooted in the social science tradition of critical realism, but we also use it to help make sense of an ever expanding and often confusing array of crisis types.

Chapter 2 provides the public manager with an overview of the environmental drivers demanding that greater attention be paid to risk and crises within public sector agencies. These drivers are provided alongside a range of justifications that public managers can use to incentivize the adoption of a systematic approach to crisis and risk management in their organization. Readers are also provided with a short synopsis of the main causes of crises and some of the key issues that crisis analysts consider in terms of causation. Chapter 3 analyses the techniques of risk assessment in broad terms and the vital role of risk communication, and Chapter 4 explores responses to risk, including the options of tolerating, terminating, transferring or treating specific threats. Business continuity planning is also discussed here as a means of ensuring that the public service organization can continue to deliver on its strategic objectives should a crisis occur.

Chapter 5 concentrates on crisis preparedness, making the case that we need to see preparations for adversity as much more than the creation of a contingency plan (however sophisticated). It goes on to document many of the issues that can lead to a lack of preparedness and to explore the now fashionable concept of resilience as one way of synthesizing and extending preparedness across different actors. Chapter 6 deals with the acute phase of crisis management, focusing on a number of key challenges that arise from the need to have networks of actors in a crisis response that are coordinated but capable of adapting to contingencies. The chapter also emphasizes how crisis management in high uncertainty is as much about symbolic actions and politics as it is about technical operations. Chapter 7 explores the aftermath and recovery period post-crisis. The challenges of evaluating crisis management policy are presented here, and the concepts of accountability and policy learning are introduced alongside an argument that these dynamics can often undermine each other in the politicized reality of a post-crisis period. The chapter also reflects upon the ways in which institutional legacies, the 'framing' strategies of actors and the idiosyncratic context of a crisis can affect the reforms put in place in its wake. Chapter 8 places risk and crisis management in today's global context. This chapter indulges in the rather risky enterprise of predicting future global threats, which are separated into three categories: growing risks, interval risks and speculative risks. Thereafter a discussion of three types of global crisis management ensues, in which the key issues that are pertinent to international humanitarian aid efforts, remote modes of crisis management and 'transboundary' forms of crisis resolution are all analysed. Finally, the Conclusion once again makes the argument that more synergy is required between the study of risk management and the study of crisis management. It is suggested that greater coherence between them will pay dividends in terms of enhancing our understanding of global collective action issues and the many ways in which politics and perceptions can hamper effective public management.

We ended the Preface of the previous edition by sharing our hope that we might help raise the profile of risk and crisis management as public sector activities. We would love to claim that the exponential growth in both these activities over recent years is due to our book but we are not that naïve. The simple fact is that political leaders and public managers have increasingly had to recognize that there is an increasing awareness of the risks and crises that characterize our societies, and that doing nothing about them is no longer an option in light of a body of crisis and risk management knowledge which illuminates the issues and prescribes action. If we have a hope for this edition, however, it would be that it begins to illuminate the new issues that public managers face in a global, interconnected world of uncertainty where nothing stands still for too long. The challenge for us all, whether interested in risk or crisis management, is to learn to adapt in this new world.

Chapter 1

Risk and crisis

Definitions, debates and consequences

LEARNING OBJECTIVES

By the end of this chapter you should:

- have a clear understanding of different types of risk in the context of public management;
- be aware of the historical development and key elements of the risk management process;
- understand the importance (and the issues surrounding) international risk management standards;
- have a clear grasp of how crises can be defined objectively and subjectively;
- have developed an appreciation of the various types of crisis that can affect public managers and policy-makers; and
- be aware of the importance of the crisis management cycle to the study of crisis.

KEY POINTS OF THIS CHAPTER

- It is crucial that risk managers create cultures of risk ownership that delegate authority across the organization.
- In the public sector, risk managers need to pay more attention to social and political risks and a variety of stakeholders.
- Risk management standards can provide an international guide to best practice but can also stifle organizational innovation.

- Crises can be defined in a number of ways but the most effective definition combines objective and subjective elements.
- The vast array of crisis definitions and types can best be understood when we consider them as a product of the language used to make sense of and influence crisis phenomena.
- A starting point for the analysis of crisis is to conceive of different phases, i.e. prevention, preparation, response and recovery/learning.

KEY TERMS

- **Risk** – the chance of something happening that will have an impact on objectives; often specified as an event or set of circumstances and the consequences (both positive and negative) that will flow from this.
- **Risk management** – the processes involved in managing risk in order to achieve objectives, by maximizing potential opportunities and minimizing potential adverse effects.
- **Risk management process** – the systematic application of management policies, procedures and practices to the tasks of communicating, establishing the context, identifying, analysing, evaluating, treating, monitoring and reviewing risk.
- **Crisis** – a set of circumstances in which individuals, institutions or societies face threats beyond the norms of routine day-to-day functioning, but the significance and impact of these circumstances will vary according to individual perceptions.

RISK AS PROBABILITY, THREAT AND OPPORTUNITY

Risks are all around us – in the air we breathe, the food we eat and the knowledge we rely upon to build our societies. Small wonder then that the word 'risk' is part of our everyday language, but what do we mean when we use the term? One meaning relates to forecasting. In this sense we are gauging the possibilities and chances of events occurring in probabilistic terms. If we define risks in this way, then it is easy to see that we are all risk managers (Wilkinson 2010).

As the speedometer on our car gets close to the legal limit we might instinctively reflect on the risk of being caught speeding by the police. When buying or selling our homes we attempt to forecast the risks and opportunities presented by variable housing markets and interest rates. When we leave the house in the morning we clothe ourselves and pack our bags in anticipation of the risks presented by our daily commutes and working lives. In these examples, the focus is on the likelihood of an event happening or not happening; of success or failure; of percentages and expectations; or, in mathematical terms, of probability. Risk also has a negative connotation. The risk management industry, for example, often refers to 'downside risk' as a means of defining threats. There is always a chance in life that we will suffer from 'the slings and arrows of outrageous fortune' regardless of our personal choices, and, unfortunately, the list of potential threats is endless. When threats do strike us, the risk is usually imposed on us involuntarily, and we may feel that it is something that is outside our control (Slovic 1987). At the same time, there are certain risks that we accept voluntarily – smoking, eating and drinking excessively, letting our insurance cover lapse, playing risky sports, or investing in property. 'Risk', in this context, tends to concentrate on the negative aspects of such actions, and in common parlance is used alongside terms such as 'threat', 'danger' and 'hazard' (Lupton 2013).

One might ask, given the many threats that we are aware of today, why anyone takes risks at all (or even gets out of bed in the morning)? Well, we voluntarily take risks, both mundane and more serious, because the gamble is often associated with the potential to create benefits, and often the bigger the gamble, the bigger the benefit. This means that in situations where our forecasts of the probability of downside risk are low but the benefits of taking the risk are tangible, we will always be incentivized to act. And as prospect theory indicates, we may even take risky decisions because there is little left to lose (Vis 2011). Hence our perception of the likelihood of a particular outcome will influence our decisions and behaviour in specific circumstances and this may, or may not, bring the result we are expecting. In other words, if we exceed the speed limit, we may reach our destination faster, and if we have good information about betting on a sporting event, the bookmaker's long odds could be exploited for serious gain. What this suggests is that there is an upside accompanying risk taking. Implicit in the idea of risk taking, as a means of deriving benefit, is that of grasping opportunity. In our everyday lives, therefore, we use the word 'risk' in three separate contexts – risk as likelihood, risk as threat and risk as opportunity. This threefold understanding of risk also exists within our organizations. We try and forecast risks so that we can exploit any opportunities that may exist and, more commonly, prevent and prepare for those downside effects.

Without an understanding of risk across these three dimensions, social and technological progress would be stymied either because of too much precaution, which would reduce innovation, or too much ignorance, which would expose us to debilitating threats. Striking a balance between these two outcomes requires policy decisions to be made as to what *is* and what *is not* considered to be 'tolerable' risk.

Before we go on to discuss some of the more crucial components of a risk management strategy, it is useful to have a common understanding of what we mean by 'risk'. To this end, we will utilize a definition that has been agreed by the International Organization for Standardization (ISO) for use in risk management standards documentation around the world. The ISO defines 'risk' simply as 'the combination of the probability of an event and its consequences' (ISO/IEC 2002). This definition takes into account both the chance element (probability or likelihood) and the potential upsides or downsides of the event (consequences or magnitude), in terms of how risk impacts on the organization's ability to achieve its objectives.

3

A final caveat is warranted here in relation to probability. One of the defining characteristics of the era that we live in is uncertainty (Beck 1992, 2009). As a consequence, risks can be ambiguous, difficult to define and may result in a range of outcomes. Uncertainty therefore exists where there is no certainty of knowledge – either because that knowledge does not exist (something has not happened before) or because we are unable to reconcile the new state of affairs with our existing data. In short, uncertainty undermines our capacity to produce reliable forecasts about the probability of many risks. We can see this issue across almost every long-term risk forecast. How might we quantify the costs and benefits of increased mobile phone and social media use? How will geopolitics affect energy supply in Europe? Will climate change bring droughts or floods? What will be the long-term impact of the global financial crisis on domestic public sectors? These are important questions for the risk manager but the answers are clouded by uncertainty, as well as our perceptions of risk and the priority we give to multiple and often interconnected risks. This is simply because our world is complicated, dynamic and difficult to reduce into predictive mathematical formulas. Risk management is far from an exact science (Hubbard 2009). Our aim in this opening chapter is to reduce a little bit of that uncertainty by defining risks and crises and outlining some of the basic characteristics of risk and crisis management.

STRATEGIC AND OPERATIONAL RISKS

The one certainty that we do have as risk managers in complex societies is that risks are ever changing. The frequency of our exposure to risk seems to be growing, the nature of the risks themselves seem to be changing to reflect modern lifestyles, and the ways in which we expose ourselves to risk as a consequence are also changing. However, what has not changed is the importance of understanding risks through a basic dichotomy, which separates those that present themselves for consideration at the strategic level from those more relevant to the day-to-day operations of an organization.

This is not to deny, of course, that there are many different categories of risk 'beyond' this simple division (see Box 1.1). Moreover, descriptions of risk are not mutually exclusive, nor are they exhaustive. Risks often have multiple dimensions and produce multiple impacts. For example, a fire in a local home for the elderly presents a *physical* risk that may result in *legal* cases – both civil and criminal – being brought against the authority, with *financial* consequences (insured and uninsured losses), and will impact on the *professional* services responsible for the well-being of the residents. The initial task of the public manager, however, is to simplify the complex world of risks that we alluded to above and a first step towards this is to broadly allocate responsibility for different types of risk.

4

BOX 1.1 ALTERNATIVE DESCRIPTIONS OF RISK

Pure – risks that either do not happen, or, if they do, have a negative impact. This term is primarily used in the context of the insurance industry, where the pure risks of fire, explosion, theft, product contamination or employee injury, etc. are the focus of insurance coverage.

Speculative – risks that may have a positive, neutral or detrimental impact. Speculative risks involve some form of gamble, e.g. investment in stocks and shares or the launch of a new product or service, whereby the outcome is uncertain and could result in either success or failure, or somewhere inbetween.

Physical – risks that have a physical dimension, such as property, equipment, people and data, where harm might occur. Such risks are largely insurable.

Intangible – risks to reputation, image, professional or market standing, which might result in tangible financial impacts on the organization.

Insurable – primarily pure, physical risks, where statistical records exist of past experience in that particular area.

Uninsurable – primarily the intangible risks, although some cover can be arranged for legal and other support for directors and officers, who find themselves the target of law suits brought by disgruntled stakeholders.

External – similar to 'environmental', these risks derive from the wider business, social or natural environments and are largely out of the control of the enterprise.

Internal – deriving from the strategic decisions or operational activities of the organization, over which individuals within the organization do have control.

Strategic risk

Strategic risks tend to be long term and fundamental in nature. These can come in three broad categories. First are those that are embedded in 'typical' strategic decisions. All strategic leaders must, of course, consider how their organization can achieve its objectives effectively and efficiently, reflect upon large-scale change initiatives and ensure that public statements will enhance their reputation. Risks can therefore emerge internally from such strategic endeavours if they are handled poorly (Drennan 2004). Second, there are recognized risks that occur at non-strategic levels of the organization.

5

This does not mean that strategic leaders have a personal responsibility for managing every organizational risk, but it does mean that they are ultimately responsible for ensuring that the correct policies, procedures and delegations are put in place and that the risks are managed appropriately across the organization. Third, there are risks that come directly from the external organizational environment. The following are examples of the types of strategic risk that might face a public service organization (PSO) and are based on a paper published by the UK Audit Commission (2001):

- *Political* – those associated with a failure to deliver either local or central government policy, or to meet the local administration's manifesto commitments, in areas such as housing, education or crime reduction.
- *Economic* – those affecting the ability of the PSO to meet financial commitments. These include internal budgetary pressures or the consequences of proposed investment decisions, including whether or not to enter into private–public partnership agreements for major construction projects.
- *Social* – those relating to the effects of changes in demographic, residential or socio-economic trends on the PSO's ability to deliver its objectives. Examples include the demands arising from caring for an increasingly ageing population or from supporting an influx of refugees or immigrant workers.
- *Technological* – those associated with the capacity of the PSO to deal with the pace/scale of technological change, or the ability to use technology to address changing demands. Increasing demands for online services and the moves towards e-government are examples here. Technological risks may also include the consequences of internal IT failures on the organization's ability to deliver its objectives.
- *Legislative* – associated with current or potential changes in national or, in the case of the United Kingdom and other countries, European law. Examples might include human rights, data protection or freedom of information legislation.
- *Environmental* – those relating to the environmental consequences of progressing the PSO's strategic objectives, for example in terms of energy efficiency, pollution, recycling, landfill requirements, emissions, etc. This will also include the impact of external environmental changes, such as those believed to be occurring as a result of global warming.
- *Competitive* – those affecting the competitiveness of the service (in terms of cost or quality) and/or its ability to deliver best value. Decisions as to whether to retain key services in-house or to outsource them to a private company bring with them both risks and benefits for the organization.
- *Customer/Citizen* – those associated with the failure to meet the current and changing needs and expectations of customers and citizens.

Operational risk

The single biggest lesson for any would-be risk manager is that the responsibility for managing risk lies with every individual employee, on a daily basis. When we discuss the operational level what we mean are those essential members of an organization that bring strategic vision to life through the implementation of policy. In public sector organizations, these are the people who face the public – our social workers, police officers and doctors, for example. Hence at the operational level, risk is present in the day-to-day functions and services of the public body. Such risks might derive from the people, property or processes involved in delivering the quality of service expected from the organization. Regardless, it is vital that the risk manager promotes the fact that risks belong to everyone and that they can never be considered the sole responsibility of one individual. In the workplace, it can be said that we are all, to a greater or lesser degree, 'risk managers'. However, when promoting the idea that risks are everyone's responsibility we need to be careful because we need to ensure that there is accountability for risk management. This means that every organization needs a risk management framework in which authority is delegated to individuals in respect of a risk. It is also crucial that this delegation is accompanied by a degree of autonomy to take decisions. In the public sector, difficulties can arise when individuals who are 'accountable' for making decisions about risk are, in fact, required to refer such decisions one or two levels above their position in the organizational hierarchy. In other words, if we wish operational staff to 'own' risks, they should be empowered to take appropriate action. Operational risks take many forms:

- *Professional* – those associated with the particular nature of each profession. These might include social work service concerns over children at risk, housing service concerns as to the welfare of tenants or education service concerns over the attainment of students.
- *Financial* – those associated with financial planning and control, income generation through local taxation or government grant, and the adequacy of insurance or other financial cover when a loss occurs.
- *Legal* – those related to possible breaches of legislation, issues of compliance with various national laws such as those on human rights, discrimination on the grounds of gender, race or disability.
- *Physical* – those related to fire, security, accident prevention and health and safety, including hazards/risks associated with employees, visitors, buildings, vehicles, plant and equipment.
- *Contractual* – those associated with the contracting out of key services and the potential failure of contractors to deliver to the agreed cost and specification. Examples can be found in school meals, transport and even in aspects of risk management such as claims handling.

7

- *Technological* – those relating to a reliance on IT systems or equipment and other machinery. This is an increasing problem as countries move towards e-government and increasing levels of public services are delivered online.
- *Environmental* – those relating to pollution, recycling and waste disposal, noise or the energy efficiency of ongoing service operations.

Both strategic and operational risks constitute the dynamic environment in which public service organizations operate today. In Chapters 3 and 4 of this book we will focus on the steps required if this risky environment is to be managed effectively.

PUBLIC SECTOR RISK

The borders that separate the public, the private and the not-for-profit sectors are increasingly blurred. The delivery of what were traditionally seen as public services today requires agencies from all three sectors. A perfect example of this are social services, which rely heavily upon governmental funding and strategic direction, as well as (and increasingly so) the private sector and voluntary bodies for service delivery. When looking at such a system as a whole it is sometimes difficult to say where one 'sector' ends and another begins. On one level, therefore, we can say that the principles of risk management are largely universal because different organizations from different sectors tend to exist together within the same policy system. We can also look across agencies from different sectors and see largely similar organizational forms, similar tasks being performed and, at a fundamental level, similar risks to people, property and processes.

However, some profound differences need to be stressed in terms of risk management in relation to the public–private distinction. The key differences rest in:

- the fundamental objective of each type of body (one is profit seeking and the other service providing);
- the networks of stakeholders that each organization needs to engage with and is accountable to; and
- the importance of the social and political environment to each.

Quite simply, the private company has a fiduciary obligation to provide profit and dividends to a relatively small number of shareholders. The public agency, however, exists to provide a service to a target group or the community in general. This is hardly startling news to anyone, but the importance of this distinction plays out in different risks. Many public sector agencies never have to worry about bankruptcy and liquidation. Private companies generally do not need to worry too much about the reform agendas of a new government. Changes in government, however, reflect public attitudes about public service funding and these can pose real threats to many public agencies. Many private companies will never need to open their finances or operational processes to public or political scrutiny, but the public sector agency is always subjected to accountability for its operations and funding. Many people are also unaware of the existence and roles performed by private companies unless they need directly to purchase a service. As a consequence, they are not subject to the kind of public debate that surrounds public service provision. Everyone has an opinion on education, health and refuse collection, for example, because these public services affect so much of our lives and we are all shareholders by virtue of the taxes we pay. Hence, while the private company might look towards technological or competitive environments to define its big risks, public agencies need to look more towards social and political environments.

A second key difference relates to the risk management process. In this regard we can see that there is less risk-taking activity in the public sector because of the lack of a profit incentive. When we also factor in decreasing levels of public tolerance of risk, allied to an increasing 'claims culture', we find explanations for why many PSOs adopt a risk-averse approach to managing risk. Many examples can be found in local government, where children's play areas have been dismantled, because of the (albeit slight) risk of injury, trees have been cut down in case they fall onto highways and schools have been turned into virtual fortresses with controlled entrances and CCTV systems in place to deter vandals, thieves and others who might seek to do harm (see Box 1.2). The challenge, particularly for public risk management, is to understand the interdependencies of risk at play and to be clear that a particular risk management strategy not only deals with the risk at hand in the way that it is intended to but also enhances the overall objectives and strategic goals of the organizations.

BOX 1.2 'CONKERING' RISK

Playing conkers is a traditional children's game. A hole is bored through the middle of a horse chestnut, and a piece of string threaded through the hole and tied in a knot at the bottom. The conker is then aimed at an opponent's conker, with the victor being the one whose nut lasts the longest without shattering into pieces. However, in 2004, the news media reported a series of stories involving this seemingly innocent pastime.

In one school, the children were only allowed to play if they wore safety goggles, brought in by the headmaster to protect the children's eyes from pieces of flying chestnut.

Another imposed a complete ban on the game because one child in the school had a severe nut allergy and they did not want to take the risk that a child would touch a conker and then their face, triggering a potentially fatal reaction.

Six trees in one local authority had their branches cut off after the council said that children could hurt themselves scrambling up the trees to collect conkers.

9

The council was also concerned for passing vehicles that might be struck by sticks thrown up to dislodge the nuts.

Reactions to such incidents suggested that a balanced approach to risk was not being taken and, in the words of one politician, it was 'the nanny state gone mad'. What these stories demonstrate are an increasingly risk-averse approach being taken by public service organizations to issues that, in themselves, appear to present a very low risk of accident or injury, but which have the potential for a legal suit to be brought against the organization, should such an incident occur.

THE DEVELOPMENT OF RISK MANAGEMENT

If we think about ancient man hunting and storing food for the winter, or the early explorers sailing the oceans, we can see that risk has been managed since the beginning of time (Bernstein 1996; Lupton 2013). The expression 'risk management' was not, however, used until 1957 (Prof. Wayne Snyder at the North American Insurance Buyers Conference in Chicago) and gained prominence in the 1960s, firstly in Canada (Doug Barlow of Massey Harris was the world's first 'risk manager') and then throughout the Commonwealth, where agricultural equipment manufacturer Massey Ferguson had a number of facilities, and the United States. Historically, industrial risks had been managed through measures such as protection against fire or flood, the training of employees in safe working practices, the installation of security equipment and the purchase of insurance. However, enlightened managers began to realize that, despite their best efforts, things would still 'go wrong' and that having an insurance policy in place that would pay out some financial compensation for a loss was only part of the solution. Indeed, many firms found to their cost that a major event such as a factory fire could put them permanently out of business, regardless of whether they had full insurance coverage for replacement of the buildings, machinery and plant.

The reason why firms experiencing such critical events often failed was that they were no longer able to produce the goods or provide the service their customers expected. While they waited to re-build and re-stock their factories, customers took their business elsewhere, sometimes never to return. Thus, the idea of 'risk management' was born. This took, as its founding principle, the identification, evaluation and control of threats to the enterprise, instead of a reliance on insurance for protection after the event. It also recognized that the true 'cost of risk' was far more than simply the cost of insurance claims and preventative measures, thus emphasizing the additional benefits to be gained from 'managing' risk.

Since the 1980s, the concept of risk management has expanded from manufacturing to commercial organizations, and been adopted by the public and not-for-profit sectors. It has also moved away from an initial concentration on the pure, tangible and insurable risks to embrace broader threats to the organization. This has involved taking a more holistic and enterprise-wide approach to the management of risk at the strategic and operational levels (Hopkin 2013).

THE ROLE OF CODES AND STANDARDS

Many models exist to describe the risk management process. In its simplest form, the management of risk involves some means of identifying, evaluating, addressing and monitoring risk. We will explore these stages in more detail in Chapters 3 and 4. To aid understanding of this process and to disseminate it more widely, a number of countries followed the lead set in 1995 by the Australian and New Zealand Standards Associations who produced the first risk management standard (AS/NZS 4360). For example, the risk management standard, developed jointly by UK risk management professional bodies the Association of Insurance and Risk Managers (AIRMIC), the National Forum for Risk Management in the Public Sector (ALARM) and the Institute of Risk Management (IRM), was published in 2003. This was a guidance document rather than a 'standard' as such, and it utilized the definitions of risk and risk-related terms approved by the ISO. This document was adopted by the Federation of European Risk Management Associations (FERMA) and translated into a number of European languages in order to enhance the understanding of, and communication about, the risk management process across European nations.

However, the original Australian and New Zealand standard (AS/NZS 4360) was revised in 1999 and 2004, and then formed the basis of standards developed by other countries, such as Canada and Japan. Ultimately, it was agreed that an international standard should be developed and a working group comprising experts from twenty-eight countries, representing all continents, developed the International Standard (ISO31000) on Risk Management – Principles and Guidelines – which was launched in 2009. Subsequently, ISO31000 replaced existing national standards, including AS/NSZ 4360, which it most closely resembled.

At the time of writing, ISO31000 has been adopted by governments in forty-one countries, from Japan to the United States, and it represents *the* standard for public sector risk management. The diffusion of the Standard around the globe is quite remarkable. The number of countries that had already adopted AS/NZS 4360 meant there was also going to be a commitment to its successor from most of the G8 and G20 nations which had pre-existing commitments to standardization. However, what was perhaps not anticipated was the spread of the new Standard into the emerging economies of Brazil, Russia, India and China. According to one member of the ISO working group that created the guidelines, this success can be attributed to the broad technical expertise used to inform the Standard and the use of national committees by the ISO, which ensured that national representatives had a voice in the formulation process. Hence the way in which the Standard was developed now allows many countries to enjoy a sense of ownership of its content (Knight 2011).

ISO31000 emphasizes the crucial importance of context (organizational culture and environmental location) and feedback mechanisms (modes of experiential learning and communication) alongside risk assessment and treatment. Hence risk managers must not only pay attention to the 'traditional' risk management process but also have cognizance of the wider organizational, cultural and environmental dynamics within which their operations are housed (see Figure 1.1).

In this regard, ISO31000 encourages a risk management process that has been defined as 'the systematic application of management policies, procedures and practices to the activities of communicating, consulting, establishing the context, and identifying, analysing, evaluating, treating, monitoring and reviewing risk' (ISO Guide 73:2009, definition 3.1). In Figure 1.2 we outline a more specific model of the process that the Standard encourages.

The first part of this process involves dialogue with stakeholders and an understanding of the way in which risks are perceived. While this is important in all organizations, it is particularly important in the public sector, where political and social dimensions of risk play a major role in influencing decisions taken. Establishing the context in which the organization operates relates to both the external environment, i.e. the economic, legal, political, social and other environments in which the organization conducts its business, as well as the internal environment, which is denoted by the aims, objectives and culture of the organization. There is a broad continuum that ranges from an 'excessive appetite' for risk-taking at one end to a complete 'aversion' to risk

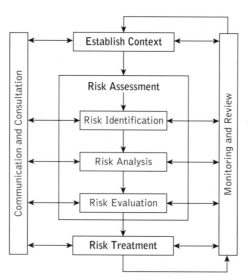

Figure 1.1 *The ISO31000 process*

Source: AIRMIC et al. (2010: 9).

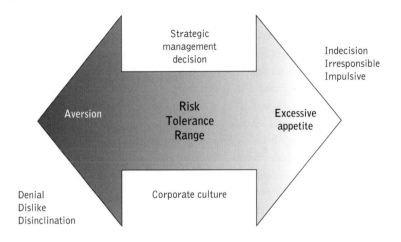

Figure 1.2 The organizational 'risk appetite'

at the other. The extent to which an enterprise is prepared to take risks in any individual set of circumstances is described as the 'risk appetite'. In Chapters 3 and 4 we will discuss how methods of risk identification and evaluation can be employed to assist the PSO in understanding its own risk appetite, and in making decisions as to how risks should be treated.

However, it would be wrong to conclude here that standardization is unproblematic. Some risk management specialists have criticized ISO31000 and the role of standards more generally. For example, Anette Mikes and Robert Kaplan, both members of the Harvard Business School, make the case that standardization of the sort encouraged by ISO31000 restricts innovation and experimentation, particularly problematic because the field of risk management is still in the process of learning about risk and its multiple dimensions. Mikes and Kaplan (2014) have produced a ten-year study, which uses more than 250 interviews with senior risk officers. They sum up the crux of the issue of standardization when they state:

> With such an abundance of principles, guidelines, and standards, scholars might conclude that risk management is a mature discipline with proven unambiguous concepts and tools that need only regulations and compliance to be put into widespread practice. We disagree. We believe that risk management approaches are largely unproven and still emerging. . . . Prematurely adopting standards and guidelines that aspire to be 'applicable to all organizations' and 'all types of risk' (as advocated, for example, by ISO31000) introduces a major risk into risk management by inhibiting companies from searching for and experimenting with innovative risk management processes that match their particular circumstances.
>
> (Mikes and Kaplan 2014: 3–4)

The counterargument to Mikes and Kaplan is of course that ISO31000 is a guide rather than a regulation. It can be used in a highly flexible manner as it is not attached to certification. Indeed, we need to emphasize that risk management standards are not designed to be 'tick-box' mechanisms that can provide assurance that risks are being effectively managed. Nor are they meant to certify that an organization is risk free. Rather they are intended to give general guidance on terminology and aid understanding of the risk management process. In doing so, they have provided a basis for both private companies and PSOs to create their own risk management frameworks. Furthermore, various training initiatives have been developed by professional institutes and educational bodies, which use the principles of these standards as the basis for their courses, thereby disseminating the content more widely and influencing a more systematic approach to the management of risk.

Nevertheless, the debate over whether standardization provides essential guidance or a one-size-fits-all straightjacket actually strikes at the heart of a risk and crisis management dilemma. How can we build policies that encourage good practice across organizations but allow those same organizations the freedom to act contingently? The question that public managers should ask themselves as a consequence is: do they see global templates such as ISO31000 as a means through which they can respond to the unique and dynamic threats that they must address?

When reflecting on this question public managers should remember that managing risk is not an end in itself. It is a means to an end, as it enables the organization to run more smoothly and deliver its services more efficiently and effectively, thereby achieving its corporate objectives. One of the proclaimed benefits of managing risk is said to be the minimization of 'surprises', yet, as we are aware, we cannot avoid the 'surprise risk' entirely. Within the organization, things will go wrong. People will make mistakes, management systems and technology will fail. Moreover, events may occur external to the organization that could not be prevented and which impact severely on its ability to operate normally. No standard, however sophisticated or popular, can prevent these events from occurring. Such episodes lead us neatly into the world of 'crisis' and crisis management.

DEFINING CRISES: SCHOOLS OF THOUGHT

The word 'crisis' is everywhere. It is used in newspaper articles, academic papers, policy documents, government reports, political language and popular speech. It is also applied to a wide variety of phenomena such as terrorist attacks, political scandals, hurricanes, chemical explosions, tsunamis, air crashes, urban riots and health scares. Crisis also seems to be a more salient topic than ever before. Over the past decade or so, many tragedies have become ingrained in popular consciousness: 9/11, the London and Madrid bombings, the Southeast Asian tsunami, the Queensland floods, the Christchurch earthquake, Hurricane Katrina, the Boston bombing, the global financial crisis, the Great East Japan earthquake, tsunami and Fukushima melt-down, the Sandy Hook school shooting and the massacre of schoolchildren on the small island of Utøya off the coast of Norway. Many of these events substantiate the fact that sophisticated public sectors, located within advanced democratic and economic settings, do not guarantee crisis protection. Every nation on earth is vulnerable.

It is easy to get lost amid the vast range of events and circumstances that are labelled as a crisis. Two broad schools of thought exist about what constitutes a crisis. We have distilled these from a wide variety of literature and we have given them our own labels. In examining these we address the apparent dichotomy (false we will argue) between those who view crises as objective phenomena and those who view crises in subjective terms as contingent on our perceptions. This then leads us to propose a third way of understanding how crises can be defined, which we have labelled a 'critical realist' perspective.

The objective school: crisis as fact

One strand of political and policy science research is characterized by positivism, which is a methodology for developing knowledge based on the assumption that the world around us can be quantified and measured (Hay 2002). Subscribers to this view argue that we, as observers of the social world, can be detached and value free and are capable of studying social phenomena as 'facts' which can be defined and measured. Applying positivism to the phenomenon of crisis would involve an assumption that crises are 'concrete' events that can be defined by a number of key characteristics. A positivist approach would be inclined towards checklists of 'crisis criteria' in order that we can 'tick the boxes' to see if a crisis exists. In many respects, this is a very sensible approach because it starts to flesh out and solidify what a crisis actually involves. Often, there is substantial agreement on three conditions that are deemed necessary for a crisis to exist (see e.g. Rosenthal et al. 2001; Farazmand 2014). These are:

Severe threat

Threat is most obvious when we talk about loss of life or property. But severe threats can manifest in many ways. For example, threats might come in the form of a slump in public confidence in the safety of our rail systems, or in a dramatic loss of funding, which threatens an organization's ability to deliver on its core goals. A simple comparison between a large natural disaster and the repeated failure of a government to deliver accurate and timely school exam results illustrates this point. No one can doubt that a life-threatening disaster is more severe in terms of threat but there are several threats lurking in the latter example that contribute towards the 'crisis' label.

15

Most obviously, thousands of school leavers will be disadvantaged through the actions of government. Also important is the fact that the policy failure could severely damage government reputation and public trust in the integrity of the education system as a whole. Hence, crisis analysts often discuss threats at the operational level (i.e. 'on-the-ground' threats to life, property, policy delivery and so on) as well as the political-symbolic level (i.e. threats to confidence in governments, threats to societal feelings of safety and security).

High levels of uncertainty

Severe threats, often appearing with varying degrees of surprise, disturb the normal routines and rhythms of organizational, social and political life. Such threats have no respect for the managerial tools and processes that traditionally create certainty for the public manager, and they subsequently pose overwhelming psychological and physical challenges. A crisis typically brings uncertainty about its causes, as well the scope and severity of its impact and will often be characterized by mixed signals and a lack of evidence about its nature. For example, an explosion in a major urban area would produce complex and interconnected uncertainties about the scale of the attack (how many casualties? what critical infrastructure is damaged?), its causes (accident? attack?) and its likely impact (containable one-off? beginning of a chain of events?).

Urgent need for action

High levels of threat and uncertainty combine to produce a 'ticking clock' for those who have the responsibility for managing major crises. Typically, governments are at the apex of crisis responses and hold ultimate responsibility for crisis decision-making, which might be focused on anything from saving lives to calming social anxiety. Partly this is a societal reflex, with citizens, the media and other stakeholders looking to government for crisis leadership. Partly it is also a product of the pivotal role of government in society, with its unique political and legislative authority, as well as its command of resources and ability to direct them in times of need. It is little wonder, therefore, that governments become key actors in 'ticking clock' narratives – such as the search for the Boston bomber or the rush to prepare vaccines for the global flu pandemic – even when they are only facilitating or legitimizing the responses of others.

From this perspective, therefore, we should be wary of 'abusing' the term crisis, or 'overusing' it to the point that it becomes devalued. Following the logic of this approach, we should show restraint and reserve the term 'crisis' for times when it really matters: when threats are high, certainty is low and decision makers are faced with seemingly impossible timescales.

The subjective school: crisis as perception

A very different tradition in the political and policy sciences is a school of thought emphasizing interpretation and construction (see e.g. Fischer 2003). The focus is on how we perceive and construct the world around us, rather than assuming it to be little more than immutable 'facts'. Translating this school of thought into crisis terms suggests that if we feel and believe that a phenomenon, event or episode is a crisis, then it is indeed 'crisis' and it is 'real' because we are using language to convey the significance of what is happening.

A simple version of 'crisis as perception' can be found in common assumptions that crises are self-evident. We don't need criteria, checklists, rulebooks or dictionaries to tell us what constitutes a crisis. A crisis just 'is' and we feel in our hearts that this is the case. This view is also implicit in many scholarly works (in particular those focusing on corporate crisis) but can be found more generally in media coverage of crises and disasters. For example, when newspaper journalists write about wars, famines and large-scale disasters such as 9/11, Hurricane Katrina or the Japanese tsunami, the term 'crisis' is assumed to be self-evident, based on the assumption of shared beliefs that these episodes couldn't be anything other than 'crises'.

A more sophisticated take on 'perceptions' focuses on the politics (large P and small p) of crisis, and a particular view that everyone's experiences are different, and that to some degree these experiences will condition their perceptions. Some people will feel more or less threatened by events, depending on factors such as their geographical location, their degree of involvement (if at all), the likely impact on their own personal circumstances and the extent to which the phenomenon comprises their core beliefs and assumption. An example of different perceptions in this regard can be seen in political crises (although is by no means confined to it), such as the so-called Arab Spring in 2010–11 during which citizens took to the streets to protest against (and in some cases overthrow) what they saw as anti-democratic regimes. For the powerful elites controlling those states, the Arab Spring was very much a crisis that posed immediate threats to their very existence. For those on the streets protesting, however, the protests were not so much a threatening crisis as an opportunity to create positive change. And for those of us viewing events from a distance there was a palpable sense of crisis without any immediate threat. Hence it is important to understand that these different perceptions do not coalesce into one indisputable definition of what is occurring. A single event can be seen as a crisis by some, an opportunity by others and even viewed with indifference by those far removed (physically and emotionally) from events. An extreme version of this argument is put forward by Bruck (1992), who suggests that there is no such thing as a crisis; it is a language construction, used by different people and different groups in order to attribute meaning to a particular set of social circumstances.

17

The critical realist school: crisis as fact and perception

The two aforementioned schools of thought clearly have some value. It is difficult to deny that many threats are 'real' (from tsunamis and nuclear meltdowns to terrorist attacks and pandemic viruses) but it is also difficult to deny that different actors vary in their perceptions of such threats. We would argue, however, that adopting either of these positions alone seriously impedes our ability to understand the phenomenon of crises and the impact they have on crisis managers, policy-makers and society more generally. If we side solely with the objective school, we will never be able to encapsulate how different perceptions lead to different understandings of events, such as the manager who ignores a high reading of contaminants in drinking water because it is considered a normal problem (in the form of a rogue reading or a transient issue which can be dealt with through normal routines). Varying perceptions *do* matter, therefore, because they condition how crisis managers respond, and what society expects of them, and ultimately how it judges them. Equally, if we side solely with the subjective school of thought, it is as though tangible threats only matter if people (or at least a significant coalition of opinion formers) think they matter. If we adopt the position that 'it's all a matter of perception', then we may be deluding ourselves that, for example, massive budgetary cuts will make no difference to front-line services, or that the collapse of several large financial institutions is nothing more than a 'market correction'.

Critical realism is something of an umbrella term for a variety of different methodological positions, but here it is our preferred position and is an attempt to reconcile 'facts' and 'perceptions', based on the existence of real and unquestionable phenomena, which may be viewed differently by different actors (see Marsh 2011). For example, we know for a fact that there are vast disparities in income and wealth, but we may view such disparities as more or less desirable, depending on our own complex and differentiated worldviews. If we apply such thinking to crisis situations, it is clear that there are extraordinary threatening conditions that may exist in themselves, regardless of whether we need to deal with them, how significant we think they are how and how we choose to label them. Such objective conditions include threats to:

■   life, e.g. flood, rail crash, bushfire, pandemic virus;
■   critical infrastructure, e.g. power blackouts, collapse of communication networks;
■   policy functioning, e.g. accidentally revealing intelligence information that severely compromises covert intelligence operations;
■   economic viability, e.g. massive organizational budget cuts;
■   political reputation, e.g. high levels of citizen dissatisfaction in opinion polls.

Despite the existence of such threats, we need to understand that their repercussions may be amplified or played down, viewed with horror or welcomed as an opportunity for reform (Boin et al. 2010). For example, a power blackout can be considered a temporary 'one-off' or the symptom of a systemic vulnerability in the electricity grid. Rail crashes can be considered bad for train operators but an opportunity for those contracted to upgrade signalling systems. Budget cuts can be seen as fatal to organizational sustainability or a galvanizing force for efficiency reforms. Severe damage to a government's reputation can be seen as a window of opportunity for opposition parties. Adopting a critical realist position, therefore, we define crisis as:

> a set of circumstances in which individuals, institutions or societies face threats beyond the norms of routine, day-to-day functioning, but the significance and impact of these circumstances will vary according to individual perceptions.

The advantage of such a definition is that it provides an insight into the tension which exists in both the phenomenon and language of crisis; that is, between very real, extraordinarily difficult circumstances, and the multitude of perceptions of these circumstances. If we wish to understand why some crises come to be labelled in one way and others defined as something different, we need to explore the relationship between objective characteristics and the meaning given to those characteristics. Such issues address fundamental methodological issues in the social sciences and we cannot hope to resolve them here. Nevertheless, armed with the basic assumption that crisis phenomena are both real *and* constructed, we have the beginnings of deeper insight into how multiple definitions of crisis are actually a product of the language that has developed around the blurred boundaries of the enigmatic phenomenon of 'crisis'.

UNDERSTANDING THE PLETHORA OF CRISIS DEFINITIONS

In this section, we use our critical realist perspective to perform three tasks. First, we map out the key characteristics that are commonly deployed in the crisis definitions used by political actors, commentators and crisis analysts. When setting out this range of factors, our own definition reminds us that we need to consider how different crisis characteristics can be defined as objective 'facts' and/or interpreted through the lenses of individual or collective opinion. Setting out this map of factors subsequently allows us to create a framework through which we can better understand types of crisis and the multiple ways that the term 'crisis' is applied. Finally, we use our definition, characteristics and framework to discuss the instrumental ways that definitions can be used by individuals to exploit the opportunities and avoid the costs associated with crises.

A map of crisis characteristics

The first set of characteristics involved in defining crises relates to what we call the 'epicentre'. This is where the 'heat' of the crisis is most keenly felt. In this regard, the essence of a crisis is often located through an interpretation of the context in which its effects are most severe. This is said to be the heart of the phenomenon. Crises can have, or may be perceived to have, one or more epicentres including: individuals, policies, institutions, societies, cross-societies, technology and the geophysical realm. A second set of characteristics relates to specific variables, which can again be objectively or subjectively defined. Most commonly, these relate to: the speed of arrival, degree of predictability, extent of preparedness, degree of intentionality to cause a crisis, degree of complexity, degree of politicization and degree of persistence after the acute stage. Let us consider each of these factors in turn. Thereafter we will combine them in a framework that will allow us to make better sense of how they come together to create crisis types.

It is important to remember, given our definition of crisis, that the factors discussed below can be contested by different political actors and commentators – not least in terms of which might be more or less significant in their eyes. This is, however, precisely our point. Each characteristic contains objective elements that can be subjectively defined.

Crisis epicentres

The realpolitik of crisis is that narratives surrounding crisis often focus – usually explicitly but occasionally implicitly – on where the crisis conditions are most severe. Sometimes the heat is on *individuals*, and therefore we write, talk and conceive of personal crises, leadership crises and so on. The ramifications of crisis may be felt elsewhere, but the focus is very much on individuals facing crisis, such as the recent case of French President François Hollande amid allegations of an affair, and Australian Prime Minister Julia Gillard amid a period of turbulence and leadership challenges in 2012–13 which eventually saw the end of her tenure. Of course, there can be reverberations from other epicentres, which can in turn produce significant threats to personal reputations and careers, as was the case with Federal Emergency Management Agency (FEMA) Director Michael Brown in the aftermath of Hurricane Katrina and Icelandic Prime Minister Geir Haarde in the wake of the global financial crisis.

We can also conceive of *policy* epicentres in the sense that the focus is on critical failures in public policy, either in terms of it being unable to deliver goals and/or widespread disagreement with the outcomes that transpired (Bovens and 't Hart 1996). A good example here is the loft insulation debacle in Australia under the 2007 Rudd government. In response to the global financial crisis, the government announced a $2-billion round of subsidies that would allow Australian citizens to insulate their homes. This was designed to stimulate aspects of the economy in the face of economic turbulence. However, the failure properly to regulate the scheme led to fraudulent claims, high levels of waste and a raft of 'builders' with no experience chasing subsidy payments. In a number of extreme cases, poor workmanship caused house fires, and four workers died installing the insulation. After a media furore, the embarrassing policy was quickly terminated and the environment minister reshuffled to a lesser post. In essence, however, this case has become known as a classic policy fiasco or policy disaster simply because – regardless of institutional and leadership context – the focus was very much on a crisis of 'policy'.

We must also consider *institutional/governmental* epicentres (Alink et al. 2001). These emerge from more deep-seated issues within larger policy areas or government more generally, in which the logic and institutions surrounding public policy have pathological weaknesses. These weaknesses are often the result of instability caused by too much change or an overt resistance to change amongst key actors, including citizens and civil society. In both cases, the result is a series of institutions that are out of step with their immediate environment. The result is what could be called a crisis-prone area of public management where many problematic focusing events take place. The Child Support Agency in the United Kingdom is an excellent example of an organization that was beset by chronic operational and reputational problems to the point that it was disbanded (King and Crewe 2013).

Another larger-scale epicentre is *society* as a whole. Here, the threat is focused on the fundamental underpinnings of a particular society, whether it be its core values, governing institutions or powerful groups whose rule seems to be facing (for better or worse) its greatest test. Academic analysis and journalistic commentary is replete with suggestions, for example, of the 'Greek crisis' and the 'Syrian crisis'.

We can also conceive of *cross-societal epicentres*. While they may originate in one or even several locations, the emphasis is on the 'heat' of crisis being felt across different sectors or even nation states. As will be explored particularly in Chapter 8, threats can escalate and shape-shift through our societies. Animal diseases translate into human disease, security crises beget refugee disasters and, of course, financial crises and debt crises mutate into riots, civil disturbance and the collapse of governments. These events are now being captured under the label 'transboundary crisis' (Boin and Rhinard 2008).

We must also have cognizance of *industrial/technological* epicentres. Here, the heat and the focus is on some form of critical technology that has failed. Of course, its impact may flow into other areas, posing immense challenges – especially for institutions. Nevertheless, the epicentre is on apparent technological failure, such as power failures, chemical spills and industrial accidents.

We must also take cognizance of *geophysical* epicentres. In understanding this category, we need to separate it, at least conceptually, from geophysical causes and geophysical symptoms. While geophysical causes refer to generic triggers such as tsunamis, mudslides, heatwaves and hurricanes, and symptoms refer to their social and infrastructural impact, geophysical epicentres refer to the abnormal forces and turbulent conflicts where threats are manifest. Geophysical epicentres refer to phenomena such as the combination of combustible materials, moisture, wind and temperature which

21

produce bushfires and the clash of tectonic plates which in turn produce earthquakes and tsunamis.

Speed of arrival

The speed at which a crisis escalates is an important indicator of its character and our attempts to understand it. Some conditions may take years to escalate and even then there are some who would not use the term 'crisis' while others would. Climate change, deforestation, public spending trends, population growth and an ageing population, for example, may arrive slowly over many years, decades and even centuries. Others are much quicker. In 2009, for example, the global swine-flu crisis took less than eight weeks to escalate from a small Mexican town in Veracruz to a WHO certified global pandemic affecting more than fifty-eight countries. Others are quicker still. The Great East Japan Tsunami also illustrates this character, arriving and creating 'disastrous' conditions within hours when it morphed into the worst nuclear crisis for a generation when the Fukushima nuclear plant malfunctioned. The 9/11 attacks on the World Trade Center were swifter still, with the two planes hitting within a period of only seventeen minutes. The speed at which a crisis arrives is a crucial variable in shaping the way in which many perceive the crisis, as well as shaping the response itself.

Degree of predictability

This issue, as with all of the factors we consider here, may be highly contested. We will come back to the ramifications of this shortly in terms of crisis types but for the moment, we should simply be aware that the assumed degree of predictability can be part of a defining process. Some crises may be considered highly predictable, at least in the eyes of some. Schwartz (2003), for example, argues that the warning signs for the types of crises we will experience in the future (migration, terrorism, climate change) are already present, although we may not be able to know precisely where and when they will occur. More certain still are accusations of 'accidents waiting to happen', and even crises which are 'inevitable'. Such language is common currency in evidence to post-crisis inquiries and investigations, which indicates how degrees of predictability have become an important feature of the vocabulary of crisis definition.

Extent of preparedness

Subjective and objective definitions of crisis also focus on the extent to which authorities are prepared, particularly through contingency plans, for crisis events. It should come as no surprise (see Chapter 5) to know that the extent and quality of preparedness can vary substantially across different types of public authorities operating in different

22

policy spheres, situated within different national, socio-political and economic contexts. Regardless of the fact that there are numerous debates on how effective preparedness actually is (Eriksson and McConnell 2011), understanding the nature of crisis involves understanding not only degrees of crisis preparedness, but also how actors perceive preparation to be important and incorporate this into their assumptions about what constitutes a crisis and what is likely to be its impact. We know from the many crisis experiences around the world that there are numerous variations that exist on a spectrum between those considered 'ill-prepared' (Hurricane Katrina, BP oil spill) and those considered 'highly prepared' (Madrid bombing, Bali bombings).

Degree of intentionality to cause a crisis

The character of crises and our perceptions of what is meaningful about them can also emerge from understandings of the extent to which (if at all) they were deliberate acts. Here we might immediately think of terrorist attacks and sabotage, but we should also think about the wilful creation of and/or inflation of circumstances to the point that crisis conditions are created. There are many reasons why the latter might happen, from creating circumstances that demonstrate effective leadership, to 'shaking the tree' of established policy/political agendas and creating an open window for policy reform and political change (Birkland 2007). Such accusations seem particularly common in 'immigration crises' and 'budgetary crises' but are by no means confined to these. Former Australian Prime Minister John Howard likened the extent of child abuse in Aboriginal communities in the Northern Territory to the lawlessness and misery of Hurricane Katrina, paving the way for what became known as the Northern Territory Intervention and a package of authoritative 'crisis' measures, including restrictions of welfare payments and bans on alcohol and pornography.

Degree of complexity

Some crises are quite discrete, linear and follow a fairly predictable trajectory of event, investigation and recommendations (rail crashes for example), but others involve higher degrees of 'coupling' that can lead to failures cascading across, physical, institutional and policy systems. International, national and subnational governing regimes all operate in dynamic and interconnected ways across multiple policy sectors, ensuring great levels of complexity. Such complexity translates into the nature of many crises themselves because they do not incubate, emerge and get resolved in hermetically sealed environments. When a volcanic eruption took place in Iceland in 2010 and an ash cloud travelled across Europe, the cause of the immediate threat was fairly self-evident. However, complexity unfolded when the cloud interacted with the complex rules and regulations surrounding European air traffic control and subsequently grounded planes across the continent. This problem is also apposite within nation states in which overlap between policy spheres (such as transport, environment, public health), as well as complex forms of governance, networks, markets and engagement with non-government actors, ensures high levels of complexity in the event of failure. As we will see, perceptions of complexity have also found their way into the language of crisis.

Degree of politicization

Another feature of crises is the extent to which they become politicized. Some crises do not ignite political conflicts, other than in the rather mundane sense of organizational politics. Here, failures and their resolution are contained largely within the boundaries of the crisis-prone organization; for example, a failed internal reorganization may create conflict around staffing issues which never become a public concern. Yet the impact of many crises can spill over beyond institutional boundaries, with emotions running high and key actors (governments, political parties, citizens, NGOs, media) all sensitized to the crisis impact and response. For example, a crisis may have touched a nerve in a nationally sensitive policy area (e.g. London riots at a time of austerity), put leaders' competence and emotional skills under the spotlight (Malaysian officials and the disappearance of flight MH370) or may have been capitalized on by critics as a means of attempting to damage the government. The extent of crisis politicization, as we will see, is also a feature of the crisis phenomenon and the language that is used by analysts and protagonists to indicate the extent to which the crisis is delegitimizing social and political values that are considered important.

Degree of persistence after the acute stage

The final dimension of crisis to consider here is the extent to which it leaves a legacy after the acute phase. There are always some legacies, even for victims' families and for the organizations that need to revisit their priorities, rules and procedures. Yet some crises have a deep, lasting and often confronting legacy that refuses to budge from institutional agendas, policy agenda and collective. Inquiries can provide forums for the airing of emotions, grievances and policy concerns, for example the 9/11 commission. Hence the aftermath of crisis filters through to the language of definition.

Fifty shades of crisis: making sense of 'crisis' types

It is easy to become bemused by the innumerable types of crisis. If we think of crisis as an 'umbrella' phenomenon that encapsulates an array of events, a modest list would include sudden crises, fast-burning crises, creeping crises, long-shadow crises, agenda-setting crises, mismanaged crisis, manufactured crises, policy fiascos/disasters, technological crises, transboundary crises, mega crises, natural disasters, accidents and emergencies.

In this section, we make sense of these types by using the characteristics we discussed above. When we combine those characteristics (see Figure 1.3), it becomes possible to distil the aspects of crisis that each type *tends* to focus upon (note that for practical purposes Figure 1.3 only selects a small sample of the crisis types outlined below). Importantly, the boundaries between these types are often blurred, but we will come back to this important qualifier after setting out the types in relation to our characteristics.

- *Sudden crises* – high speed of arrival, any epicentre is possible, e.g. hostages taken, terrorist attacks, power blackout.
- *Fast-burning crises* – high speed of arrival, low persistence after the acute stage, any epicentre possible but more likely to be individual, policy, institution, societal or industrial/technological, e.g. heatwaves, water contamination episodes.
- *Creeping crises* – any epicentre possible but especially societal. Particular emphasis on low speed of arrival, high predictability and low level of preparedness, e.g. climate change, obesity, ageing population.
- *Long-shadow crises* – any epicentre is possible but it is particularly likely to be at societal level; high level of persistence after the acute stage, e.g. race riots in major cities, nuclear meltdowns.
- *Agenda-setting crises* – epicentre most likely to be at individual, policy, institutional, societal, industrial/technological levels, with high level of politicization and high levels of persistence after the acute stage, e.g. mass shootings, major budget short-falls.
- *Mismanaged crises* – epicentre most likely to be individual, policy and institutional, with emphasis on low level of preparedness and high level of adverse politicization, e.g. any crisis attracting substantial criticism for ineffective crisis management.
- *Manufactured crises* – emphasis on high level of intent to cause a crisis. Epicentre most likely to be policy or institutional, e.g. any crisis where there is an accusation of creating and/or inflating the threat to one of critical proportions.
- *Policy fiascos/disasters* – epicentre is likely to be policy (and also at times individual and institutional) with an emphasis on a high level of predictability and high degree of politicization, e.g. any substantive policy where the repercussions of apparent substantial failure to meet policy goals attract high levels of adverse politicization for policy makers and accusations of 'they should have seen it coming' and the near inevitability of failure.
- *Technological crises* – epicentre is technological although it may also spread to policy, institutional, societal and even cross-societal levels. Emphasis will often be on high levels of complexity, e.g. failure in critical IT infrastructure.
- *Transboundary crises* – epicentre is cross-societal, although it made also encompass other epicentres, particularly policy, institutional, societal, technological and

25

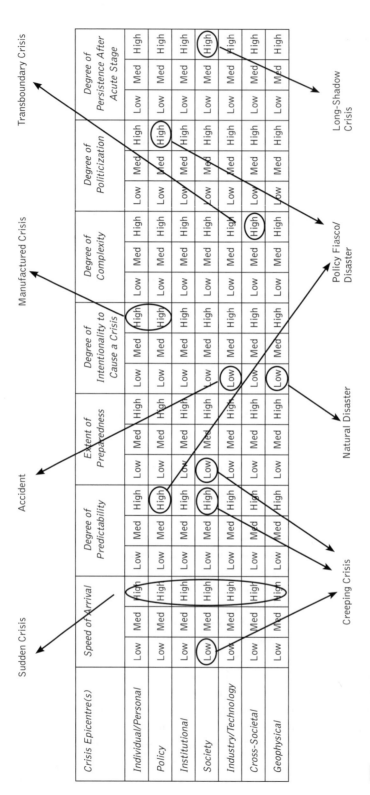

Figure 1.3 Points of emphasis: a roadmap to help understand tendencies in the framing of crisis types

geophysical. Emphasis also on high level of complexity, e.g. pandemics, economic meltdowns.

- *Mega crises* – all epicentres are possible but emphasis likely to be on societal, cross-societal, technological and geophysical. Emphasis also likely to be on high level of complexity and high level of politicization, e.g. global failure of internet.
- *Natural disasters* – epicentre is geophysical although it can spread to all other epicentres. There is high emphasis on natural causes and no intentionality to cause harm. Debates will also revolve around speed of arrival, degree of predictability and level of preparedness, e.g. tsunamis, bushfires, earthquakes, mudslides.
- *Accidents* – epicentres tend to involve aspects of technology although they may also be societal. Emphasis is on little or no intentionality to cause failure, e.g. major chemical spillages, 'friendly fire' in times of war.
- *Emergencies* – emphasis on individual and institutional epicentres, with high speed of arrival, high degree of predictability and high level of preparedness, e.g. fires, road crashes.

Crucially, there is no definitive way to classify a crisis as a single type. However, our critical realist definition, with its emphasis on objective threats and varying perceptions, suggests that we should not try to do so. The reason for the blurred boundaries between the types is precisely *because* individuals will often view the same circumstances in different ways, emphasizing or deemphasizing characteristics to fit with their perceptions. Indeed, many crises seem to have a legitimate claim to reside in several categories. A nuclear meltdown could lay claim to be a 'sudden crisis' if we emphasized the speed at which it happened, or an 'agenda-setting crisis' if we wanted to emphasize the legacy it left behind in terms of future changes to energy policy.

The politics of definition

The attribution of a particular set of characteristics as constituting a certain crisis type – by policy-makers and experts to families and the media – is a political act. Amid many potential and often conflicting labels to choose from, the framing of a crisis as type 'X' often means that a perception of its origins and impact will influence what should be done in response. Varying perceptions, therefore, are not only a manifestation of our attempts to understand, but also to influence. We can think about this if we identify some of the adverse consequences of crisis:

- human costs – loss of life, scarred survivors, family trauma;
- critical infrastructure costs – failures in networks such as transport, IT, water, energy;
- policy costs – the failure of core policies;

- economic costs – loss of revenue, loss of markets, job losses;
- political-symbolic costs – damage to organizational/governmental legitimacy, damage to strategic policy direction; and
- personal costs – possible investigations, damage to reputation and loss of employment.

We can also think of some of the opportunities afforded by crisis, including:

- opening up debate on serious issues, in a way that was previously not possible;
- bringing about organizational change and learning to ensure better prevention and preparedness for future threats;
- bringing about policy change and learning;
- boosting the fortunes of effective leaders;
- being the catalyst to punish weak and/or ineffective leaders; and
- providing opportunities for some organizations to 'prove' themselves and lobby for longer-term increases in funding.

Threats can cause damage in the short term, but opportunities may emerge for medium to longer-term learning, change and reduction of vulnerabilities. Yet such outcomes are neither predetermined nor liable to be acceptable to all. For this reason, actors often attempt to define issues in ways that can generate support for their positions and their desired outcomes so that they can exploit opportunities and reduce costs. From a conceptual point of view, therefore, we need to understand 'agency' (the capacity of individual actors or groups to act instrumentally within the broader institutional structures of society) and 'framing' (the process through which agents use language instrumentally to pursue goals). These concepts allow analytical purchase on how crises can be defined into existence through language, how support can be generated for a selective view of events and how legitimacy can be attached to particular solutions as a consequence of the definition or crisis type applied. Here we identify four particularly important ways in which this may happen.

1. FRAMING PHENOMENA AS BEING OF 'CRISIS' PROPORTIONS

One aspect of framing relates to the application of the term 'crisis' itself. It can be an attempt to break through the normal routines, rhythms and problems of political life, and using the term 'crisis' can create conditions of extraordinary drama and urgency. Opposition parties often use this tactic to attack their counterparts in government, to claim that the regime and its policies are in a deep mess of their own making. The language of crisis may also be deployed by others actors (advocacy groups, NGOs, think tanks) to destabilize the legitimacy of the status quo and be heard above all the other voices competing for government's valuable agenda time. From the United Kingdom to Australia and Sweden to Canada, political discourse is replete with 'crises' of health care, refugee policy, civil liberties, homelessness, budgets, local democracy, community care and so on. Using the term 'crisis' frames events in such a way as to imply that they are so extraordinary and unacceptable that reform is needed for a better future.

The framing of the crisis epicentre is a key means of elevating a set of circumstances in this regard. If crisis is portrayed as being embedded in institutions and the values and structures of society more generally, it is being positioned at (some might argue inflated to) a level where it is a direct challenge to core beliefs (Brändström and Kuipers 2003). In 1996, after the arrest of notorious Belgian child serial killer Marc Dutroux, several hundred thousand people marched in the so-called 'white march', condemning the police and judicial systems as incompetent and even as being complicit in not cracking down on a nationwide child sex ring. In essence, the epicentre was framed as the very public institutions that are meant to be safeguards against inhumane and criminal practices. Emphasizing certain crisis characteristics through use of a certain crisis type is also a means of elevating an issue. An exemplar is the use of 'creeping crises' on issues such as climate change, where no unequivocal critical point ever seems to be reached (in terms of the classic objective criteria of high threat, lack of information and little time to act), yet active interventions are nevertheless promoted by the mere attribution of the label 'crisis', because the definition implies that a predictable threat exists and we are ill-equipped to deal with it.

2. FRAMING PHENOMENA AS NOT BEING OF 'CRISIS' PROPORTIONS

The most direct way of playing down an event is simply not to use the term 'crisis' at all, and instead write/talk of business as usual (Boin et al. 2009). In the early stages of the 2009–10 MPs' expenses crisis in the United Kingdom, the initial response of the Leader of the House Harriet Harman was that it was an issue that could be dealt with through routine and minor regulatory reforms. But at times this approach may be politically unviable because there is sufficient momentum, through events and a gathering coalition, to label events as a 'crisis'. Government may then resort to using the term 'manufactured crisis', paying lip-service to crisis terminology and recognizing there is a significant perception of a threat, but accusing critics of manufacturing a crisis for ulterior motives. Alternatively, they may use the tactic of framing a crisis epicentre that is not so deeply embedded in social values (Brändström and Kuipers 2003). For example, amid accusations of a 'crisis of government' because of political scandals or corruption at the heart of a regime, senior political elites may refer to a 'personal crisis' for the minister involved. Alternatively, if they are accused of presiding over a 'mismanaged crisis', blame can be attributed to officials, as was the case with Sweden's troubled response to the 2004 Asian tsunami (in which some 30,000 Swedish citizens were affected).

3. FRAMING RESPONSE AND AFTERMATH AS A TIME FOR STABILITY

This narrative also relies upon a specific framing of the crisis epicentre. The 'time for stability' narrative generally accords with an optimistic view of failure (Bovens and 't Hart 1996), in the sense that the basic institutions and values of society are considered fundamentally robust, meaning that we should not get caught up in swift, knee-jerk reactions to replace them. Many corruption scandals would fit this category, where the focus is often on sanctions against those involved and a refinement of policies and procedures, rather than opening out the possibility of institution-wide corruption, or the possibility that deeper social values may cultivate corrupt behaviour. The attribution of particular crisis types, with their emphasis on particular aspects of a crisis, can also aid the 'playing down' of events and the shoring up of policies, institutional structures and societal values. Even the term 'natural disaster' has a stabilizing role, because of its emphasis on a geophysical epicentre with no intent in itself to cause harm.

4. FRAMING THE RESPONSE AND AFTERMATH AS AN OPPORTUNITY FOR CHANGE

All things being equal, the more localized the epicentre and the less embedded it is in the fabric of institutions and society, then the easier it is to make the case for change. This is reflected in the language of crisis and the crisis type. Framing events as a 'personal crisis' for an official who oversaw a 'policy disaster', or the introduction of a new IT system that produced a 'technological disaster', creates a wider window for reform (new official, new policy, new IT system) than, for example, situating these failings within governing strategies ('crisis of government') or societal values ('crisis of capitalism). Beyond the epicentre, emphasizing certain characteristics of crisis can also, all things being equal, create greater opportunities for reform. Examples include playing up high levels of politicization through the term 'agenda-setting crisis'.

Overall, the multiplicity of types of crisis and innumerable definitions is not something we should bemoan – confusing as they may be at times. Crisis language and terminology are part of the fabric of crises themselves. The many variations of crisis are a product of the language we use to make sense of and even shape a phenomenon that by its very nature seems to shape-shift and continually surprise us.

THE CRISIS MANAGEMENT CYCLE

We have attempted in this chapter to make sense of the various definitions and types of crisis. How can we now move beyond this and make sense of the entire crisis life cycle? A useful way of studying a crisis, the default in many respects, is to divide it into different phases in a crisis management cycle. As indicated in Figure 1.4, these are:

- prevention – thinking the unthinkable, risk analysis, threat assessment, mitigation strategies;

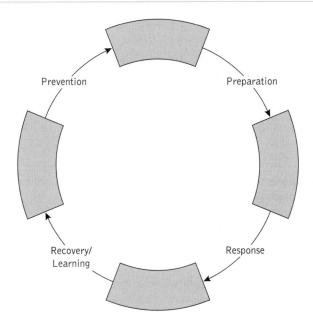

Figure 1.4 *The crisis management cycle*

- preparation – contingency planning, simulations, training, education;
- response – emergency working, operational deployment of resources, communications; and
- recovery – debriefing, counselling, rebuilding, inquiry, accountability, learning.

A few points must be made about this model. The first is that it is not necessarily
an accurate reflection of the reality of crisis management in its entirety. The cycle
should instead be understood as a general approximation of policy-making, which
allows us to simplify and learn about a complex activity. The second point is that in
each stage of the cycle a broad distinction can be made between operational and
political functions. For front-line workers and crisis managers, operational consequences involve saving lives, restoring order and recovery programmes. For institu-
tional/policy and political elites, they may ultimately be held accountable for
operational matters, and the success of 'local' issues is certainly something they
would wish for. However, the consequences for elites are wider. They must consider
short and long-term institutional, political and social repercussions. For example,
will the organization survive the crisis? What form should an inquiry take? Do we
need better regulation? Is there a limit to how much government can protect the
public? One corollary of operational-symbolic consequences is that the management
of crises is not simply the responsibility of public sector operatives, administrators
and policy workers – it is also the role of elected politicians. Crisis management

31

activities, therefore, may range from saving lives to the political 'selling' of the response.

In many respects, slicing up crisis dynamics in this way is a useful first step in understanding crisis experiences. The categories gives us a broad indication of the types of activity that occur at different periods, and often post-crisis inquiries will use such categorizations in their reports because they are convenient, easy to understand and give the appearance of objective detachment. The approach shares much in common with the wider 'policy cycle' approach to public policy-making (see e.g. Cairney 2012; Hill 2013), which portrays a logical sequence from problem definition through to implementation and evaluation. There are three issues with such an approach that are worth noting:

1. Cyclical models often present an image of policy-making that is clear, linear and simple. We know this is not always the case. Policy-making can be messy and complex.
2. Cyclical models often do not pay enough attention to the 'darker' sides of policy-making, which deal with issues such as political machination, self-interest, power and exclusion.
3. Cyclical models do not pay enough attention to normative issues. That is, what kinds of policy we should be putting in place to enhance our societies. They are instead focused on the process rather than the outcomes of policy.

Nevertheless, the cycle of crisis management still represents the dominant way of understanding these complex, highly uncertain events. It is well understood and widely used and as such we also use it to structure our crisis management chapters.

CONCLUSION

We would hope by now that we have conveyed the impression that risk and crisis are complex and often contested phenomena, and that the task of managing both is equally complex. This is true, of course, because we inhabit complex societies in which we have built complex systems around us that we don't always understand perfectly. These complex systems mean that 'typical' risks and crises (workplace health and safety or natural disasters, for example) are becoming harder to control and that new threats continue to appear on our horizon as we develop. We cannot therefore deny that risk and crisis management are two of the hardest managerial endeavours.

However, the reader should be assured that there is a wealth of useful knowledge that can help us cut through some of the complexities noted above. We now live in an era in which we are more aware of the risks and crises that we face than ever before. As a consequence, we have more sophisticated knowledge about risk and crisis management than at any point in human history. For sure, increased knowledge brings about increased awareness of complexities but it also brings about a shared ownership of the fundamentals in terms of practice. In the basic definitions of risk and crises, in the principles found in international risk management standards, and in the crisis management cycle, for example, we see a shared understanding between academics and practitioners about the essence of risk and crisis management. This shared understanding allows us to face a world of uncertain threats together.

 EXERCISE 1.1

Select a public service organization with which you are familiar. Find out whether it has produced a policy on risk management. How is risk and risk management defined in the context of this organization? How might a crisis emerge from the risks it faces and how might that crisis be defined?

DISCUSSION QUESTIONS

1. Can a risk also be an opportunity?
2. Is management of risk in public service organizations different from that in the private sector?
3. Is the term 'crisis' overused?
4. Can you think of a crisis where values have been threatened rather than property or lives? Were these events worthy of the label crisis?
5. Choose a crisis and map out the scale, complexity of cause and degree of politics. Where would you place this crisis on Figure 1.3?

REFERENCES

AIRMIC, Alarm and IRM (2010) *A Structured Approach to Enterprise Risk Management and the Requirements of ISO 31000*. Available at: <http://www.airmic.com/guide/structured-approach-Enterprise-Risk-Management-ERM-requirements-ISO-31000> (accessed 18 May 2014).

Alink, F., Boin, A. and 't Hart, P. (2001) 'Institutional Crises and Reforms in Policy Sectors: The Case of Asylum Policy in Europe', *Journal of European Public Policy*, 8: 71–91.

Audit Commission (2001) *Worth the Risk: Improving Risk Management in Local Government*, London: Audit Commission.

Beck, U. (1992) *Risk Society: Towards a New Modernity*, London: Sage.

Beck, U. (2009) *World at Risk*, Cambridge: Polity Press.

Bernstein, P. (1996) *Against the Gods: The Remarkable Story of Risk*, New York: John Wiley.

Birkland, T.A. (2007) *Lessons of Disaster: Policy Change after Catastrophic Events*, Washington, DC: Georgetown University Press.

Boin, A. and 't Hart, P. (2003) 'Public Leadership in Times of Crisis: Mission Impossible?' *Public Administration Review*, 63: 544–553.

Boin, A. and Rhinard, M. (2008) 'Managing Transboundary Crises: What Role for the European Union?' *International Studies Review*, 10: 1–26.

Boin, A., 't Hart, P. and McConnell, A. (2009) 'Towards a Theory of Crisis Exploitation: Political and Policy Impacts of Framing Contests and Blame Games', *Journal of European Public Policy*, 16(1): 81–106.

Boin, A., McConnell, A., 't Hart, P. and Preston, T. (2010) 'Leadership Style, Crisis Response and Blame Management: The Case of Hurricane Katrina', *Public Administration*, 88(3): 706–23.

Bovens, M. and 't Hart, P. (1996) *Understanding Policy Fiascos*, New Brunswick, NJ: Transaction.

Brändström, A. and Kuipers, S. (2003) 'From "Normal Incidents" to Political Crises: Understanding the Selective Politicization of Policy Failures', *Government and Opposition*, 38(3): 279–305.

Bruck, P. (1992) 'Crisis as Spectacle: Tabloid News and the Politics of Outrage', in M. Raboy and B. Dagenais (eds), *Media, Crisis and Democracy*, London: Sage, pp. 108–19.

Cairney, P. (2012) *Understanding Public Policy*, Basingstoke: Palgrave.

Drennan, L. (2004) 'Ethics, Governance and Risk Management: Lessons from Mirror Group Newspapers and Barings Bank', *Journal of Business Ethics*, 52: 257–66.

Eriksson, K. and McConnell, A. (2011) 'Contingency Planning for Crisis Management: Recipe for Success or Political Fantasy?' *Policy and Society*, 32(2): 89–99.

Farazmand, A. (2014) 'Crisis and Emergency Management: Theory and Practice', in A. Farazmand (ed.), *Crisis and Emergency Management: Theory and Practice*, Boca Raton, FL: CRC Press, pp. 1–9.

Fischer, F. (2003) *Reframing Public Policy: Discursive Politics and Deliberative Practices*, Oxford: Oxford University Press.

Hay, C. (2002) *Political Analysis*, Basingstoke: Palgrave Macmillan.

Hill, M. (2013) *The Public Policy Process*, 6th edition, Essex: Pearson.

Hopkin, P. (2013) *Risk Management (Strategic Success)*, London: Kogan Page.

Hubbard, D.W. (2009) *The Failure of Risk Management: Why It's Broken and How to Fix It*, Hoboken, NJ: John Wiley & Sons.

International Organization for Standardization [ISO] and International Electrotechnical Commission [IEC] (2002) *Guide 73: Risk Management Vocabulary – Guidelines for use in Standards*, Geneva: ISO.

International Organization for Standardization [ISO] (2009) *ISO Guide 73: Risk Management Vocabulary*, Geneva: ISO.

King, A. and Crewe, I. (2013) *The Blunders of our Governments*, London: Oneworld.

Knight, K.W. (2011) 'Risk Management – New Work Reinforces a Solid Toolbox'. Available at: <http://www.iso.org/iso/home/news_index/news_archive/news.htm?Refid=Ref1585> (accessed 21 May 2014).

Lupton, D. (2013) *Risk*, 2nd edition, Abingdon: Routledge.

Marsh, D. (2011) 'The New Orthodoxy: The Differentiated Policy Model', *Public Administration*, 89(1): 32–48.

Mikes, A. and Kaplan, R.S. (2014) 'Towards a Contingency Theory of Enterprise Risk Management', Harvard Business School Working Paper, Boston, MA.

Perry, R.W. and Quarantelli, E.L. (eds) (2005) *What is a Disaster? New Answers to Old Questions*, Philadelphia: Xlibris.

Quarantelli, E.L. (ed.) (1998) *What is a Disaster? Perceptions on the Question*, London, Routledge.

Rosenthal, U., Boin, R.A. and Comfort, L.K. (2001) 'The Changing World of Crisis and Crisis Management', in U. Rosenthal, R.A. Boin and L.K. Comfort (eds), *Managing Crises: Threats, Dilemmas and Opportunities*, Springfield, IL: Charles C. Thomas, pp. 5–27.

Schwartz, P. (2003) *Inevitable Surprises: Thinking Ahead in a Time of Turbulence*, New York: Gotham.

Slovic, P. (1987) 'Perception of Risk', *Science*, 236: 280–5.

Vis, B. (2011) 'Prospect Theory and Political Decision-Making', *Political Studies Review*, 9(3): 334–43.

Wikinson, I. (2010) *Risk, Vulnerability and Everyday Life*, Abingdon: Routledge.

FURTHER READING

Risk management

Bernstein, P.L. (1996) *Against the Gods: The Remarkable Story of Risk*, New York: John Wiley.

For a historical perspective on risk, and humankind's attempts to control it, from the times of the Ancient Greeks to the present day, this book is essential reading. Bernstein clarifies many of the concepts relating to risk, such as probability, game theory and rational versus irrational decision-making, by telling tales of mathematicians, merchants, gamblers and philosophers in a narrative style that makes history come to life and helps us understand the risk issues of today.

Beck, U. (1999) *World Risk Society*, Cambridge: Polity Press.

A classic. The essays by this social theorist bring a sometimes controversial perspective to an understanding of risk in modern society. Beck argues that increasing globalization and the impact that this has on our environment create new 'world problems' that require a new way of thinking. This is an important book when considering the sociological and political dimensions of risk and the impact, on all of us, of major global changes.

There are a number of books that explore aspects of the risk management process and the contexts in which risk is managed. Primarily these focus on the private for-profit sector. Nonetheless, there are many risk issues that are common to both the private and public sectors and these books are therefore worth reading. Examples include: Hopkin, P. (2013) *Holistic Risk Management in Practice*, London: Witherby; Waring, A. and Glendon, A.I. (1998) *Managing Risk: Critical Issues for Survival and Success into the 21st Century*, London: International Thomson Business Press; and Pickford, J. (ed.) (2001) *Mastering Risk, Volume 1: Concepts*, Harlow: Pearson Education. For a book focusing specifically on risk in public service organizations, read Fone, M. and Young, P.C. (2005) *Managing Risks in Public Organizations*, Leicester: Perpetuity Press.

Crisis management: a quick 'go-to' guide

We now know that the public managers who find themselves in a crisis will have to make quick decisions under conditions of uncertainty. In recognition of this we have prepared a 'go-to' guide below through which public managers can quickly identify a relevant text that may help them define the nature of the crisis that they are facing.

Quick prescriptions (for a basic 'how to' in terms of crisis identification and management)

Farazmand, A. (2001) *Handbook of Crisis and Emergency Management*, New York: Dekker; Nudell, M. and Antokol, N. (1988) *The Handbook for Effective Crisis Management*, Lexington: Lexington Books; Regester, M. (1989) *Crisis Management: What to Do when the Unthinkable Happens*, London: Hutchinson; Seymour, M. and Moore, S. (2000) *Effective Crisis Management: Worldwide Principles and Practice*, Continuum: London; Mitroff, I. (2001) *Managing Crises before they Happen*, New York: AMACOM; and Fink, S. (2002) *Crisis Management: Planning for the Inevitable*, Lincoln, NE: iUniverse.

Crisis types (for a more thorough discussion of the term 'crisis' and its various types)

FIASCOS AND INSTITUTIONAL CRISES

Bovens, M. and 't Hart, P. (1996) *Understanding Policy Fiascos*, New Brunswick: Transaction; Dunleavy, P. (1995) 'Policy Disasters: Explaining the UK's Record', *Public Policy and Administration*, 10(2): 52–70; 't Hart, P. and Gray, P. (1998) *Public Policy Disasters in Western Europe*, London: Routledge; Alink, F., Boin, A. and 't Hart, P. (2001) 'Institutional Crises and Reforms in Policy Sectors: The Case of Asylum Policy in Europe', *Journal of European Public Policy*, 8(4): 286–306; Boin, A. and 't Hart, P. (2000) 'Institutional Crises and Reforms in Policy Sectors', in H. Wagenaar (ed.), *Governmental Institutions: Effects, Changes and Normative Foundations*, Boston: Kluwer, pp. 9–32; McConnell, A. (2003) 'Overview: Crisis Management, Influences, Responses and Evaluation', *Parliamentary Affairs*, 56(3): 393–409; Stark, A. (2011) 'The Tradition of Ministerial Responsibility and its Role in the Bureaucratic Management of Crises', *Public Administration*, 89(3): 1148–1163.

NATURAL DISASTERS

Rosenthal, U., Charles, M.T. and 't Hart, P. (eds) (1989) *Coping with Crises: The Management of Disasters, Riots and Terrorism*, Springfield: Charles C. Thomas; Rosenthal, U., Boin, R.A. and Comfort, L.K. (eds) (2001) *Managing Crises: Threats, Dilemmas and Opportunities*, Springfield: Charles C. Thomas; Quarantelli, E.L. (ed.) (1998) *What is a Disaster? Perspectives on the Question*, London: Routledge; and in a follow-up: Perry, R.W. and Quarantelli, E.L. (eds) (2005) *What is a Disaster? New Answers to Old Questions*, Philadelphia: Xlibris; Wisner, B., Blaikie, P., Cannon T. and Davis, I. (2004) *At Risk: Natural Hazards, People's Vulnerability and Disasters*,

London: Routledge; Kapucu, N. and Ozerdem, A. (2012) *Managing Emergencies and Crises*, Boston, MA: Jones & Bartlett.

TRANSBOUNDARY CRISES

Wachtendorf, T. (2009) 'Trans-System Social Ruptures: Exploring Issues of Vulnerability and Resiliency', *Review of Policy Research*, 26: 379–93; Boin, A. (2009) 'The New World of Crises and Crisis Management: Implications for Policymaking and Research', *Review of Policy Research*, 26(4): 367–77; Boin, A. and Rhinard, M. (2008) 'Managing Transboundary Crises: What Role for the European Union?' *International Studies Review*, 10: 1–26. Ansell, C., Boin, A. and Keller, A. (2010) 'Managing Transboundary Crises: Identifying the Building Blocks of an Effective Response System', *Journal of Contingencies and Crisis Management*, 18(4): 195–207.

Chapter 2

Risk and crisis management

Drivers and barriers

LEARNING OBJECTIVES

By the end of this chapter you should:

■ be aware of the justifications for the practice of risk and crisis management in the public sector;

■ have developed an understanding of the drivers and barriers to effective risk and crisis management;

■ be aware of the factors through which crises can be caused; and

■ have developed an understanding of sense-making processes that can identify potential threats as they develop.

KEY POINTS OF THIS CHAPTER

■ Risk and crisis management must be justified as a means of achieving the core business of a public sector organization.

■ Key benefits include enhanced quality management, increased partnership working, better internal coordination, effective implementation and greater efficiencies.

■ A range of external drivers motivate the practice of risk and crisis management, including inquiries, legislation, regulatory principles, audit and inspection regimes, and the expectations of society.

■ Potential barriers to effective risk and crisis management relate to efficiency concerns, organizational values, political constraints and a lack of understanding and training.

- Crises may be caused by human error, technological failure, management systems failure or societal/governmental behaviour. More commonly, a crisis involves a combination of these factors.
- Enhanced sense-making processes can help an organization identify, prevent or moderate crises before they strike.

KEY TERMS

- **Corporate governance** – the way in which an organization is managed. Many countries around the world now have codes or standards for corporate governance, to which publicly listed companies are expected to adhere. These codes and standards have also been adopted by many public service organizations.
- **Enterprise risk management (ERM)** – an integrated approach to the management of all of the risks that the organization faces. This is also referred to as holistic, integrated or enterprise-wide risk management.
- **Responsive regulation** – a model of regulation which promotes guidance and principles rather than legal enforcement. This model was a key factor in the development of the global financial crisis.
- **Sense-making** – identifying problems at an early stage as they begin to manifest into larger threats. Making sense of threats as they emerge requires constant environmental scanning, willingness to think about worst-case scenarios and a capacity to collate and interpret multiple sources of information.
- **Social responsibility** – consideration of the social and environmental consequences of any organizational decision or action. Closely linked to the concept of sustainability.

ADOPTING A SYSTEMATIC APPROACH TO RISK AND CRISES

The largest justification for engaging in processes of risk and crisis management is as self-evident as it is convincing. As more and more of the risks and crises typified in Chapter 1 become prevalent in our public sectors, the need to mitigate threats and prepare properly for catastrophes seems compelling. We have to ask, therefore, why, if this justification is so profound, is it that public organizations still neglect to adopt systematic approaches to risk and crisis management?

One answer to this question relates to the pressures of leadership within busy public organizations, particularly those that do not appear to be risky or crisis prone. Managers who are responsible for our hospitals, schools and public transport systems, for example, must prioritize the efficient and effective delivery of their core services (Stevenson 2013). This is a hard enough task in itself and, as a consequence, a range of issues surrounding risk and crisis management can be deprioritized or even squeezed

39

off organizational agendas completely. What this means is that would-be risk and crisis managers must be able continually to justify their activities by showing how their work complements the core business of any public organization. Yet incentivising risk and crisis management practices in this way is no easy task. One of the largest hurdles can be seen in the simple fact that when risks or crises are prevented effectively, nothing actually happens! There is a lack of a definable output which can be used as evidence of success and this means that risk and crisis managers can struggle to justify their existence (Boin and 't Hart 2003). Consequentially, we provide a number of clear rationales in this chapter which public managers can use to promote risk management practices to organizational decision-makers and colleagues.

A second answer to the question of why some organizations systematically protect against risks and crises and others don't relates to the complexities of the internal and external organizational environment. Just as there are a wide range of threats and opportunities facing public service organizations, multiple environmental influences provide the motivation for, and drive the practices of, risk and crisis management. These drivers are often a combination of what might be described as 'push' and 'pull' factors. Aspects of the external environment, such as the need to comply with health and safety legislation or the need to be seen to be acting in socially responsible ways around climate change, can certainly push organizations into forms of risk management. However, there may be a number of factors within an organization, such as the need to ensure high levels of efficiency or a conservative organizational culture, which can pull public managers away from making changes that privilege risk and crisis preparedness (Stewart 2009). This chapter therefore provides an understanding of the drivers and the barriers that can push and pull the creation of a risk and crisis management agenda in a public body.

A third answer to our opening question is more straightforward. One reason why public sector organizations may not prepare for the worst might simply be that there is a lack of understanding about the way in which crises can be created (and therefore avoided). Failures to understand deeper causes of crises, how they incubate and how they then translate into reality mean that the public manager is left without a road map that can help them take those vital first steps towards increased safety. For this reason, we also include a discussion of the causes of crises in this chapter and a discussion of sense-making processes. These sections provide a blueprint for thinking about how action can be taken to moderate or prevent crises.

JUSTIFYING RISK AND CRISIS MANAGEMENT

In recent years, there has been a growing awareness of the risks arising from failing to act on opportunities to deliver better and more cost-effective public services (NAO 2011) and that a certain amount of risk-taking is inevitable if an organization is to achieve its objectives and improve its performance (OGC 2004). In this context, the management of risk and the preparations for managing a crisis have to be seen as part of everyday good management. There are strong relationships with other management initiatives, such as those relating to quality assurance and enhancement. Furthermore, the increasing use of partnership agreements, both internally and externally (the latter often with private providers), has produced a further driver for addressing risk issues. Clear financial benefits can be achieved and this is one of the most persuasive arguments for senior executives who may be reluctant to invest time and money in risk and crisis management initiatives. Unfortunately, it is the actual experience of a crisis that proves to be the strongest incentive for change in some organizations. Yet directors and managers will still need to be convinced that there is a clear cost–benefit case before committing resources to risk management measures. In preparing such a case, it is important to remember that costs and benefits are not confined to financial measurement and that, equally, the cost of *not* taking a particular course of action must be considered. Let us explore here the rationales that can be used to build a case for risk and crisis management.

Ensuring organizational quality

If risk management is viewed as yet another management 'fad', or as the responsibility of a named individual (such as the 'risk manager'), it is likely to fail, quite possibility to a substantial degree. The management of risk must be accepted as a normal part of everyone's job, from the CEO to the most junior employee in the organization. It therefore needs to be integral to all functions, processes and initiatives within the PSO. One way to ensure that this process takes place is to show how risk management is coterminous with quality assurance. Many employees in a public service organization are likely to be familiar with aspects of quality assurance/enhancement. Even if the organization has not chosen to follow a total quality management (TQM) route, it is possible that it will have sought to achieve 'kite marks' and quality standards that are externally validated and publicly recognizable. Such approaches seek to ensure, whatever the individual, department or organization is seeking to deliver, that it does it 'right first time' and that in doing so it avoids waste and inefficiency. The management of risk can be viewed as an inherent part in the process of managing quality (Toft and Reynolds 1997) because, unless threats to the achievement of the delivery objectives are identified, evaluated and appropriate controls put in place, it is less likely that services can be delivered with the level of quality intended.

Integration across organizations

No organization can operate as a silo in today's complex public sector environment. Any public body that does not have the capacity to build strong partnerships across public, private and voluntary sector borders will certainly struggle to fulfil their mission. This is because today's social problems are themselves complex and need to be

41

addressed through more sophisticated ways of joint working than those that have defined public services in previous eras. The global reach of 'joined-up government' and 'whole of government' initiatives and the increasing respect given to network management as a coordination tool both pay testimony to the fact that partnership working is the order of the day – particularly in local government. An obvious example is in the area of child protection, where those responsible for education, social welfare and health all have to be involved in ensuring the well-being of an individual child, who may be at risk. A second example can be found in the complicated network of actors – both private and public – who come together to build and then supervise large infrastructure projects for public sectors, such as schools and hospitals. One of the largest issues within these complex networks relates to the incongruence that can exist between the different organizational cultures, objectives and attitudes of the respective parties. In this area, however, the practice of risk management can provide a mechanism through which the differences of various partners can be bridged (Jennings 2012). One of the largest examples of this benefit can be seen in the preparations for so-called 'mega-events', such as the Olympic Games (see Box 2.1).

Integration within the organization: enterprise risk management

Whether at the planning stage of a new project or as part of day-to-day strategic and operational management, risks need to be managed in an integrated fashion, encompassing potential threats at each level of the entire organization (Fraser and Simkins 2010). Risk management can therefore be a powerful tool for enhancing synergies within an organizational structure. This is where enterprise risk management (ERM) becomes important because, as Lam (2003) highlights, ERM means that:

- the organization requires to be integrated;
- the risk transfer strategies require to be integrated; and
- risk management requires to be integrated into the business processes of the company.

If we translate these three elements into the public sector environment, we can see that 'integration of the organization' is equally applicable to this sector. Both at the national level and at the local level, the value of operating the organization as an integrated entity is now being recognized. With regard to integrating 'risk transfer strategies', decisions are required to be taken at the highest levels as to the risk 'appetite' of the organization, as this will determine the extent to which it is prepared to retain as opposed to sharing risk, by outsourcing or by insurance. We will deal with this issue in more depth in Chapter 4. However, what we can say here is that the concept of ERM is much more embedded now than it was in 2007 when the first edition of this book was written. One consequence of this is that there is now more of a holistic approach to risk management across public and private sectors. By this we mean that risk management can no longer

BOX 2.1 PARTNERING AROUND THE GAMES: AN OLYMPIAN EFFORT

In preparing for an Olympic Games, host cities need to coordinate a huge range of very different partners with very different objectives. In preparations for the London Olympics, a number of organizations were responsible for ensuring that the games were delivered on time and within budget. At the national government level, the Government Olympics Executive was created to provide strategic direction and accountability to the taxpayer. At the operational level, the London Organizing Committee was created as a private company to take the key implementing decisions. This body was complemented by the London Development Agency, the Mayor's Office, the Olympic Park Legacy Company and the Olympic Delivery Authority, who all had to quickly plug into and work alongside the pertinent central and local government agencies. All of this, moreover, was done under the watchful gaze of the International Olympic Committee. We must also consider the athletes and their organizations in this complexity. The British Olympic and Paralympic Associations, for example, were less concerned with project management issues than they were with the performance of their member athletes. And finally, we cannot forget the massive number of private sector companies in this mix, all seeking to make profit from the many contracts and mass-marketing opportunities that these events bring.

Will Jennings is a risk analyst who has examined the coordination of Olympic Games preparations. His analysis shows that the shift from an insurance approach to an integrated and comprehensive form of risk management in preparation for such 'mega-events' enhances the degree of coordination across partnerships. As more and more organizational objectives and performance measurements are framed in the language of risk, a 'colonizing effect' is said to take place in which the narrative of risk management crosses organizational boundaries affects the perceptions of different actors and effectively brings organizations together around a common understanding of threat and mitigation. From this view, the language of risk can bring organizational strangers together around common purposes.

Source: Rothstein et al. (2006); Jennings and Lodge (2011); Jennings (2012).

be seen as a distinct activity located at the periphery of the organization. It is now, more than ever before, a 'whole-of-organization' or 'organization-wide' competence. And, although 'enterprise' has a corporate feel to it, it is important for public managers to understand that, at its essence, the concept of ERM can be understood in this cross-sectoral manner.

In turn, this means that public sector organizations are generally much more aware of the importance of understanding organizational culture as a means to integrate risk management within an organization. Therefore, they are now more focused on understanding how this culture influences 'appetite' for risk (the extent to which an organization wishes to take risks to ensure returns of some sort) and the relationship between this appetite and management decisions.

An additional benefit of the ERM approach is the ability to provide evidence, through regular and relevant risk reporting, that the organization is taking the issue of risk seriously and that assessment and evaluation of risk is being undertaken in a systematic, comprehensive and coordinated manner. Such reporting provides some degree of assurance to stakeholders that the CEO and senior executives are conducting their responsibilities in line with current expectations of good governance and, in particular, may reassure funding bodies that financial resources are being used efficiently and effectively. A key feature of this approach is the establishment of both a philosophy and a culture of risk management, with the objective of creating a set of organizational goals and expectations that each manager and employee can use to help frame their specific risk management responsibilities and decision-making. This approach is the antithesis to a centralized risk management function, which runs the danger of being viewed as 'the department that does risk management'. Instead, it reinforces the need for risk to be dealt with at its source, by the people closest to it and within the ethos and values set by the organization.

Finally, the integration of risk management into the 'business processes' of the organization needs only the addition of the words 'and services' to make it applicable to a public service organization. The PSO has the objective of delivering a service or services to the public, and the integration of risk management into the daily operations of the departments that provide these services is essential. At the same time, PSOs themselves are supported by a range of business processes, including administration, IT, human resources and finance, which, in turn, need to address their own risk issues if they are to provide the level and quality of support that the PSO needs and expects.

As discussed in Chapter 1, managing risk is not simply about reducing loss, but is also a means of maximizing opportunities and ensuring successful achievement of organizational objectives. In order to achieve efficiency gains and supply innovative services or new modes of service delivery, risk management needs to be integrated with, and supported by, the business processes of the organization. Thus, ERM/ORM requires a structured and disciplined approach that aligns strategy, processes, people, technology and knowledge with the purpose of evaluating and managing the uncertainties the organization faces (DeLoach 2000) and that puts in place policies and processes to deal with such uncertainties. Rather than being viewed as a separate, stand-alone function, risk management is best viewed no differently than sound general management (Toft and Reynolds 1997; Culp 2001). This narrative should be continually emphasized and promoted at all times in every aspect of the PSO.

Enhancing implementation

Every new venture is a trade-off between loss and opportunity and involves competing demands for resources not only within but also between projects. We also know that organizational decision-makers have a tendency to underestimate the challenges of implementation (Hill and Hupe 2009). What seemed like a simple process at the strategic planning table can somehow become something far more tortuous as more actors, interdependencies and resource demands materialize across the life of a project. Adopting a risk management approach, however, enables better decision-making at the strategic level, by providing information about risks that might affect programme implementation. At the project level, risk analysis should be an integral part of the project life cycle, with each stage of the project being broken down into its component parts, and the risks to the successful achievement of each stage assessed and treated (Chapman and Ward 1997). This is not just a matter of safeguarding against an unlikely failure, however; it must instead be understood as a standard way in which reliability and efficiency can be promoted from the bottom up.

The big one: saving money

This is a big argument especially during those periods of austerity when public sectors need to retrench. Risk management can create financial savings in such contexts, particularly with regard to insurance premium costs and claims against the PSO. Insurance companies base the premiums they charge for policy covers such as fire, theft, employee injury or public liability on the experience of the public sector as a whole. These premiums are then adjusted according to the level of risk that the individual PSO presents.

In practice, this means that those organizations with better than average protection against the risks insured (i.e. better risk controls) and/or better than average claims experience (i.e. fewer and less costly claims) compared with similar organizations are likely to be able to negotiate lower premiums and better cover than those with a poorer history. Taking this one step further, the PSO may find that it is able to reduce losses to such an extent that buying insurance cover is no longer necessary or financially sensible. Such losses that do occur can be budgeted for as part of normal operational costs, and absorbed in this way, with insurance being purchased only for what might be described as 'catastrophic' events.

Financial benefits can also accrue from a reduction in actual claims against the organization. These benefits accumulate not only from costs saved in compensation payments but also from the hidden cost of time spent administering such claims. Enhanced street lighting, replacement of broken paving stones and better street cleaning have been shown to protect the public from trips, slips and falls that might result in successful claims for compensation. Similarly, improved staff training and education along with robust supervision results in fewer mistakes being made within professional service providers.

45

ENVIRONMENTAL DRIVERS

The previous section has outlined a range of factors that can incentivize the practices of risk and crisis management within an organization. This section moves the discussion onwards by reviewing a number of drivers that are located in the organizational environment. Inquiries about previous events can certainly act as a spur for action. A second factor relates to the need to comply with legislation. Failure to do so will result in criminal and, in some cases, civil charges being brought. Third, we can see many principles, often created by quasi-governmental or professional institutes, against which the organization and its officers are expected to abide. Finally, pressure from consumer groups and non-governmental organizations (NGOs) may be responsible for changing attitudes towards the management of issues that fall within the general heading of 'social responsibility'. Hence compliance with inquiry recommendations, legal instruments, regulatory principles and social expectations are likely to form key planks in any public audit and inspection regime, and the results will be open to scrutiny by wider stakeholders and the general public. We will deal with each of these aspects in turn.

Learning from previous events

When things are going relatively smoothly, organizations can become complacent about the need for proactive management of risk. Unfortunately, the absence of an extreme and damaging event in the past does not mean that it will fail to happen in the future. Sometimes organizations are simply lucky. However, when that luck runs out, the results can be disastrous. In such circumstances, mistakes in judgement may be made that, in the case of vulnerable children or the elderly for example, can prove fatal. In order to manage such risks, it is essential that lessons are learned from previous events and that recommendations for improved practice are put in place. Inquiry reports often prove the driver for change and improvement in the management of risk and crises in this sense (see Box 2.2). Depending on the gravity of the problems, inquiries can range from independently contracted consultations that tend to focus on managerial issues, to legislative inquiries that seek political explanations, through to full judicial inquiries where issues of corporate manslaughter and criminality could be put on the table. These inquiries will be discussed further in Chapter 7, where we will see that change and learning after a crisis is not always inevitable. However, the smart public manager would do well to search out, and give respect to, the recommendations of inquiries in their field. Failure to view inquiries as an impetus for reform, even if the recommended changes are small-scale, opens up an organization to accusations of blame and culpability when its luck runs out.

BOX 2.2 THE UK FUEL PROTESTS: A CRISIS FORESEEN

The UK fuel crisis began at the Stanlow refinery on the night of 7 September 2000, when approximately 150 farmers and hauliers blockaded the site's exit in protest over the high cost of fuel taxation. The apparent success of the Stanlow blockade encouraged further protests around the UK and by 11 September most of the country's oil refineries were effectively closed. By 13 September, widespread panic buying by motorists meant that 90 per cent of petrol stations – reliant upon a cost-efficient 'just in time' delivery strategy – had run out of fuel. Commuting via public transport had become difficult; fuel rationing was implemented; supermarkets had reported panic buying of groceries; schools began to close; and, according to the government at least, fuel shortages within the NHS meant that lives were at risk.

The fuel protests were begun by groups such as Farmers for Action and the People's Fuel Lobby, who viewed themselves as political 'outsiders' prepared to take direct action. In the run-up to the crisis, these groups had engaged in a number of smaller protests, including a 'go-slow' demonstration in central London during which lorries were driven at walking pace around Parliament Square while a parliamentary debate on fuel duty was taking place in the House of Commons. In July of that year, the Environment, Transport and Regional Affairs Committee published an inquiry report which recorded a 'vigorous campaign against what they [hauliers] perceived as unfair levels of taxation, particularly on fuel and Vehicle Excise Duty, which included attempts to disrupt the flow of traffic in cities and towns, and on motorways' (HC 296: 2000, para. 1). This inquiry, which clearly identified the threat of a potential crisis in the near future, was ignored by the government. This decision to ignore the inquiry, whether intentional or unintentional, would return to haunt the government in September as the stand-off between the protestors and the Treasury brought the country to a standstill.

What the fuel protests show is that public inquiries must always be treated seriously as insights into the potential for the escalation of problems to crisis proportions.

Source: HC 296 (2000); Robinson (2002); Stark (2010).

Compliance with legislation

As society has developed, so too has the extent to which legislation is used to control aspects of our personal and professional lives. The process of industrialization in the nineteenth and twentieth centuries led to increasingly stringent expectations relating to health and safety in the workplace. This had an impact not only on directors and managers, but also on the behaviour of individual workers. For example, while it may be incumbent on management to provide personal protective equipment such as hard hats or fluorescent jackets to workers that need such protection, there is also an obligation on the individual to use the protective equipment or clothing that is made available to him/her. If this is not provided, the organization may be in breach of health and safety legislation, while the worker who chooses not to use such equipment is likely to find that any subsequent claim for injury is reduced because of this contributory negligence.

While it may be easier to see the relevance of such legislation in a manufacturing environment than in an office environment, the principles remain the same. Many PSOs will be involved in 'risky' activities to a greater or lesser degree. Examples can be found in building and roads maintenance, waste collection and disposal, school sports and other activities involving children, such as day trips and group holidays. Even the office environment is not without its risks, with trailing computer and phone cables and problems associated with visual display units being just a few examples. Accountability for the death of an employee or someone in the care of the organization can result in criminal charges being brought against individuals, their line managers and senior executives, depending on the exact nature of legislation relating to corporate manslaughter in the country concerned.

In addition to raising concerns about health and safety, industrialization also increased levels of pollution and, as a result, highlighted the need to control such emissions. From smog-filled air to contaminated rivers and streams, legislative controls were deemed necessary to limit the damage that industrial organizations were doing to the environment and public health. Today, there are additional concerns relating to the dangers inherent in the disposal of nuclear and biological waste, the toxic gases in domestic appliances, asbestos removal and the dumping of plastics and other non-biodegradable substances in landfill sites.

To the list of physical risks associated with health and safety or environmental pollution we can now add a range of less tangible risks that often present themselves in office and other workplace environments. Examples include bullying and harassment, gender or racial discrimination, age discrimination, pensions entitlement and human rights. The latter issue has raised debates over the extent to which employers are entitled to invade the privacy of their employees, for example by monitoring telephone calls or email usage, or dictating dress codes. Many of these employment risks have resulted in employees taking legal action against their employers in special industrial tribunals and courts.

48

A further risk arises from the need to protect sensitive information and ensure that it is used only for the purpose for which the information was originally gathered. This duty has now to be balanced, in many countries, with the demands for 'freedom of information' and a public 'right to know'. Public service organizations that fail in any of these statutory duties risk criminal penalties ranging from fines to imprisonment. In addition, they are likely to suffer reputation damage and increased scrutiny of their activities by government agencies, including their primary financiers.

Compliance with regulation

While the law regulates many aspects of our personal and professional lives, as well as the way in which organizations conduct their business, some dimensions are subject to recommended principles and codes of best practice, which are expected to be followed unless exceptional circumstances dictate otherwise. Critical to the study of risk drivers in the public sector, therefore, are regulatory practices relating to corporate governance and public sector 'morality'.

Influential in the development of many codes of corporate governance has been the report of the UK committee chaired by Sir Adrian Cadbury, *Financial Aspects of Corporate Governance* (1992). Cadbury outlined three fundamental principles of good corporate governance: openness, integrity and accountability. The implication of the report for senior executives lay in the emphasis it placed on their responsibility for ensuring that the necessary internal controls over all the corporate activities were in place and functioning effectively. This significantly raised the profile of risk management in many organizations and acted as a driver in its implementation.

A subsequent report from a committee chaired by Nigel Turnbull in 1999, *Internal Control: Guidance for Directors on the Combined Code*, went on to emphasize the changing nature of risks facing the business enterprise and the role of internal control in managing those risks appropriately rather than trying to eliminate them (Financial Reporting Council 2005). Turnbull recognized that profits were, in part, the reward for risk-taking in business. Without innovation, society cannot hope to progress, but innovation brings with it some degree of risk, which requires to be managed in order to achieve a successful outcome.

This view was echoed in a speech made by the Auditor-General for Australia in September 2005 when he referred to Principle 7 of the Australian Stock Exchange (ASX) *Corporate Council's Principles of Good Corporate Governance and Best Practice Recommendations* (issued in March 2003), which mandates the requirement to establish a sound system of risk oversight and management and internal control by identifying, assessing, monitoring and managing risk. In his opinion, risk management was a cornerstone of good corporate governance, and resulted in better service delivery, more efficient use of resources, better project management, as well as helping to minimize waste, fraud and poor value-for-money decision-making (McPhee 2005).

49

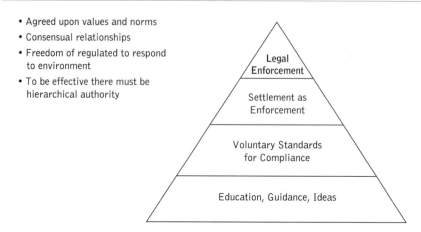

- Agreed upon values and norms
- Consensual relationships
- Freedom of regulated to respond to environment
- To be effective there must be hierarchical authority

Legal Enforcement

Settlement as Enforcement

Voluntary Standards for Compliance

Education, Guidance, Ideas

Figure 2.1 *Responsive regulation pyramid*

Source: Adapted from Parker (2002) and Ayres and Braithwaite (1992).

Over the past two decades, an influential system of corporate governance has also proceeded through what is known as responsive regulation (Ayres and Braithwaite 1992). This system is interesting because it seeks to balance a small amount of legislative authority, usually enforced by a regulatory agency, with a 'light touch' approach that attempts to steer organizations by promoting good practice and principles. Responsive regulation therefore promotes a small number of sticks and a large number of carrots in order to incentivize self-regulation. This is encapsulated in Ayres and Braithwaite's (1992) pyramid. What the pyramid shows is that regulators often seek to create flexible regimes which will trade on goodwill and sound values first and then enforce punitive measures second (see Figure 2.1).

A typical example comes from the United Kingdom in the form of the old Financial Services Authority (FSA), which provided the financial industry with a broad set of principles through which it was expected to regulate itself. A second example, also from the United Kingdom, comes in the form of the Press Complaints Commission, which, prior to the Levenson Inquiry, also sought to regulate with a light touch. It is telling that each of these regulatory models have been entangled in two of the biggest crises that the United Kingdom has faced recently – the global financial crisis and the 'phone hacking' scandal – and both are in the process of being fundamentally reformed so that the respective regulatory agencies have more 'teeth' to punish those who derogate from regulatory principles. In the case of the former, that means punishing investment bankers who are prepared to exploit moral hazard and in the latter, reporters, editors and newspaper owners who ignore ethics in the search to fill column inches.

These changes in regulatory regimes reflect pre-existing research which has shown how responsive regulation will only work effectively if a regulator has the capacity to sanction those who transgress. A comparison between two responsive regulatory regimes in Australia, for example, found that the more effective regulator was the one with a greater capacity to operate at the top ends of the responsive pyramid (legal enforcement) as this promoted a tougher image, which in turn encouraged self-adherence to regulatory principles (Parker 2002). As one study of regulatory governance has noted wryly, 'self-regulation works if, as well as speaking softly, the state carries a big stick' (Bell and Hindmoor 2009: 90). Hence regulators who speak softly can be a driver of risk management practices if the principles they promote are relevant. Regulators who carry the threat of sanctions, however, cannot be ignored.

In the public sector, good governance tends to be encouraged through a range of principles enshrined in various documents, which attempt to instil the public sector with a 'public service ethos' – a morality rooted in a widely held view that public servants should embody the principles of neutrality, integrity and servitude to a public that sits above party political interests (Rhodes et al. 2009). These values are often collated in informal codes of practice and guidance. In the European Union, for example, the public service ethos is enshrined in the *Code of Good Administrative Behaviour*, while in the United Kingdom it is expressed through the Civil Service Code. In Australia, the concepts of accountability, responsibility, transparency, ethics and probity were described by the former Secretary to the Department of the Prime Minister and Cabinet, Dr Peter Shergold, as 'values intrinsic to professional public service' and first articulated in the Public Service Act 1999.

In seeking to enhance confidence in local democracy and promote ethical governance both at committee and at individual levels, local authorities have arguably moved ahead of the private sector (Kirkbride and Letza 2003). A significant development in the United Kingdom was the establishment of an Independent Commission on Good Governance in Public Services, which produced *The Good Governance Standard for Public Services* in 2004 (see Box 2.3). The Standard is intended to complement existing codes and guidance, and is to be used by all organizations and partnerships that work for the public using public money. It comprises six core principles of good governance, each with supporting principles and suggestions about how these might be put into practice. Explicit within this is the need to manage risk.

Compliance with audit and inspection

The remits of internal, external and government-funded auditing agencies have considerably widened in recent decades. Once focused primarily on financial matters, audits have expanded to include non-financial issues and management practices. Indeed, the prevalence of auditing cultures has led to arguments that they are now a defining feature of our societies and our political systems (Power 2008). Within the public sector, the need to ensure accountability and transparency in the utilization of public funds is obviously paramount. However, inspections are now being conducted into the overall

51

BOX 2.3 THE GOOD GOVERNANCE STANDARD FOR PUBLIC SERVICES IN BRITAIN

The Standard produced by the UK's Independent Commission on Good Governance in Public Services in 2004 promotes a risk management system that addresses the full range of organizational activities and responsibilities. It recommends the implementation of an effective risk management system and suggests the following steps be taken by the governing body of a PSO:

- identifying key strategic, operational and financial risks;
- assessing the possible effects that the identified risks could have on the organization;
- agreeing on and implementing appropriate responses to the identified risks (internal control, insure, terminate, modify, accept);
- putting in place a framework of assurance from different sources, to show that risk management processes, including responses, are working effectively;
- reporting publicly on the effectiveness of the risk management system through, for example, an annual statement on internal control, including, where necessary, an action plan to tackle any significant issues; and
- making it clear that the governing body carries ultimate responsibility for the risk management system.

Source: Adapted from Section 4.3 of the Good Governance Standard, Independent Commission on Good Governance in Public Services (2004).

performance of such bodies, particularly, in the case of the United Kingdom, those in the local government sector. Such assessments measure how well councils are delivering services for local people and allocate a rating that can be used to benchmark improvements in services within and between these local government organizations. The extent to which potential risks are identified and managed forms a key element in these assessments. By publishing the outcomes, it is expected that less well-performing authorities will be challenged to match the pace of those that are improving more quickly and achieving better results.

Compliance with the expectations of society

As previously discussed, there is an expectation that a PSO will act in an ethical manner and ensure that it has robust corporate governance processes in place. With a broad range of stakeholders, there is also an expectation that the organization will act in a manner that is socially responsible.

Social responsibility is a term that is used to describe an organization's obligation to be sensitive to the needs of all its stakeholders and is closely linked with the concept of 'sustainability'. This requires consideration of the social and environmental consequences of any decision, in addition to its financial and economic dimensions. In some countries, regulation relating to environmental and social issues has increased, with some of this being driven at a supranational level, for example by the European Commission and the United Nations. Pressure from NGOs and local issue groups on proposals for waste disposal, the installation of mobile phone masts or wind farms, open cut mining, genetically modified crops and nuclear power stations have led to greater consultation and communication with those stakeholders who are most likely to be affected by such developments (see Box 2.4). The message from one of the largest international NGOs, Friends of the Earth, to 'think globally, act locally' also brings a focus on wider issues such as climate change and nanotechnology. The public service organization now needs actively to manage the broader social and environmental risks arising from its activities and to demonstrate to its stakeholders that it is behaving in a socially responsible manner. PSOs that are perceived as not treating their employees well, not being energy efficient, or careless in their attitude towards waste management, may find that this is costly not only in financial terms but also in terms of the esteem in which they are held by the community.

BOX 2.4 NON-GOVERNMENTAL ORGANIZATIONS

A non-governmental organization (NGO) is an organization which is independent of government. This means that the NGO can pursue its own objectives, structure itself freely and create and implement its own policies as long as it remains within legal parameters. The term often refers to lobby or advocacy groups, whose aim it is to influence government policy-making and/or implementation, but NGOs come in a variety of shapes and sizes, including private companies and voluntary bodies. They range from small, local community action groups campaigning against, for example, the location of mobile phone masts, to national trade unions, to large, multinational groups such as Greenpeace and Friends of the Earth. However, NGOs can also be directly involved in the formulation and implementation of risk and crisis management. For example, private consulting companies, such KPMG or Deloitte & Touche routinely provide evidence for policy-makers upon which risk management policies are built, while humanitarian relief organizations, such as the Red Cross or Medicine Beyond Borders, implement disaster management policies on behalf of governments and international actors like the UN.

BARRIERS TO EFFECTIVENESS

In an ideal world, there would be no barriers to effective risk and crisis management. The necessary resources would be in place, organizations would be structured around an awareness of the qualities required to respond to threats, staff would be trained to identify risks and to manage any crises that might occur and politics would not be an issue. Unfortunately, this is simply not the case for most public sector organizations.

The reality is that most PSOs are under considerable budgetary constraints, and competition for funds within the organization is likely to be fierce, especially in light of austerity measures and debt management programmes coming in the aftermath of the global financial crisis. As such, the pursuit of efficiency is an inevitable reality for all PSOs. This can be problematic in at least two ways. The first relates to prevention measures, which often rely upon redundant resources. Redundancy in this regard describes auxiliary resources, which are not optimally efficient, yet may be crucial as a backup in terms of identifying faults and preventing failure. The second, often superfluous, safety check that catches the one in 1000 fault is the most obvious expression of redundancy in action. Nine hundred and ninety nine times, the second safety check is wasteful and inefficient – it is redundant and does nothing. Yet that single 'catch' can be absolutely crucial in preventing disaster. Hence as an organizational value, redundancy has a pedigree amongst certain crisis analysts as a means of preventing accidents and disaster and promoting 'high reliability' (La Porte and Consolini 1991; Sagan 1993). The problem, however, is that being highly reliable often means being highly inefficient, at least in the short term, which is a price that few PSOs can afford to pay. What this means is that there are organizational values within public sector organizations that pull public managers away from effective risk prevention.

We can say the same thing about crisis management. Consider, for example, the need for adaptation in the face of fast-paced threats. Crisis managers must be able to innovate just as quickly as the crises that they are required to control. Yet it has been shown that the pursuit of efficiency within public management processes can mean that the organizational apparatus surrounding the crisis manager will be more intransigent than adaptable (Stark 2014). Hence when public services are made too lean through efficiency savings they cannot always promote the 'rapid customization' that is essential to good crisis management (Ansell et al. 2010). In effect, organizations that pursue efficiency to an extreme will become error prone because of this lack of adaptability (Landau and Chisholm 1995).

Other organizational values, often taken for granted as virtuous, can also cause problems. Highly procedural forms of organization, for example, may be extremely effective at dealing with routine and small-scale emergencies (Moynihan 2009). However, there is a real danger that too much proceduralism can stifle innovative leadership in crises and create deterministic forms of procedure that can mean a lack of adaptive capacity (Stark 2014). Hence crisis management can be viewed in terms of an organizational paradox because 'on one hand, emergency response requires meticulous organization and planning, but on the other hand it is spontaneous. Emergency managers have to innovate, adapt, and improvise because plans, regardless of how well done, seldom fit circumstances' (Waugh Jr and Streib 2006: 132). A lack of organizational 'nimbleness', caused by problematic organizational values, can therefore be a real impediment to effective crisis management.

A further inhibitor is a lack of understanding of the language of risk and of the tools and techniques that can be employed to identify, evaluate and treat threats to the achievement of the organization's objectives. The management of risk needs to be undertaken at the source. In other words, staff at every level in the organization need to be aware of, and trained to deal with, the risks that occur in their everyday employ-ment. This also applies to directors and senior executives in the organization, who are furthermore required to think beyond their immediate areas of expertise and consider broader strategic threats to the whole enterprise. Effective education and training in the management of risk is necessary throughout the organization, as is appropriate prepara-tion and training for the management of crises.

Conflicts may also exist between long-term and short-term political goals, requiring difficult decisions to be made today by elected members and their executive that may impact on the future well-being of the communities they serve, as well as their future careers. Improving air quality, for example, by excluding private cars from sections of a city or implementing congestion charging, may be good for the long-term health of the local community. However, such issues are often highly emotive and politically charged. This can result in compromises being made that fail to achieve the original aims.

UNDERSTANDING THE CAUSES OF CRISES

Two questions are addressed in this section. The answers to each one are designed to provide public managers and policy-makers with an understanding of how to think about the threat of crises from an early stage, so that they can begin meaningfully to prepare for the worst. The first question is why do crises occur? This is obviously a crucial ques-tion that public managers and policy-makers must consider if they are to have any hope of preventing, moderating or coping through catastrophes. Perhaps more significantly, we also want to ask, why does history often repeat itself in terms of the human errors that help cause crises? Addressing this question moves the discussion onwards from an understanding of causation generally to an understanding of what actions can ensure that public managers are part of the solution to crises rather than part of the problem.

At a general level, we can identify two causal pathways through which crises arrive at the doorstep of the public organization. One is a slow-paced pathway where seem-ingly benign issues translate gradually into risks, which in turn incubate and become transformed into crises. These crises tend to be endogenously created, meaning that the risks, vulnerability and subsequent hazards will come from within an organization or policy sector. This is not to say that the crisis events themselves will not be fast-paced or sudden but rather that hindsight will identify a long process of internal incubation within a discrete set of institutions (Turner 1978; Alink et al. 2001). The second causal pathway is typically seen in the natural disaster. In these events, a very sudden trigger event, such as an earthquake or a flood, presents a hazard to a community. This hazard will materialize into a disaster if there is a level of social vulnerability, which will typically have developed over a long historical period. In this sense, causation emerges through the combination of a short, sharp but external threat in conjunction with a lack of social protection within a community, which may be the result of a diffuse range of factors, such as poverty or race relations (Wisner et al. 2004). Focusing more specifically on issues of public management, we can say that crises can occur because of a failure in one or more of the following elements:

- human behaviour (human error);
- technology;
- management systems;
- government behaviour.

Human error

Generally, human beings make decisions and take action based on the best information available to them at the time. That said, human beings are not logical, detached machines. They make misjudgements despite good intentions, get tired and careless, make mistakes due to lack of training, override systems when they are insufficiently supervised, and sometimes deliberately commit sabotage or fraud in the work environment. Almost all crises feature elements of human error.

One strand of research, conducted by political psychologists with an interest in crisis management, is particularly illuminating in this area ('t Hart 2010 offers a good overview of this field). For example, motivational theories of psychology have been applied to examine the specific leadership traits of American presidents. These analyses have led to conclusions that certain styles of leadership can encourage forms of 'policy drift' which, in turn, increase vulnerability to crises and hamper preventative crisis management efforts (Cottam et al. 2004; Preston 2008). Applying such perspectives to public management indicates that certain leadership behaviours can have a bearing on the frequency and nature of the crises that a public sector experiences. A second example from the psychological literature can be found in the concept of 'groupthink', where incentives and pressures for group harmony and cohesion can override a group's ability to assess problems, process information and take decisions. The erroneous rationalizations arising from a groupthink situation can lead to symptoms of invulnerability, overconfidence, excessive optimism, unquestionable belief in morality and a process of self-censure during decision-making. Janis (1982) has argued that groupthink cultures caused some of the worst crises in US history, including the Bay of Pigs episode, Pearl Harbour and the escalation of war in Vietnam. The theory has also been used in explanations of contemporary policy failures, such as the Iran–Contra scandal (see Box 2.5).

56

BOX 2.5 GROUPTHINK AND THE IRAN–CONTRA CRISIS

The Iran–Contra affair is the perfect example of a relatively modern groupthink situation causing a crisis. In the mid 1980s, with the approval of the then President of the United States, Ronald Reagan, Colonel Oliver North and a small group of White House officials and career military men began to sell weapons, through various private middlemen, to Iran in an attempt to gain leverage in the Middle East. The arms sales were conducted so that the US administration could broker the release of American citizens being held hostage in Lebanon. However, the plot thickened as it emerged that this group then used the funds that it received from the selling of the weapons to fund Nicaraguan Contra rebels who were waging a terrorist war against a communist government. Paul 't Hart's account of this affair indicates how this small group of decision-makers fell victim to a groupthink process because:

- The group was isolated from surroundings and public scrutiny.
- Members of the group were either 'in or out' depending on their ideological views.
- Secrecy bound them together and emphasized the need to stick together.
- They believed they were acting heroically in the best interests of the United States.
- Their mandate from the president led to a belief that they were invulnerable to blame.
- Initial successes (two hostages were released) emboldened them and their cause, leading to the Contra funding.

These factors ultimately led the group down a path to conviction that their actions were right despite the political, democratic and ethical issues involved. What the Iran–Contra affair shows is that human error can emerge from a decision-making process where group dynamics are put before more rational, clear-headed evaluations of right and wrong.

Source: 't Hart (1994).

Technological failure

Failures in technology can have physical impacts, as well as an impact on the continuity of services. In safety-critical environments such as nuclear power plants, chemical factories, space shuttles, airplanes and railways, risk controls must be sufficiently robust to enable 'fail-safe' situations. These systems are highly complex and, according to Perrow (1999), will inevitably experience accidents of one kind or another. The questions that society has to ask itself are: do the benefits outweigh the risks, and are there any alternatives? Double and triple backups, manual and automatic overrides, 'dead man's handles' and automatic shutdowns are all examples of features built into safety-critical systems in an attempt to protect life, should one part of the technology fail. However, redundancies such as these are not foolproof. Within many PSOs, failure in power or IT systems can effectively disable the organization and prevent it from being able to conduct its operations. This situation becomes increasingly grave as organizations move towards greater provision of e-services. When technological failure does occur, plans need to be in place that will firstly protect life, and then protect property and ensure continuity of the service.

In large, complex organizations, imbalanced goals and ineffective learning combined with pressure to achieve targets can lead to shortcuts being taken and mistakes being made. Analysis of the Columbia Space Shuttle disaster found that many historical, social, political and technological factors interacted across different organizational technologies to create unsafe conditions, unrealistic expectations and faulty decision-making (Starbuck and Farjoun 2005). Given the complexity of many organizations, where multiple and unexpected interactions of failures are possible, if not inevitable, these can be viewed as 'normal accidents' or 'system accidents' (Perrow 1999: 4).

Management systems failure

There is no doubt that we live in a 'blame' society with the media always eager to attribute responsibility for failure to one or more individuals within an organization. Thus it was the sailor who failed to close the bow doors of the roll-on roll-off ferry who was to blame for it sinking; the pilot who shut off the wrong engine who was to blame for the crash; the social worker who did not insist on entering the house to inspect conditions who was responsible for the child's death. And so on.

Although human error may well have been a component in these scenarios, it was only part of the picture. Where there is human error, even in circumstances where the situation has been caused by deliberate or negligent action on the part of an individual, there are often signs that management systems are inadequate. Lack of robust policies and guidance documents, lack of training and supervision of staff, poor record-keeping, inadequate communication (vertically and horizontally within the organization), cultures of mistrust between employees and management, the swift application of blame for mistakes and an inability to learn from previous incidents all contribute to the

58

emergence of crisis situations. The organizational model for managing safety views human error more as a consequence than a cause (Reason 1997). Errors are perceived as symptoms of latent conditions that exist in the system as a whole, rather than as merely the result of individual human inadequacies. However, we must be careful here. Following on from Chapter 1, we must learn to disentangle political accusations about systemic failure from real systemic problems or smaller-scale (and less blameworthy) issues. When isolated or relatively benign issues are framed as symptoms of a larger systemic mess, opportunistic actors can politicize minor issues into full-scale crises (Brändström and Kuipers 2003). In such situations, deeper causes of crisis can be masked by rhetorical political explanations.

Government behaviour

The attitudes and actions of society in relation to government behaviour may also influence the likelihood of crises occurring. Decisions about spending on infrastructure such as roads and railways (where these are under public control), water treatment, waste disposal, health and social services are balanced against issues of cost and public willingness to pay. While it is likely that a straw poll would find almost everyone in favour of improvements in all of the above public services, it would almost equally find resistance to the idea of increased taxation to pay for such improvements. Government, therefore, has the difficult task of balancing varying and sometimes conflicting demands from citizens for increased levels of service and safety, sometimes at no extra cost. Failure of government or government-funded agencies adequately to maintain critical infrastructure, such as rail tracks, has been a factor in several major rail crashes around the world. The introduction of new computer systems, without adequate testing or training, has resulted in disruption, huge financial costs and public dissatisfaction. These were labelled as 'policy fiascos' in Chapter 1, and are characterized by decisions that are associated with negative impressions of the individuals and agencies responsible (Bovens and 't Hart 1996). Case study 2.1 gives an example. If these impressions exist on a large scale, PSOs will not have the legitimacy and credibility to prevent problems being perceived in a negative light and, inevitably, problematic events will be labelled as crises.

IDENTIFYING CRISES BEFORE THEY ARRIVE

As we noted above, many crises emerge from an incubation period during which problematic decisions or failures to act heighten the potential for a problem to develop. When organizations fail to see the warning signs that are present in this period, or alternatively identify relevant problems but undervalue their significance, there is a much greater likelihood of a crisis occurring (Fink 2002). Every day we are surrounded by hundreds if not thousands of small risky events, on which we have to make decisions

CASE STUDY 2.1 THE AUSTRALIAN LOFT INSULATION DEBACLE

In response to the global financial crisis, the Rudd government introduced a series of policies across 2008 and 2009 that were designed to stimulate the Australian economy. One of these measures was a Home Insulation Program (HIP) through which citizens received a subsidy of $1600 dollars in order to insulate their house. This subsidy effectively meant that most homeowners could have their buildings insulated for free, as claims of $1600 dollars or less were directly paid to the installers. The policy had three objectives: (1) to stimulate the building industry; (2) to increase employment; (3) to promote energy efficiency.

However, the implementation of the HIP can be considered to be an example of a policy fiasco:

- Four inexperienced workers died while installing insulation.
- A large number of fraudulent claims by homeowners and builders ensued.
- Over 200 fire incidents were reported as a consequence of poorly installed insulation, and $1 billion dollars had to be spent implementing a number of remedial policies, including safety checks in homes.
- The scheme was cancelled with less than half of its $2.45-billion budget allocation being spent.
- The Australian Energy Minister, Peter Garrett, was shuffled out of his post.

Numerous investigations into the HIP have identified that:

- The scheme was implemented without adequate consultation with industry experts.
- A risk management review conducted for the Department of Environment as it established the policy had identified nineteen potential risks, including the issue of fraud, waste and inadequate levels of training in the building industry, but it was ignored by ministers.
- The concerns of officials in the Department of Environment about the speed at which the policy was to be rolled out were also ignored by ministers.
- The government had not identified a clear set of qualifications for builders who wished to be registered for the scheme nor had it anticipated the volume of demand for the scheme amongst homeowners.

This is a particularly interesting case study because it shows how a knee-jerk reaction to a larger crisis led to a series of hasty decisions through which a domestic policy fiasco developed. However, in many ways the Rudd government was caught between a rock and a hard place. Without economic stimulus policies like the HIP, they would have almost certainly been criticized for a slow or neglectful response to the global financial crisis. Yet their quick response, conducted as it was with minimal regard to proper risk management, created a completely new and unanticipated crisis domestically.

Source: Auditor-General (2010); Lewis (2012).

and take action. Most of these are of little consequence, or may appear to be, yet when combined with other factors they can take on a more serious dimension. What this means is that the process of 'sense-making' is an absolutely crucial aspect of preventative crisis management, which must be taken seriously by crisis managers (Boin et al. 2005). Fink (2002) takes the view that when an organization is not actually in a state of crisis, it is instead in a pre-crisis mode when, if it is vigilant, it may see something that needs to be addressed quickly, before it escalates and contributes to the creation of an acute crisis. For some crises, there is little or no warning stage. Arguably, the terrorist attacks of 9/11 would be an example of this. Few could imagine the new methods of destruction that would be employed on that day. However, for the majority of serious incidents, subsequent investigations normally reveal a catalogue of small events and failings that, had their significance been fully understood and addressed, might have prevented the incident from occurring. An example here can be seen in the lack of prudential regulation and global oversight of the banking industry prior to the credit crunch of 2007–8. Looking back with hindsight, we can now observe the development of a 'perfect storm' as relaxed mortgage rules spurred on exponential increases in housing market prices, which in turn encouraged investment banks to leverage huge sums of money in order to trade in mortgage-backed securities with little in the way of regulatory scrutiny or credit agency oversight. Ultimately, what emerged, according to one prominent economist, was a system 'designed to encourage risk taking – but it encouraged excessive risk taking. In effect, it paid them [bankers] to gamble. When things turned out well, they walked away with huge bonuses. When things turned out badly – as now – they do not share in the losses' (Stiglitz 2008). Thus, a risk-inducing system was created and was only identified as such after that risk had escaped to paralyse markets and governments around the world.

Therefore, if we seek greater capacity to prevent future crises from occurring, a collective state of vigilance (Fink 2002) or mindfulness (Weick and Sutcliffe 2001) is recommended. And this state must be one which not only makes sense of problems within an organization but also one that is capable of identifying problems as they emerge across the partnership networks which we discussed above. This is no mean feat for any public organization. Most PSOs still remain ill-equipped to horizon scan for threats in their environment and identifying potential threats from within an organization, as we have already stated, requires putting together many small pieces of a larger mosaic of risk. On both counts, sense-making functions are more likely to be seen as a distraction from the achievement of core organizational goals rather than an essential concern. Problems can also arise, however, if systems that are put in place to manage crises create a sense of organizational complacency. In this regard, the 'normalization of risk' (Boin et al. 2005) can mean that public managers adopt a 'we have got this covered' attitude to potential threats and stop looking for, and thinking about, worst-case scenarios. Sensing risks and crisis is a perpetual process which should not stop once a system or policy has been put in place.

In their study of high reliability organizations (HROs) such as aircraft carriers, nuclear power plants and fire-fighting crews, Weick and Sutcliffe (2001) found that these organizations were able to maintain reliable performance because of certain key characteristics. They describe these as:

- Preoccupation with failure – treating any lapse as a symptom that something is wrong with the system, encouraging reporting of errors, learning lessons from near misses and being wary of complacency.
- Reluctance to simplify interpretations – knowing that the world is complex, unstable and unpredictable, they encourage individuals to look beyond their own boundaries and to be sceptical of received wisdom.
- Sensitivity to operations – scrutinizing normal operations in order to reveal deficiencies in supervision, safety procedures and training, hazard identification, etc. and encouraging continuous adjustments that will prevent errors from accumulating and enlarging, encouraging people to speak out about their concerns.
- Commitment to resilience – developing capabilities not only to detect problems but also to be able to continue working when things go wrong.
- Deference to expertise – decisions are delegated to those on the front-line and with the most expertise (not necessarily the most experience) in that field.

(Adapted from Weick and Sutcliffe 2001: 10–17)

All organizations, whether they are HROs or PSOs, develop their own cultural beliefs about the world in which they operate. They create rules, regulations and procedures based on a set of expectations, which may or may not be met. When unexpected events occur, they may be so small that they are hardly noticed, or their potential for damage may not be fully realized. A recurring source of misperception lies in the temptation to define an unexpected event as unproblematic in order to preserve the original expectation (Weick and Sutcliffe 2001: 49), such as defining a water contamination episode as a unique 'one-off' set of circumstances rather than symptomatic of an underlying vulnerability in the capacity to produce safe drinking water.

Key factors in any sense-making process are the ability to learn from what has happened in the immediate past, listen to worst-case predictions and listen to a range of voices in the organizations that will be affected in a crisis. In 2010, the Australian

Meteorology Bureau predicted that a La Niña weather pattern in the Indian Ocean would result in high weather pressure. If this was coupled with a large monsoonal rainfall, it would create a high risk of flooding throughout Australia. Between July and December of that year Australia experienced its wettest period on record and as a consequence many parts of the country, particularly in the state of Queensland, suffered flooding throughout 2010. These events, however, were a minor prelude to the major flash flooding that occurred between December 2010 and January 2011 across Queensland, in which the scale and severity far exceeded the earlier flood events. A total of thirty-eight people were killed, over 13,000 households were completely flooded and the cost of reconstruction was counted in billions of dollars

Amidst this tragedy were a few success stories relating to sense-making and crisis preparation. In the rural region of Banana Shire, located in the hinterlands of north Queensland, residents who had suffered from flooding in the months prior to the 'big one' had lobbied their local government for increased crisis management measures in anticipation of future floods. Sensing the risk, and keen to respond to local electorate concerns, the local council put in place a number of devolved crisis management units within isolated communities in preparation for any future event. When the floods returned, these localized units managed to coordinate local evacuations and other emergency response measures effectively, leading to calls from the official inquiry for their model to be replicated across the state (Stark and Taylor 2014). This instance of sense-making, which proceeded through a local authority willing to listen to its public, stands in stark contrast to other stories of local government performance pre-flood, which were all too often characterized by neglect of crisis management measures and a lack of awareness of the growing threat caused by the monsoonal rainfall. What this case shows is that participatory forms of governance, which allow citizens to air concerns and voice grievances about the risks they face, can perform a crucial role in horizon scanning, sense-making and crisis management preparation (Stark and Taylor 2014).

CONCLUSION

The pressures on organizations to address issues of risk and crisis management are increasing. Such pressures emanate partly from the internal operations of the organization and the need to maximize efficiency and quality in service delivery, and partly because of the requirement to comply with government and the expectations of citizens, insurers and others. Compliance, on its own, is not enough if an organization is to address the broad range of risks it faces as it attempts to achieve its corporate objectives and fulfil its role in the community. A belief in the wider benefits to be gained from attempting to manage risk in a holistic, enterprise-wide manner, and the development of plans to deal with a crisis situation, is now gaining ground. Although the impetus for addressing risk issues in many organizations has come through the adoption of codes of corporate governance, there is now a greater awareness that governance has to be balanced with performance if the enterprise is to be successful. Awareness and management of risk are essential elements in achieving the desired performance outputs.

When crises occur, it is usually due to a combination of factors relating to human, technological, management and governmental interactions. While crises always have the capacity to come as 'bolts from the blue', we do have some capacity to identify potential crises as they incubate. Sensitive organizations, with the capacity to collate and assess a range of data about threats, will be able to see some (although not all) crises coming before they wreak havoc. Later in this book, we will examine how organizations can better prepare themselves to deal with crises in other ways (Chapter 5), and learn lessons from such events (Chapter 7). However, in the following chapter, we will start to explore some of the techniques that can be applied to identify and assess risks, and consider issues of public perception and willingness to tolerate situations that bring both societal benefits and pose potential threats.

EXERCISE 2.1 LEARNING LESSONS FROM A CRISIS

Choose an example of a crisis situation within a public service organization and consider the following issues:

1. What factors contributed to the development of the crisis?
2. Could action have been taken to: a) identify the crisis as it emerged; b) deal with the crisis while it was happening?
3. What damage or loss resulted?
4. What lessons were learned?

DISCUSSION QUESTIONS

1. Based on your own experience in a public service organization, or on your general knowledge of this sector, what do you believe is the most powerful justification for risk and crisis management, and why?
2. Can a private sector approach such as enterprise risk management be successfully transferred to a public service organization? Give reasons.
3. What are the key pieces of legislation that are driving risk and crisis management in your organization?
4. How would you scan the horizon for potential crises? Would you use existing organizational tools or create unique processes to perform 'sense-making' functions?

REFERENCES

Alink, F., Boin, A. and 't Hart, P. (2001) 'Institutional Crises and Reforms in Policy Sectors: The Case of Asylum Policy in Europe', *Journal of European Public Policy*, 8: 71–91.

Ansell, C., Boin, A. and Keller, A. (2010) 'Managing Transboundary Crises: Identifying the Building Blocks of an Effective Response System', *Journal of Contingencies and Crisis Management*, 18(4): 195–207.

Auditor-General (2010) *Home Insulation Program*, Audit Report no. 12 2010–11. Canberra: Australian National Audit Office.

Ayres, I. and Braithwaite, J. (1992) *Responsive Regulation: Transcending the Deregulation Debate*, New York: Oxford University Press.

Bell, S. and Hindmoor, A. (2009) *Rethinking Governance: The Centrality of the State in Modern Society*, Melbourne: Cambridge University Press.

Boin, A., 't Hart, P., Stern, E. and Sundelius, B. (2005) *The Politics of Crisis Management: Understanding Public Leadership under Pressure*, London: Cambridge University Press.

Boin, A. and 't Hart, P. (2003) 'Public Leadership in Times of Crisis: Mission Impossible?' *Public Administration Review*, 63: 544–53.

Bovens M. and 't Hart, P. (1996) *Understanding Policy Fiascos*, Edison, NJ: Transaction Publishers.

Brändström, A. and Kuipers, S. (2003) 'From "Normal Incidents" to Political Crises: Understanding the Selective Politicization of Policy Failures', *Government and Opposition*, 38(3): 279–305.

Chapman, C. and Ward, S. (1997) *Project Risk Management: Processes, Techniques and Insights*, Chichester: John Wiley & Sons.

Cottam, M.B., Dieter-Uhler, E., Mastors, E. and Preston, T. (2004) *Introduction to Political Psychology*, Mahwah, NJ: Lawrence Erlbaum Associates.

Culp, C.L. (2001) *The Risk Management Process: Business Strategy and Tactics*, New York: John Wiley & Sons.

DeLoach, J.W. (2000) *Enterprise-Wide Risk Management*, London: Financial Times, Prentice Hall.

Financial Reporting Council (2005) *Internal Control: Revised Guidance for Directors on the Combined Code*, London: Financial Reporting Council.

Fink, S. (2002) *Crisis Management: Planning for the Inevitable*, Lincoln, NE: iUniverse.

Fraser, J. and Simkins, B.J. (eds) (2010) *Enterprise Risk Management: Today's Leading Research and Best Practices for Tomorrow's Executives*, Hoboken, NJ: John Wiley & Sons.

't Hart, P. (1994) *Groupthink in Government: A Study of Small Groups and Policy Failure*, Baltimore, MD: Johns Hopkins Press.

't Hart, P. (2010) 'Political Psychology', in D. Marsh and G. Stoker (eds), *Theory and Methods in Political Science*, 3rd edition, Basingstoke: Palgrave.

HC 296 (2000) *The Road Haulage Industry, Fifteenth Report of the Environment, Transport and Regional Affairs Committee*, Session 1999–2000, London: Stationery Office.

Hill, M. and Hupe, P. (2009) *Implementing Public Policy*, Thousand Oaks, CA: Sage.

Independent Commission on Good Governance in Public Services (2004) *The Good Governance Standard for Public Services*, London: OPM and CIPFA.

Janis, I . (1982). *Group-Think*, Boston: Little Brown.

Jennings, W. (2012) 'Mega-Events and Risk Colonisation: Risk Management and the Olympics', Centre for Analysis of Risk and Regulation, Discussion Paper 71.

Jennings, W. and Lodge, M. (2011) 'Governing Mega-Events: Tools of Security Risk Management for the London 2012 Olympic Games and FIFA 2006 World Cup in Germany', *Government and Opposition*, 46(2): 192–222.

Kirkbride, J. and Letza, S. (2003) 'Corporate Governance and Gatekeeper Liability: The Lessons from Public Authorities', *Corporate Governance*, 11(3): 262–71.

La Porte, T.R. and Consolini P.M. (1991). 'Working in Practice, But Not in Theory: Theoretical Challenges of High Reliability Organizations', *Journal of Public Administration Research and Theory*, 1: 19–47.

Lam, J. (2003) *Enterprise Risk Management: From Incentives to Controls*, Hoboken, NJ: John Wiley.

Landau, M. and Chisholm, D. (1995). 'The Arrogance of Optimism: Notes on Failure-Avoidance Management', *Journal of Contingencies and Crisis Management*, 4: 67–80.

Lewis, C. (2012) 'A Recent Scandal: The Home Insulation Program', in K. Dowding, and C. Lewis (eds), *Ministerial Careers and Accountability in the Australian Government*, Canberra: ANU E Press.

McPhee, I. (2005) Risk and Risk Management in the Public Sector, a Speech to the Public Sector Governance and Risk Forum, Australian Institute of Company Directors in conjunction with the Institute of Internal Auditors Australia. Available at: <http://www.anao.gov.au/~/media/Uploads/Documents/risk_and_risk_management_in_the_public_sector.pdf> (accessed 3 June 2014).

Moynihan, D.P. (2009). 'The Network Governance of Crisis Response: Case Studies of Incident Command Systems', *Journal of Public Administration Research and Theory*, 19(4): 895–915.

National Audit Office [NAO] (2011) *Managing Risks in Government*. Available at: <http://www.nao.org.uk/wpcontent/uploads/2011/06/managing_risks_in_government.pdf> (accessed 18 May 2014).

Office of Government Commerce [OGC] (2004) *Management of Risk: Guidance for Practitioners*, London: HMSO.

Parker, C. (2002) 'Regulating Self-Regulation: The ACCC, ASIC, Competition Policy and Corporate Regulation', in S. Bell (ed.), *Economic Governance and Institutional Dynamics*, Melbourne: Oxford University Press.

Power, M. (2008) *Organized Uncertainty: Designing a World of Risk Management*, Oxford: Oxford University Press.

Preston, T. (2008) 'Weathering the Politics of Responsibility and Blame: The Bush Administration and its Response to Hurricane Katrina', in Boin, A., A. McConnell and P. 't Hart (eds), *Governing after Crises: The Politics of Investigation, Accountability and Learning*, Cambridge: Cambridge University Press

Rhodes, R.A.W, Wanna, J. and Weller, P. (2009) *Comparing Westminster*, Oxford: Oxford University Press.

Perrow, C. (1999) *Normal Accidents: Living with High-Risk Technologies*, Princeton, NJ: Princeton University Press.

Reason, J. (1997) *Managing the Risks of Organizational Accidents*, Aldershot: Ashgate.

Robinson, N. (2002) 'The Politics of the Fuel Protests: Towards a Multi-Dimensional Explanation', *Political Quarterly*, 73(1): 58–66.

Rothstein, H., Huber, M. and Gaskell, G. (2006) 'A Theory of Risk Colonization: The Spiralling Regulatory Logics of Societal and Institutional Risk', *Economy and Society*, 35 (1): 91–112.

Sagan, S.D. (1993) *The Limits of Safety: Organizations, Accidents and Nuclear Weapons*, Princeton, NJ: Princeton University Press.

Starbuck, W.H. and Farjoun, M. (2005) *Organization at the Limit: Lessons from the Columbia Disaster*, Malden: Blackwell Publishing.

Stark, A. (2010) 'A New Perspective on Constituency Representation: British Parliamentarians and the "Management" of Crises', *Journal of Legislative Studies*, 16(4): 495–514.

Stark, A. (2014) 'Bureaucratic Values and Resilience: An Exploration of Crisis Management Adaptation', *Public Administration*, 92(3): 692–706.

Stark, A. and Taylor, M. (2014) 'Citizen Participation, Community Resilience and Crisis-Management Policy', *Journal of Australian Political Science*, 49(2): 300–315.

Stevenson, A. (2013) *The Public Sector: Managing the Unmanageable*, London: Kogan Page.

Stewart, J. (2009) *Public Policy Values*, Basingstoke: Palgrave Macmillan.

Toft, B. and Reynolds S. (1997) *Learning from Disasters: A Management Approach*, 2nd edition, Leicester: Perpetuity Press.

Turner, B.A. (1978) *Man-Made Disasters*, London: Wykeham.

Waugh Jr, W.L. and Streib, G. (2006) 'Collaboration and Leadership for Effective Emergency Management', *Public Administration Review*, 66: 131–40.

Weick, K.E. and Sutcliffe, K.M. (2001) *Managing the Unexpected: Assuring High Performance in an Age of Complexity*, San Francisco: Jossey-Bass.

Wisner, B., Blaikie, P., Cannon T. and Davis, I. (2004) *At Risk: Natural Hazards, People's Vulnerability and Disasters*, London: Routledge.

FURTHER READING

Fone, M. and Young, P.C. (2005) *Managing Risks in Public Organizations,* Leicester: Perpetuity Press.

For an in-depth analysis of public sector risk, this book is an essential read. The authors explore conceptual issues relating to risk, uncertainty and the management of public risk, before proposing an organizational framework that enables the alignment of risk management with the organization's goals and objectives. Written for both academics and practitioners, the book also provides an insight into the political, economic, legal and other environments in which public sector organizations operate, and gives practical guidance on key risk management issues.

Bovaird, T. and Löffler, E. (eds) (2003) *Public Management and Governance,* Abingdon: Routledge.

This edited book covers a range of topics relating to the management and performance of public service organizations. Part III of the book focuses on governance as an emerging trend in the public sector and includes chapters on ethics and standards of conduct.

67

Toft, B. and Reynolds, S. (2005) *Learning from Disasters: A Management Approach*, 3rd edition, Leicester: Perpetuity Press.

First published in 1999 and now in its third edition, this book demonstrates how organizations can learn from mistakes and failures. Disasters are examined as systems failures and the authors show how a failure of hindsight, i.e. an inability to learn from one's own and from others' experience, can lead to catastrophic situations. Well-illustrated with numerous case studies, this is an essential read for any student of risk or crisis management.

Chapter 3

Assessing, evaluating and communicating risks

LEARNING OBJECTIVES

By the end of this chapter you should:

- be aware of a range of techniques for identifying potential sources of risk;
- understand the difference between risk identification and risk evaluation;
- appreciate the significance of subjective risk assessment (risk perception);
- be aware of the debates surrounding acceptable levels of safety; and
- understand the role of risk communication in the assessment of risk.

KEY POINTS OF THIS CHAPTER

- Assessing risks involves both the identification and the evaluation of potential threats.
- A range of techniques, both quantitative and qualitative, can be used to identify risks. These include brainstorming, historical data analysis and physical inspections.
- Risk evaluation requires an assessment of both the likelihood and the impact of a risky occurrence. This can be displayed on a risk matrix.
- Individuals filter the information they receive before coming to a judgement on risk. Decisions on acceptability of risk involve values as well as facts.
- Citizens are reluctant to accept information from sources that are deemed to have vested political and/or economic interests.
- Risk communication strategies should value different areas of expertise and experience.
- The media plays a major role in influencing public perceptions of risk.

KEY TERMS

■ **Acceptable risk** – the acceptability of risk depends on which kinds of risks and which group of people are being considered. As there is no single conception of risk, there is no way to get everyone to accept 'it' (Douglas and Wildavsky 1982: 4).

■ **Risk communication** – communication intended to supply laypeople with the information they need to make informed, independent judgements about risks to health, safety and the environment (Morgan et al. 2002: 4). This also denotes the process of debate between all stakeholders on a risk issue.

■ **Risk evaluation** – the process of comparing the level of risk (the chance of something happening that will have an impact on objectives) against risk criteria (the terms of reference by which the significance of risk is assessed, including associated costs and benefits, legal and statutory requirements, socio-economic and environmental aspects, the concerns of stakeholders, priorities, etc.). (Adapted from AS/NZS 4360:2004.)

■ **Risk identification** – the process of determining what, where, when, why and how something could happen.

■ **Risk perception** – the way in which an individual or group views a risk. This is influenced not only by objective facts but also by values and beliefs.

■ **Tolerable risk** – to tolerate a risk is not necessarily to accept it, instead it reflects a willingness to offset the costs with the benefits.

■ **Risk culture** – the values, beliefs, knowledge and understanding of risk that is shared by a group of people with a common purpose, such as employees or groups within an organization (IRM 2012).

THE CHANGING FOCUS ON RISK ASSESSMENT

The prerequisite for managing risk is an understanding of the organization, its purpose, processes, culture and the context in which it operates (Hutter and Power 2005). It is within this context that all decisions regarding the assessment and treatment of risk will be made. The assessment of risk is itself a two-part process, encompassing elements of identification and evaluation. A range of techniques may be used to provide a comprehensive and systematic approach to assessing risks. Some have been drawn from engineering and scientific disciplines, others from the business management and decision science domains. This is reflected in Strydom's (2002) view that the principal disciplines from which risk research or risk analysis originally grew were:

1. A combination of systems and planning theory arising out of military and space research, including knowledge of systems failures, probabilities of risk and extent of loss.

2. A variety of business management, planning, decision-making and game theories, plus cost-benefit analysis, where choice between alternatives is calculated in monetary terms.
3. A descriptive theory of decision-making behaviour under conditions of risk.

When the focus of risk assessment moves from risks with a single source (such as the release of toxic chemicals from an industrial plant with largely local consequences), to multiple sources (such as carbon dioxide emissions that may have a global impact), the need for interdisciplinary and integrated approaches grows (Renn 2008). Rayner (1992) describes this change as a move from conventional risk management, which is largely contained within disciplinary 'silos', to risk management that is more holistic and integrated in its approach. This approach was described in Chapter 2 as one of 'enterprise risk management'.

However, no matter how detailed and factually accurate a risk assessment might appear to be, judgements on the acceptability and tolerability of individual threats will be strongly influenced by human factors and the culture of the organization. Moreover, industrial and societal developments mean that risks are constantly changing. Eliminating one source of danger may introduce another. Douglas (1985) gives the example of asbestos, which was hailed as a great discovery and used for the prevention of fire damage, only for it to be found – many years later – to be a source of lung disease when fibres are ingested. Similarly, lead pipes enabled the steady supply of water to domestic premises, until they had to be replaced when the dangers of lead poisoning became apparent. Such examples have had a major impact on public service organizations, which have had to replace potential sources of danger, often at considerable cost, both in terms of disruption and finance. As the risk environment has changed so too have public concerns and debates about risk issues (see Box 3.1).

How risks are perceived by individuals and social groups and the factors that influence such perceptions have been the subject of much research in the fields of psychology and sociology (Slovic 2010). Why does the public fear certain types of low probability risk, yet apparently tolerate others that provide a greater likelihood of injury and loss? To address this question we need to understand not only the factors that influence individual risk perception, but also the ways in which information about risk is communicated to, and discussed with, the public.

RISK IDENTIFICATION

The identification of potential risks is the first stage of the risk assessment process. This requires a systematic approach, involving techniques that may be largely quantitative or qualitative, or that contain elements of both. The importance of the risk identification stage cannot be underestimated. Fink (1986) noted that when the early warning signs of potential threats are ignored or misinterpreted a crisis may result.

71

BOX 3.1 CHANGING PUBLIC DEBATES SURROUNDING RISK

The role of the public in debates on risk has expanded since the early days of nuclear power. Strydom (2002) views this development as having taken place over four stages:

1. *Nuclear energy, safety research and risk assessment debate* – debate about risk relating to the civil nuclear power industry became politicized in the 1960s and 1970s, and broadened into a wider public risk discourse; risk research was motivated by economic and political concerns and there was a shift of focus from the probability of objectively calculable risk to the social acceptability of risks.

2. *Nuclear and environmental opposition and social acceptability of risk* – new concerns about global environmental problems became more prominent than issues of nuclear power, although the latter was still a concern; debates in the 1970s drew attention to the difference between data produced by experts and the meaning given to such data by individuals and social groups; emergence of risk comparisons raised the question of the acceptability of risk.

3. *Public concern and the problem of risk perception* – confidence and trust in those making technical decisions was low; public perceived connection between economic interests and scientific, technological development and implementation; the supposition that the public was either ignorant or irrational led risk experts to focus on ways in which they could stimulate learning and bring the public round to accepting given risks through risk communication, although this tended to be top-down rather than a constructive debate.

4. *Full-scale public risk discourse* – a series of major incidents in the 1970s and 1980s (Seveso, Three Mile Island, Bhopal, Chernobyl, etc.) heightened public concern and led to a fully developed public risk discourse; the role of the media came under scrutiny; a focus on new problems relating to the global environment and sustainability brought the focus back to old issues and a recontextualizing of the nuclear technology threat.

In summary, the discourse changed from one based mainly on expert risk calculation and assessment to allow more open and wide-ranging participation in the debate by individuals and social groups.

Source: Adapted from Strydom (2002: 13–34).

Early detection of such signals is pivotal if action is to be taken in time to reduce either the likelihood or the magnitude of the threat, and preferably both (Hensgen et al. 2003). The difficulty lies in the weakness of many of these signals and the ambiguity surrounding them. Indeed, Hensgen et al. (2003) point out that, initially, signals are always ambiguous, for if all things were certain, there would be no need for signalling. In hindsight, certain signals may appear to be clear, but at the time, these could have been lost in the surrounding 'noise' of competing signals and therefore not attracting the attention they deserved at the time it was most needed. It is only through the optimal processing of signals and consequent action being taken that risks can be managed and crises avoided, or reduced in their effect.

A range of techniques can be brought to the systematic identification of both possible opportunities and the potential risk factors associated with them. These techniques include individual and group activities, desk-based exercises, physical inspections and computer modelling. No single method can provide a comprehensive perspective and therefore several may be used together in order to provide a more complete picture. A number of these techniques are described below.

Brainstorming

Many organizations utilize 'brainstorming' workshops as a means of encouraging creative thinking. Such sessions can be used by public service organizations to help identify opportunities for development, new strategies for delivery and other changes that might be necessary to ensure the continuing growth and success of the organization. At the same time, the brainstorming technique generates the opportunity to explore potential threats, both large and small, that might prevent the PSO from achieving a particular objective. For example, brainstorming can be used in an attempt to identify threats at the strategic level of the organization, such as changes in legislation or client expectations, major fraud or inadequate pension funds. It can also be used to explore threats at the operational level involving, for example, the effective functioning of individual departments such as the salaries section of a finance office, or a key service such as the entire social work provision of a local government authority. A brainstorming exercise will generate random lists of potential threats, which can then be grouped into categories of risk and used as the basis for further exploration and evaluation.

Questionnaires and surveys

Questionnaires and surveys can be used to gather information from various individuals and parts of the organization about current performance and performance improvement. Additionally, these methods can assist in the identification of factors that have led, or may lead, to loss-producing situations, and record how these are presently being treated. The results may allow for comparisons to be made between departments or locations, and indicate areas requiring further investigation. Questionnaires are also used to explore the attitudes of employees to the risks that are present in their working environment. This information can then be compared with data on the actual losses or accidents that have been experienced. Any discrepancy between the perceived experience and the actual data can then be explored further and may indicate that additional training and/or more effective communication is necessary.

Historical data analysis

Historical data in the form of accident records, loss histories and insurance claims can be useful in highlighting current areas of weakness and trends over time. The value of such information is, of course, dependent on its completeness and accuracy and it is worth remembering that past trends are not necessarily good indicators of experience in the future. Such analysis should therefore be tempered by considering the current and likely future changes that may impact on these historical trends. For example, changing demographics in the workforce, including gender balance, ethnic or age profiles, may be significant. Likewise, the organization's policies and procedures may have changed, with certain practices having been abandoned or radically altered, with a concomitant effect on the threats posed. An example might be the reduction in liability claims arising from school trips, where a reluctance on the part of schools or education departments to expose both students and staff to the risk of injury and/or claims of negligence, has resulted in fewer trips actually taking place than in the past.

Physical inspections

Physical inspections are an essential part of the assessment of fire, health and safety risks. Simply walking through an organization's premises will identify situations and materials that could cause a hazard. Typical office risks include trailing computer and phone cables, high-level storage, poor or harsh lighting and blocked windows and doors (particularly hazardous when these are the main or fire exit doors). Less obvious may be the threat posed by locating information technology hubs or essential documents on the ground floor of a building that could be affected by flood. By moving critical infrastructure and storing documents on a higher floor, the risk can be reduced to a more acceptable level. Likewise, having a systematic approach to the backup and storage of vital data will minimize disruption should IT systems fail.

Flow charts

More quantitative techniques are found in the risk engineering and safety functions of organizations, where flow charts are used to explore the 'flow' of liquids, solids and production processes. This technique can also be used for the routine flows of money, people and information that a public service organization will experience on a daily basis. For example, a social welfare office will have clients arriving throughout the day;

may be distributing food, finance or other materials needed for daily living; and may also be receiving cash for loan repayments or housing rental charges. By charting the flow in the form of a diagram, areas of duplication and potential bottlenecks may be identified. Such an approach will aid the identification of critical areas that require attention if delivery of the service is to continue flowing smoothly. A quantitative element can be added to such charts by estimating how likely a failure is to occur at each of the key points of the flow, and the impact that this might have. Specialist software allows such data to be modelled and makes it possible to test the impact of proposed changes before they are implemented.

Risk registers

Once identified, risks may be classified into categories or types of threat. Entering these on a risk register allows a number of related issues to be addressed. Issues include the 'ownership' of the risk, current preventative measures in place to treat it and recommended action for the future. The register can also be used to note when actions have been undertaken and by whom. There must be sufficient data to make collating the information worthwhile, but each organization will need to decide its own content requirements for each entry (OGC 2002).

RISK EVALUATION

Lists of potential threats are of little value in isolation and need to be supplemented by an estimation of the likelihood (probability) of their occurrence (Gupta 2013). This estimation can be expressed in a number of different ways, e.g. as an occurrence over time (once every ten years) or as a statistical probability (one in a million chance). In turn, these estimates can be grouped and expressed on a grading scale as 'high', 'medium' or 'low' risk, or ranked from one to five, where one represents 'almost certain to occur' while five may be an 'extremely rare occurrence'. Although effort is made to ensure that estimates are accurate and based on sound, available and objective information, risk evaluation – by its very nature – involves a subjective component, where even small variations in perceptions can produce large variations in probability rankings (Fischhoff 2012). Decisions on where to rank risks on a grading scale will rest with the organization itself, and be dependent on its risk appetite. Organizations with little appetite for risk-taking are likely to set the criteria for a 'high' probability risk at a lower level than a more risk-taking organization. An example of descriptions used to assess the likelihood of risk is shown in Table 3.1.

Assessing risks in terms of likelihood is important but is only part of the overall risk evaluation process. Risks categorized as low likelihood, for example, may differ considerably in terms of their potential impact on the organization. Therefore an evaluation of the impact or magnitude of damage associated with each type of risk also needs

75

Table 3.1 *Describing the likelihood of risk*

Factor	Score	Description
Almost Certain	5	Almost 100% chance of occurrence; experienced once a year or more often
Very Likely	4	More than 75% chance of occurrence; has occurred in recent years; circumstances frequently encountered, i.e. daily/weekly/monthly
Likely	3	40–74% chance of occurrence; expected to occur in next 1–2 years; circumstances occasionally encountered, i.e. once/twice a year
Unlikely	2	10–39% chance of occurrence; has not occurred in recent past but may occur once every 5+ years
Rare	1	Less than 10% chance of occurrence; may never happen or may occur only under exceptional circumstances

to be made. A rating scale is developed that reflects the organization's view of the magnitude of risk, from the insignificant to the catastrophic. Some scales will include specific financial levels of loss within each category. An example is given in Table 3.2.

The scores for both likelihood and magnitude can be combined (multiplied) and displayed on a risk matrix. These matrices generally show levels of probability on the vertical axis and levels of severity on the horizontal axis. As can be seen in Table 3.3, a further evaluation of the 'overall' level of risk can be made by allocating descriptions of 'low', 'medium' and 'high' to the combined scores. This indicates how serious the organization considers the threat to be, and the urgency with which action should be undertaken. Such an evaluation is not based solely on the numerical value in a cell of the matrix, but takes other factors into account.

For example, in Table 3.3, both the top left and bottom right scores are '5'. The score in the top left cell represents an event that is almost certain to occur on a daily basis, but is considered insignificant in its impact, and has therefore been evaluated as 'low'. On the other hand, a score of '5' in the bottom right of the matrix represents a rare event with potentially catastrophic results, and has been rated as 'high'. The latter provides a signal that action either to prevent a catastrophe or reduce its impact should be taken at the earliest opportunity. Applying the colours of a traffic light to such a matrix emphasizes the key areas requiring attention. Thus, threats falling within 'green' (low-risk) boxes may require less attention than those in the 'amber' (medium-risk) and 'red' (high-risk) zones.

In identifying and evaluating the range of threats to which the public service organization might be exposed, there is a danger that these may be viewed as isolated or independent of one another. While statistical procedures seek a numerical value (based on a combination of likelihood and impact) for each individual threat, the reality is that

Table 3.2 *Describing the magnitude of risk*

Magnitude	Score	Description
Catastrophic	5	The consequences would threaten the survival of the project or service as well as the organization itself. The risk might cause significant problems for service recipients, paid and voluntary staff, other stakeholders (e.g. financiers, elected officials) and perhaps for the general public. The organization would face a significant loss of revenue.
Major	4	The consequences would threaten the ability of the organization to continue the project or service. The organization is likely to face a loss of revenue and the event/circumstances would require attention by senior management.
Moderate	3	The consequences may not threaten the organization's survival, but would require some changes in structure or delivery. Some revenue loss may occur.
Minor	2	The consequences threaten only the efficiency or effectiveness of the service and organization, not its survival. The consequences can be handled by mid- to senior-level managers, and clients are likely to be unaffected.
Insignificant	1	The consequences would have a negligible impact on the organization, and the risks can be handled by existing routine procedures

Source: Table adapted from Herman et al. (2004: 24).

many of these threats are interrelated and may impact in many different ways across the organization and require a coordinated, enterprise-wide response.

RISK PERCEPTION

Despite a rigorous system of risk identification and evaluation, it is still possible that a small action, seemingly insignificant at the time, may prove to be the catalyst for a major incident. Most notably, these can arise out of a 'fault in the human technology of an organization' (Hensgen et al. 2003: 68), which is why an understanding of the human element in both the assessment and management of risk is vital.

The problem for policy-makers is that approaches for objectively quantifying risk (e.g. actuarial analysis, probabilistic risk assessment, and epidemiology/toxicology) all assume that risks can be assigned a value that represents their 'harmfulness', independent of any social, economic, political or cultural context (Jaeger et al. 2001; Fischbacher-Smith 2012).

Table 3.3 *Evaluating the overall level of risk*

Magnitude		Insignificant	Minor	Moderate	Major	Catastrophic
	Score 1		2	3	4	5
Likelihood						
Almost Certain	5	5 Low	10 Medium	15 High	20 High	25 High
Very Likely	4	4 Low	8 Medium	12 High	16 High	20 High
Likely	3	3 Low	6 Medium	9 Medium	12 High	15 High
Unlikely	2	2 Low	4 Low	6 Medium	8 Medium	10 High
Rare	1	1 Low	2 Low	3 Low	4 Medium	5 High

Key:

Low = low risk; routine procedures in place to address risk issues.
Medium = moderate risk; management need to address specific risk issues; responsibility for the management of key risks should be clearly assigned.
High = high or extreme risk; requires attention by senior management and decisions taken to reduce likelihood and/or impact of serious threats.

According to Adams (1996), the search for a numerical measure to attach to the loss associated with a particular adverse event encounters the problem that people vary enormously in the importance that they attach to similar events. Risk assessment cannot therefore be reduced to a simple product of mathematical probabilities and consequences because this ignores the fact that it is essentially a human and social phenomenon (Pidgeon et al. 1992). Judgement is inherent in, and essential to, all forms of risk assessment and objective attempts to assess risk by quantifying its probability and estimating the severity of its impact are faced with the argument that, in essence, all risk is subjective (Slovic 1992; Russell and Babrow 2011). Thus, judgement arises in the choice of risks to assess, in estimates of their probability and consequences and in the categorization of such outcomes on scales of 'high to low' or 'one to five'.

Threats from the use of technologies in civil nuclear energy production or the creation of genetically modified crops may present risks that scientists can only express in minute percentages or ratios. These small probabilities are 'conceived' rather than directly 'perceived' by the public (Fisk 1999) and may be viewed as risks that are not worth taking. Douglas and Wildavsky (1982: 64) describe the way in which feasible limits for low levels of risk are set as depending 'not on what nature will withstand, but on what people will stand for'. Douglas (1985), discussing the conflicting views that exist over the safety of nuclear power production, further highlights a 'tragic difference' between what the nuclear community (i.e. scientists and engineers) believe is an exaggerated public perception of the actual dangers, in contrast to their own view of the scientific 'facts', and a public which suspects that the safety of a particular technology has been exaggerated by the scientists. We therefore need to look further for an explanation of the deep divide between these sets of beliefs.

Individuals filter the information they receive and make judgements based on a combination of their own experience, personal values and beliefs, and those of others close to them. When trying to estimate risk, they may recall past events or try to imagine what might occur in the future. There is no single, scientific and authentic risk narrative that sits outside individual experience (Russell and Babrow 2011). Frequently, probability is judged by how easily examples come to mind. Psychologists refer to this as the 'availability bias', which is a means of describing the systematic errors that are found when people are asked to give quantitative estimates of risks (Morgan et al. 2002). There is therefore a distortion in perception of risk if certain events are particularly memorable or have attracted media attention. Thus, the risk of death from diabetes, which is relatively frequent, is likely to be underestimated unless the individual has had personal experience of the disease in a friend or family member, while that from rabies is overestimated, due to media coverage of such rare incidents.

Individuals also apply a form of cost-benefit analysis to risk issues, balancing for example the (low) probability of being involved in an air crash with the (high) benefit of cheap international travel. This can create a gap between perceived and desired risks, with the threats posed by medical technologies (e.g. exposure to X-rays and prescription drugs) being considered as high in benefit, low in risk and therefore acceptable, while lower levels of radioactivity and chemical hazards from an industrial setting (e.g. nuclear power and pesticides) are viewed as high in risk, low in benefit and unacceptable (Slovic 1999). One explanation for this discrepancy might be that the medical use of radioactivity is for the overall benefit of the patient, while its use in an industrial setting is perceived to have no direct individual benefit. What does, however, seem clear is that quantitative risk assessments conducted by 'experts' do not appear to allay the fears of the general public regarding certain types of technological risk.

A significant factor influencing these judgements is 'dread risk'. The higher a hazard scores on this perceived scale, the more people will want to see it reduced and regulated. 'Dread' was one of the characteristics that Fischhoff et al. (1981) used to highlight individuals' attitudes towards a variety of unfortunate events that might cause them harm. Sometimes referred to as 'fright factors', these are illustrated in Box 3.2. These fright factors demonstrate that the key to the acceptability or otherwise of risk is not simply a matter of objective scientific calculations.

This can also create a gap between regulators and the regulated, as each views risk from a different perspective or, as Fisk (1999) describes it, each is legitimately sampling from a different world. While the statutory duty of a regulator is to make decisions that will protect society as a whole, the average citizen will be more concerned with the risks facing them, their families and friends. Experts reciting risk statistics,

BOX 3.2 FRIGHT FACTORS

Why do some risks cause more fear and anxiety than others, even when scientific estimates of their likelihood are low? Authors such as Fischhoff (Fischhoff et al. 1981) and Slovic (1990) have identified a number of negative attributes of hazards that appear to influence risk perception and acceptability. These include the following:

1. To be *involuntary* (e.g. exposure to pollution or nuclear radiation) rather than voluntary (e.g. participating in dangerous sports or recreational drug use).
2. As *inequitably distributed* (some benefit while others suffer the consequences, e.g. the location of a landfill site).
3. As *inescapable* by taking personal precautions (e.g. the individual has no control over the situation, such as when travelling as a passenger in a commercial aircraft).
4. To arise from an *unfamiliar or novel* source (e.g. genetically modified crops).
5. To result from *man-made rather than natural* sources (e.g. chemical, biological and nuclear technologies).
6. To cause *hidden and irreversible* damage, e.g. through onset of illnesses such as cancer and lung disease many years after exposure, such as in the case of shipyard workers and miners.
7. To pose some particular danger to *small children or pregnant women* or more generally to *future generations* (e.g. the release of toxic dioxins from waste incinerators).
8. To threaten a form of death (or illness/injury) *arousing particular dread,* cancer being one of the most notable.
9. To damage *identifiable rather than anonymous victims,* i.e. making the risk seem more 'personal' and likely to impact on family and friends.
10. To be *poorly understood by science* and further generate fear of the unknown.
11. As subject to *contradictory statements* from responsible sources (or, even worse, from the same source) such that trust in the reliability of risk information is lost.

Source: Adapted from Bennett (1999: 6).

including expected annual mortality rates, are unlikely to change people's attitudes and perceptions, because shifts in public attitudes have led to much less willingness to leave problem-solving to the experts (Coles 1999).

A study into the Australian public's perception of environmental health risk found that many of the environmental health issues faced by modern society were viewed as presenting a high risk to health (Starr et al. 2000). In particular, people were concerned with pollution of the environment in Australia as well as global issues, such as climate change and ozone depletion. The majority appeared unwilling to wait until the government alerted them to a specific environmental health problem before taking action, preferring instead to observe the environment around them and act accordingly. While 80 per cent of the respondents considered government departments to have moderate or greater responsibility for protecting the public against environmental health risks, more than 60 per cent viewed individuals, local councils, doctors, community groups and industry as having a similar responsibility.

Decisions on environmental policy often appear to shift the burden of risk from one party and impose it on another. The decision to site a new landfill waste disposal site would be an example of this. While there may be an overall benefit for the local community, there could be a detriment to households living in the vicinity of the site, with potential health risks, a reduction in the aesthetic environment, increased road traffic and, consequently, a negative impact on the value of their properties. There would be little surprise if affected individuals were to protest about the fairness of such a decision, but this would not be an argument that was solely predicated on risk grounds (Fisk 1999). The challenge for local authorities charged with making the final decision on planning permission is how to balance the views of all the stakeholders and come to a decision that will be acceptable to the majority, if not all, of the interested parties.

WHAT IS ACCEPTABLE RISK?

Risk is an essential element in our daily lives and risk-taking is crucial if we are to progress as a society. Few people expect life to be entirely free of involuntary danger but the question of 'how safe is safe enough' has become increasingly relevant (Renn 2008). According to Rayner (1992: 95), policy-makers' constituents care about the key issues of trust, liability and consent. Specifically, they want to know:

1. Are the institutions that make the decisions that manage and regulate the technology worthy of fiduciary *trust*?
2. Is the principle that will be used to apportion *liabilities* for an undesired consequence acceptable to those affected?
3. Is the procedure by which collective *consent* is obtained for a course of action acceptable to those who must bear its consequences?

In practical terms, individuals, organizations and government are faced with the need to take decisions involving current and potential future hazards and, as a consequence, have to decide what is and is not acceptable (Pidgeon et al. 1992). Thus, the acceptability of risk is a decision problem, involving values as well as facts – both those that are generally agreed upon and those that are contested. There can be no single number that would represent acceptable risk for society as a whole. At best, it might be possible to find the most acceptable alternative in a specific problem that will represent the values of a particular constituency (Fischhoff et al. 1981).

Decisions on safety and security have a major subjective component and are influenced by economic and political concerns (Strydom 2002). During the public inquiry into the Sizewell B nuclear plant in the United Kingdom, which took place between 1983 and 1985, the chairman of the inquiry criticized the use of the term 'acceptable risk', arguing that the phrase 'tolerable risk' might better reflect the reluctance that individuals commonly showed towards certain hazardous activities. This was taken up by the UK Health and Safety Executive (HSE), which, in a report on the tolerability of risk from nuclear power stations, advised that:

> Tolerability does not mean acceptability. It refers to the willingness to live with a risk to secure certain benefits and in the confidence that it is being properly controlled. To tolerate a risk means that we do not regard it as negligible or something we might ignore, but rather as something we need to keep under review and reduce still further if and as we can.
>
> (HSE 1988: 1)

The HSE statement makes it clear that the toleration of risk is a balancing act, where there is a trade-off between the possible risks and the possible benefits arising from a particular use of technology. A slightly different approach is taken by Renn (2008), who distinguishes sharply between risks that are 'tolerable' in pursuit of other benefits, and risks that are 'acceptable' because they are so low that they are not worth the cost of pursuing. Regardless, instrumental in the process of evaluating acceptable/tolerable risks is effective monitoring in an attempt to reduce risk to levels 'as low as reasonably practical', known as ALARP (see Box 3.3). However, decisions as to whether to permit the development of a nuclear power station, the installation of mobile phone masts, the construction of a new flood barrier or similar contentious proposals, is ultimately a political one.

As individuals, members of various groups (family, work, social, etc.) and communities (local and national), we make decisions every day on what we regard as 'acceptable' risk, and act accordingly. For government and other public service organizations, such assessments and decisions will impact on a broad range of stakeholders and this is likely to provoke a range of responses. Take, as an example, the decision to consider developing a new nuclear power station. One side of the argument is that this technology produces clean and sustainable energy that is essential if society is to meet continuing demands for electricity. Its construction would provide employment and bring demand for other resources into the local area. Another side concerns value for money and more aesthetic issues, such as the impact on local scenery – particularly if the site is one of natural beauty. Opposition to such a development would be drawn not only from individuals in those communities most closely affected

BOX 3.3 ALARP

ALARP is the abbreviation of 'as low as reasonably practicable'. At its core is the concept of 'reasonably practicable' – this involves weighing a risk against the trouble, time and money needed to control it. It is a concept that is widely used in the health and safety sector, with regard to workplace risks.

Using the words 'reasonably practical' allows goals to be set for duty-holders, without being too prescriptive. This flexibility has advantages but also has drawbacks. Deciding whether a risk is ALARP can be challenging because it requires duty-holders and us, as individuals, to exercise judgement. This can be done by reference to existing, established 'good practice'. Where a hazard is high, complex or novel, good practice can be built upon, using more formal decision-making techniques to inform judgements.

A definition of 'reasonably practicable' was set out by the UK Court of Appeal (in its judgement in *Edwards v National Coal Board* [1949] 1 All ER 743). In essence, making sure a risk has been reduced ALARP is about weighing the risk against the sacrifice needed to further reduce it. The decision is weighted in favour of health and safety because the presumption is that the duty-holder should implement the risk-reduction measure. To avoid having to make this sacrifice, the duty-holder must be able to show that it would be grossly disproportionate to the benefits of risk reduction that would be achieved.

Examples might be:

- To spend £1m to prevent five staff suffering bruised knees is obviously grossly disproportionate; but
- To spend £1m to prevent a major explosion capable of killing 150 people is obviously proportionate.

Source: Adapted from the UK Heath and Safety Executive (2006).

but also from wider and well-established pressure groups, which have a history of opposing such developments. Who decides what level of risk is acceptable and how the needs of society as a whole can be balanced against the needs of individuals and their communities?

More recently the issue of tolerable risk has been expressed through the concept of risk 'appetite', which has been defined as 'the amount of risk, on a broad level, that an organization is willing to take on in pursuit of value' (KPMG 2008: 3). Obviously, the appetite that any organization enjoys will be dependent on a number of variables including age, core business, environment and reputation. Hence the well-established, one-dimensional service deliverer that operates in a stable environment and relies upon reputation will probably have a conservative risk appetite. Here we are likely to find many public organizations, who, more often than not, deliver one or two core services and operate in a space which is more protected from market forces (but more sensitive to public and political opinion). For these organizations, the incentives for a large risk appetite will be dulled. Conversely, we might look to a young private sector organization in a highly dynamic environment where entrepreneurship is prized (think social media technology) and see that a large appetite for risk is the default strategic position. This all begs the question, of course, of how such an appetite should be gauged in the first instance. This is where we run into problems of ambiguity, imprecision and competing values. However, what we do know is that effectiveness comes from appetite being incorporated into an organization's strategy. This often comes in the form of what is known as an appetite statement, which connects a strategic attitude to risk tolerance to the value and missions of the agency. Statements of this nature can be qualitative or quantitative. In the case of the latter, sophisticated econometric models now exist which attempt to forecast risks and then create definable attitudes to specific scenarios. The problem with these is twofold: (1) organizations lean towards them because they are scientific in nature but they tend to exclude more qualitative risks which cannot be counted; (2) econometric models cannot hope to capture the complexity of modern risks. In the case of the former, risk managers can create qualitative appetite statements that determine categories of risks and then establish on a broad scale whether they are more or less tolerable. For most organizations the categories can begin at a general level; all organizations are concerned with reputation, all are concerned with income (whether grant-funded or market-driven), all need to worry about regulatory issues and most need capital investment. Hence these can be scaled as risks in an appetite statement (low to high priority in relation to risk taking). The key issue for all managers in this regard is determining how qualitative categories, such as reputation, can be measured. For public managers specifically, the question is what categories of risk are more or less tolerable in a public sector as opposed to a private concern? We would return to our discussion in Chapter 1 and emphasize the variety of stakeholders and the increased concern with political and social environmental issues in public sectors. Regardless of qualitative or quantitative character, all appetite statements must reflect an acknowledgement that risk-taking can be a virtue. This simple statement reflects a core private sector principle but is one which it is often difficult to accept in the public sector. What is required therefore is an understanding of how risk appetite can be effectively promoted in public sector terms.

THE PRECAUTIONARY PRINCIPLE

While it is sensible to take precautions to prevent adverse outcomes from arising out of our daily activities, both personal and occupational, the concept of the 'precautionary principle' takes this one step further. Since the 1970s, this principle has increasingly been applied to public policy decisions on environmental and health hazards. Essentially, the decision whether or not to invoke the precautionary principle is exercised where scientific information is insufficient, inconclusive or uncertain, and where there are indications that the possible effects on the environment, or human, animal or plant health may be potentially dangerous and inconsistent with the chosen level of protection (Commission of the European Communities 2000). This involves judgements not only about short- to medium-term risks but also about the longer-term impact on future generations.

Within the European Communities, the only explicit mention of the precautionary principle is in the environment field (Article 174 of the EC Treaty); however, its scope is perceived as being much wider. Indeed, the Commission considers that the European Community is entitled to prescribe the level of protection that it considers appropriate with regard to the environment, human, animal and plant health, and this has become a central plank of Community policy. As different expressions, such as 'precautionary approach' and 'precautionary measures' are also used in some treaties and agreements, the European Environment Agency attempted to clarify some of the key terms used in discussions of the precautionary principle. These are illustrated in Table 3.4.

Table 3.4 *Clarification of terms used in discussion of the precautionary principle*

Situation	State and dates of knowledge	Examples of action
Risk	'Known' impacts; 'known' probabilities, e.g. asbestos causing respiratory disease, lung and mesothelioma cancer, 1965–present	Prevention: action taken to reduce known hazards, e.g. eliminate exposure to asbestos dust
Uncertainty	'Known' impacts; 'unknown' probabilities, e.g. antibiotics in animal feed and associated human resistance to those antibiotics, 1969–present	Precautionary prevention: action taken to reduce potential risks, e.g. reduce/eliminate human exposure to antibiotics in animal feed
Ignorance	'Unknown' impacts and therefore 'unknown' probabilities, e.g. the 'surprises' of chlorofluorocarbons (CFCs) and ozone layer damage prior to 1974; asbestos mesothelioma cancer prior to 1959	Precaution: action taken to anticipate, identify and reduce the impact of 'surprises', e.g. use of properties of chemicals such as persistence or bioaccumulation as 'predictors' of potential harm; use of the broadest possible sources of information, including long-term monitoring; promotion of robust, diverse and adaptable technologies and social arrangements to meet needs, with fewer technological 'monopolies' such as asbestos and CFCs

Source: EEA (2002: 9–10).

At the international level, the principle was first recognized in the UN General Assembly's 1982 World Charter for Nature and subsequently incorporated into the 1992 Rio Declaration, which stated in Principle 15 that:

> In order to protect the environment, the precautionary approach shall be widely applied by States according to their capability. Where there are threats of serious or irreversible damage, lack of full scientific uncertainty shall not be used as a reason for postponing cost-effective measures to prevent environmental degradation.

This principle has been progressively consolidated into international environmental law with, for example, the World Trade Organization (WTO) highlighting the close links between international trade and environmental protection and the need to achieve sustainable development.

The Commission document on the precautionary principle clearly embraces the concept of 'acceptable' risk. This affects two distinct aspects of the principle: first, the political decision to act or not to act (the decision to do nothing being a response in its own right), and second – if action is required – what measures to take. Recourse to the precautionary principle therefore presupposes that potentially negative effects arising from a particular product or process have been identified, but that there is no scientific certainty about the exact nature of the threat, either because of the insufficiency or the imprecise nature of the evidence. Where action is deemed necessary, some general principles of risk management should apply, in that the measures should be:

- *proportional to the chosen level of protection* – a total ban may not be a proportional response to a potential risk in all cases but it may be the sole option in some;
- *non-discriminatory in their application* – comparable situations should be treated in the same way, and different situations should not be treated in the same way, unless there are objective grounds for doing so;
- *consistent with similar measures already taken* – measures taken should be of similar scope and nature to those already taken in equivalent areas where scientific data is available;
- *based on an examination of the potential benefits and costs of action or lack of action* (including, where appropriate and feasible, an economic cost-benefit analysis) – this involves both the long and the short term, with the scope of such an analysis being much broader than economic factors alone, encompassing non-economic considerations such as the efficacy of possible options and their acceptability to the public;
- *subject to review in the light of new scientific data* – measures should be periodically reviewed in the light of new scientific information and amended as necessary; and
- *capable of assigning responsibility for producing the scientific evidence necessary for a more comprehensive risk assessment* – this is already done in many countries, where the

manufacturers of products deemed dangerous a priori, such as medical treatments, are required to demonstrate their safety before gaining a licence for distribution. This reverses the burden of proving injury, by treating them as dangerous until demonstrated otherwise.

(Commission of the European Communities 2000)

In its analysis of fourteen case studies relating to health and the environment, occurring between 1896 and 2000, the European Environment Agency (EEA) found that, in many of the cases, adequate information about potential hazards was available (EEA 2002). Unfortunately, this information was often discounted or undervalued and in some cases effectively ignored because it conflicted with short-term political or economic exigencies. The study highlighted the importance of trusted and shared information and noted that 'public acceptability of risks requires public participation in the decisions that create and manage such risks, including the consideration of values, attitudes and overall benefits' (EEA 2002: 5). This view was incorporated within a list of 'twelve late lessons' that were drawn from the fourteen events studied. These lessons are shown in Box 3.4.

A major concern about the cautious approach advocated by proponents of the precautionary principle is that it may stifle innovation and prevent great developments in the future (Smith and Toft 1998). The contrary view is that the potential consequences of many current activities are greater than at any time in the past, with nuclear energy, carbon emissions, nanotechnology and genetic modification all capable of catastrophic impacts on the planet and its various inhabitants. According to Smith and Toft (1998), the aim of the public sector should be to minimize such risks to society rather than to encourage them, adding a warning that by the time we fully understand the complexity and scale of the problem, it might be too late. Proponents of the 'precautionary principle' would therefore advocate restricting any new developments until issues of safety and security could be adequately assessed and addressed. However, it can equally be argued that a lack of scientific certainty is not a sufficient reason to delay implementation if the delay might result in serious or irreversible harm (Jaeger et al. 2001).

Although accepted as part of many national and international treaties, there does seem to be divergence in the way that the precautionary principle is utilized in European policy and law, and in the United States. The conventional wisdom is that Europe endorses the precautionary principle and seeks proactively to regulate risks, while the United States opposes the precautionary principle and waits for more evidence of actual harm before regulating (Wiener 2003). In fact, both the United States and Europe would be considered at the highly precautionary extreme of the global spectrum (compared, for example, with rapidly developing industrial nations in Asia, or Aids-affected African states). Wiener (2003) finds more points of similarity than difference in US and European approaches to risk assessment, with cost-benefit analysis being utilized to ensure proportionality of response. He suggests that the main difference lies in the choice of risks over which a precautionary approach is advocated. Europe appears to be

BOX 3.4 LATE LESSONS FROM EARLY WARNINGS

1. Acknowledge and respond to ignorance, as well as uncertainty and risk, in technology appraisal and public policy-making.
2. Provide adequate long-term environmental and health monitoring and research into early warnings.
3. Identify and work to reduce 'blind spots' and gaps in scientific knowledge.
4. Identify and reduce interdisciplinary obstacles to learning.
5. Ensure that real-world conditions are adequately accounted for in regulatory appraisal.
6. Systematically scrutinize the claimed justifications and benefits alongside the potential risks.
7. Evaluate a range of alternative options for meeting needs alongside the option under appraisal, and promote more robust, diverse and adaptable technologies so as to minimize the costs of surprises and maximize the benefits of innovation.
8. Ensure use of 'lay' and local knowledge, as well as relevant specialist expertise in the appraisal.
9. Take full account of the assumptions and values of different social groups.
10. Maintain the regulatory independence of interested parties while retaining an inclusive approach to information and opinion gathering.
11. Identify and reduce institutional obstacles to learning and action.
12. Avoid 'paralysis by analysis', by acting to reduce potential harm when there are reasonable grounds for concern.

Source: EEA (2002: 193–4).

more precautionary than the United States about risks arising from genetically modified foods, hormones in beef, toxic chemicals, phthalates in toys (e.g. babies' teething rings), climate change, marine pollution, guns, teenage consumption of illegal drugs and antitrust/competition policy. In contrast, the United States appears to be more precautionary than Europe about new drug approval, lead in gasoline, the ozone layer, particulate matter (from automobile emissions), nuclear energy, teenage consumption of alcohol and tobacco, speed limits on major highways, mad cow disease, choking hazards embedded in food, 'right to know' disclosure requirements, potentially violent persons, terrorism and weapons of mass destruction (Wiener 2003: 225–9). Thus, both the United States and Europe take a precautionary approach to the regulation of many risks, but they concentrate their efforts on different risks, in line with their own unique historical, cultural and other experiences. It is this diversity in precautionary particularity, not precautionary principle, that Wiener suggests is worthy of further attention.

RISK COMMUNICATION

Individuals dealing with complex risk issues rely, in part, on expert evaluations and advice from government. However, there may be a difference between the content of expert data and the meaning given to it by the public (Strydom 2002). This has been described as a 'crisis in confidence' (Slovic 1992) with the public reluctant to simply accept a scientific opinion, especially when this may be contradicted by other experts (Bennett et al. 2010). Information may be judged, first and foremost, not by its content but by who the message is from, and whether the recipient trusts the source (Bennett 1999). Thus, the actual level of danger posed by mobile telecommunication masts, or the flood threat arising from global warming, may be unclear, as mixed messages are relayed to the public by experts who are sometimes viewed as less than impartial, for example as representing government or industrial interests. Nonetheless, when it comes to risks that are potentially widespread, long-term and unavoidable, the public want to know that an everyday activity such as eating genetically modified foodstuffs is completely safe (Langford et al. 1999).

Risk communication is not simply an 'add-on' to risk assessment, but needs to inform thinking throughout the whole process (Coles 1999). There is a difference between providing information and genuine communication. Issues of trust, and the credibility of the source of information are critical to the acceptance of such messages, which otherwise may be treated with considerable suspicion (Smith and Tombs 2000; Bennett et al. 2010). However, trust is a two-way process and authentic communication involves sustained relationships in which mutual trust and respect are nurtured (Otway 1992). Openness has to be balanced with issues of confidentiality, particularly where data or information are commercially sensitive. This has implications for dialogue on risk matters, and on public participation in risk decision-making (Bradbury et al. 1999).

Trust and accountability are also significant in getting people to change their attitudes and behaviour. Healthy eating campaigns may be ignored if the public does not trust the agency delivering the message, while the take-up of preventative vaccination may fail if the risks and benefits are not well communicated. Trusted sources such as consumer organizations are seen as both knowledgeable and concerned with public welfare. In contrast, distrusted sources such as the government and government agencies are perceived to distort information, to have been proven wrong in the past and to provide biased information (Frewer 1999: 25).

Research undertaken by the United Kingdom's National Consumer Council (NCC 2002) into consumers' views on risk found a strong sense of dissatisfaction with the way in which government and other official bodies handled issues of risk and uncertainty. The lack of trust in government appeared based on a number of key factors:

- a belief that those in government are motivated by personal or political gain; that parties and politicians constantly 'spin' information, and make decisions reactively rather than proactively;

- a sense that there is a web of 'conspiracies' between politics, business and the media such that decisions on policy are based more on money than on consumers' needs; and
- a view that government and politicians have a poor track record, based on broken promises and bad decisions.

Moreover, there was a pervading view amongst consumers that government tended to treat them in a patronising manner; a feeling of being ignored by those in power was commonplace. Public consultation was seen as 'tokenistic' and 'pointless', particularly by those individuals in lower income groups, and this resulted in feelings of exclusion from the real debates.

When dealing with sensitive risk issues, there is therefore a need for finely tuned communication strategies (Covello 2010). Bennett (1999) notes a progressive change in the literature on this issue. He describes this as a move:

- from an emphasis on 'public misperceptions' and a tendency to view any deviation from expert opinion as a result of ignorance or stupidity;
- via empirical research into what concerns individuals and why;
- to an appreciation that both expert and lay opinions should inform one another.

Communication strategies that are top-down are less likely to be effective than strategies that include constructive two-way debate (Strydom 2002). However, too much information can be confusing, particularly if it is complex and sometimes contradictory. According to Otway (1992: 227), the main product of risk communication is not information but the quality of the social relationships it supports. In this respect, risk communication is not an end in itself, but an enabling agent that facilitates the continuous evolution of relationships between the parties.

This changes the focus from one in which the expert is 'right' and the lay person is 'wrong' to one in which differences in expertise and experience amongst all the stakeholders are acknowledged and the different contributions that each can bring to the communication process are valued. Moreover, these experiences and understandings are continually in a process of change, so the process of communication itself is constantly changing. Thus, it is not a linear approach to risk communication but one that is multi-way and values both sides of the argument that is most likely to result in some form of consensus (Bradbury et al. 1999).

When public service organizations fail to acknowledge the legitimate viewpoints of all concerned parties, controversy and conflict can ensue, bringing with it adverse publicity, extensive media coverage and often an escalation of resistance to the changes being proposed. 'Public participation can thus be viewed as a means of developing consensus among policy makers, technical experts, and the range of affected stakeholders' (Bradbury et al. 1999: 124).

90

The NCC study found that consumers wanted improvement in the way in which government agencies communicated with them on risk issues. Their findings suggested that:

- government provide a lead – but let people make up their own minds;
- greater consumer input be included in the decision-making processes about risk issues, and more meaningful consultation;
- there should be greater openness and honesty on the part of the government and its agencies, including better communication where facts are uncertain;
- dialogue between government and the consumer should be increased; and
- government should find new ways to listen to consumers.

(NCC 2002)

From past experience, it appears that the public gives much more attention to bad news than it does to good. Slovic (1999) refers to this as the 'asymmetry principle', meaning that there is a kind of unevenness to the processing of risk information. Given sufficient attention by the media, a single poor outcome in a vaccination programme, particularly if it involves a child, will carry much greater weight in forming public opinion on the merits of such a programme than a thousand positive outcomes. According to Slovic (1999: 46–9), when it comes to issues of trust, the playing field is not level. Instead, it is naturally inclined towards distrust for the following reasons:

1. Negative (trust-destroying) events are more visible or noticeable than positive (trust-building) events.
2. When events do come to our attention, negative (trust-destroying) events carry much greater weight than positive events.
3. Sources of bad (trust-destroying) news tend to be seen as more credible than sources of good news.
4. Distrust, once initiated, tends to reinforce and perpetuate distrust.

Thus, adverse events in a system, where there is already concern about safety, will be magnified both in terms of the publicity they attract and the fears that will be reinforced within an already anxious public.

The media plays a major role in creating perceptions of risk and, since it is generally believed that 'good news does not sell newspapers', the focus is more likely to be on the negative aspects of a situation than the positive. A possible risk to public health, for example, is more likely to become a major story if certain 'triggers' are in place. Bennett (1999: 17) identifies the following triggers as being significant:

1. Questions of *blame*.
2. Alleged *secrets and attempted cover-ups*.
3. *Human interest* through identifiable heroes, villains, etc.

91

4. Links with *existing high-profile issues or personalities*.
5. *Conflict*.
6. *Signal value*: the story as a portent of further ills ('what next?').
7. *Many people exposed to* the risk, even if at low levels ('it could be you').
8. Strong *visual impact* (e.g. pictures of suffering).
9. Links to *sex* and/or *crime*.

Newspaper headlines such as 'Eau no' for the Perrier water contamination incident and 'Frankenstein foods' for stories relating to genetically modified crops, brought attention to issues of the alleged risk to public health which the scientific evidence did not fully support. Yet, the resultant economic loss not only to the companies directly involved but also to related businesses was considerable. In the case of GM crops, arguments over the potential benefits of such technology appeared to get lost in a debate which focused almost entirely on the threats that it might pose to non-GM farming, wildlife and humans.

Special interest groups, whether local, national or international, play a major role in communication about specific types of risk. Plans to build a new waste incinerator or to allow open-cast mining are typical of the types of development, requiring government planning consent that are likely to generate hostile reactions from local communities and expand beyond the immediate area of impact to become issues of national concern and media interest.

The UK government has recognized the fact that the public's need for information may be different from that of other stakeholders and that these needs may vary according to the different stages of the risk management process (UK Resilience 2006). It identified three core communication needs: information, assurance and involvement. First, there is a need for *information* about the nature of the risk, the reliability of risk assessments, who is responsible for managing the risk and what options are open to them to control their exposure to the risk or mitigate the consequences. Second, *assurance* is required that advice and decisions are based on robust information and analysis, that action is being taken to reduce uncertainty, that the necessary procedures are in place to manage the risk and that those responsible for assessing and managing the risk are exercising leadership, acting competently and in the public interest. Finally, there needs to be an opportunity for *involvement* in the process of assessing the risk, and in deciding what action to take.

Increasing public participation in the risk debate does not, however, ensure success in reducing distrust or enhancing and creating trust (Earle and Cvetkovich 1995; McComas et al. 2010). There is some evidence that this may simply help to polarize attitudes, as people tend to select information that is consistent with an already held view (Frewer 1999).

Coles (1999) highlights the considerable use of public consultation and participation in the decision-making process in Australia and New Zealand. The Food Agency (ANZFA), which is similar to the United Kingdom's Food Standards Agency, can include individuals with relevant expertise on the project teams that review a product's safety. Once their assessment is published, the individual states develop their own policy, with regard to regulatory control and use. Coles found that one consequence of the wide consultation that was carried out on sensitive risk matters in Australia and New Zealand was that it became very difficult for government to pursue a policy that was not supported by the consultation exercise. However, on a positive note, public participation could help achieve both creative solutions and consensus, and minimize adverse public and media reactions. This, in turn, could lead to greater public trust of government and risk regulators.

Evidence that risk communication is not always as effective as industrialists, government and regulators might wish is found in the large number of campaigns that are fought by local residents and special interest groups against proposals to site certain types of development that might pose a health and safety hazard, or otherwise result in a detriment to the area. An example is shown in the case study below. An appreciation of what causes concern may allow the organization to undertake some forward planning, in the form of proactive risk management, rather than find itself in a situation of near continuous crisis management (Bennett 1999).

CASE STUDY 3.1 WIND FARMS: SUSTAINABLE 'GREEN' ENERGY OR A BLOT ON THE LANDSCAPE?

What do Scotland and Tasmania share in common? One answer is that both regions experience some of the strongest winds in the world. The opportunity therefore exists to capitalize on this natural resource and produce electricity by harnessing wind farms. In Scotland, government policy has, for a number of years, supported the development of onshore wind power. Not only is it argued that wind farms generate a significant source of renewable energy but also that they bring many opportunities to communities, for example by creating jobs associated with designing, constructing and maintaining wind farms. Additionally, they can result in continuing income when developers and communities agree some form of shared ownership or financial benefit. While acknowledging that 'wind farms must always be very carefully sited to ensure that none are built which have unacceptable impacts on the environment or local amenity', the Scottish government also stated that 'Ministers have no limit to the amount of wind farms they would like to see in Scotland – as many as possible, but wind farms will not be given the go-ahead at any price.'

On the other side of the world, King Island Tasmania is buffeted by the so-called Roaring Forties. Australia wants to generate 20 per cent of its electricity from renewable sources by 2020 and Hydro Tasmania's proposal to build a 200-turbine wind farm would go some way to helping meet that target.

So, here we have a risk – the declining availability and rising price of fossil fuels, allied to a growing global population with huge demands for energy – and a proposed solution – wind farms. Such schemes are, however, not without their opponents and protests have arisen at local, national and international levels.

The European Platform Against Windfarms (EPAW) was founded in 2008 by a small number of like-minded associations and groups from four EU countries. It now has almost 700 member organizations from twenty-three countries.

The aim of EPAW is to support its members in their opposition to more wind farm proposals. Opposition takes a number of forms, including:

- questioning the effectiveness of wind farms, both in terms of electricity generated and financial benefits;
- concern about damage caused directly or indirectly to flora, fauna and landscapes;
- concern about damage to tourism, the local economy, individuals' quality of life, their health and a lowering of property values.

Although the European Commission declined EPAW's request for a moratorium on the approval of new wind farm projects, the association's stated aim is to continue until they achieve this goal.

Meanwhile in Australia, a spokesperson for the Clean Energy Council took the view that opponents to these projects were 'a very small minority (that had) become very vocal and essentially created a perception that communities are opposed to wind farms. We know that not to be the case.' Nonetheless, certain politicians and political parties have sided with the protesters and vowed to introduce more rigorous planning regulations in future.

Providing facts to communities and individuals, who might be affected by wind farms, is vitally important in helping them make an informed decision about the risks and opportunities that wind farms might bring. Even so, when it comes to the construction of 60m-high turbines, which radically change the local landscape, the temptation to say 'not in my back yard' (NIMBY) and find multiple reasons to oppose such developments, is often overwhelming and can outweigh any arguments relating to the 'greater good' of society as a whole.

Sources: Online resources accessed on 10 May 2014. Business, industry and energy – onshore wind www.scotland.gov.uk, Guardian Sustainable Business blog – 'Anti-Wind Farm Campaigners Threaten Australia's Renewable Energy Target' www.theguardian.com, European Platform Against Windfarms www.epaw.org

CONCLUSION

The assessment of risk involves more than a scientific calculation of the potential harm that might ensue. Risk evaluation requires an acknowledgement and understanding of the significance of public perception and attitudes towards risk and it requires a sure understanding of culture. Although many of the examples used in the risk perception literature are industrial or technologically based, the findings of research in this field are equally relevant within a public sector environment. No public service organization can expect proposed changes to infrastructure or service provision to be met with universal acceptance. The greater the controversy over such proposals, the greater and more organized the protest is likely to be. Changes involving the closure of hospitals, schools or fire stations, or the construction of new housing and industrial developments, can – if genuine public participation in the risk debate has not occurred – result in major disruption, political intervention and, for some elected members, defeat at the polls.

Effective communication is vital and has to be two-way if the public is fully to engage in the debate. In this way, trust between the parties can be better established and a consensus is more likely to be reached. Assessing risks is not, however, an end in itself. It is the immediate precursor to taking action both to prevent threats and to reduce their impact should an adverse event occur. In Chapter 4, we will examine a variety of techniques for treating risks, and the preparation of continuity plans that will assist the PSO in continuing to deliver its objectives during a crisis situation.

 EXERCISE 3.1

You are Director of Education in a local or state government authority. Due to changing demographics, the number of school-age children has been declining and is set to decline further in the next ten years. Difficult decisions have to be made regarding efficient use of resources and the favoured option is to close a school in one of the suburban areas and merge it with another, larger school closer to the city centre. The larger school has good physical resources but is located within an area of socio-economic deprivation.

■ What are the key risk issues that you and your team will have to consider when making this decision?
■ How is this decision likely to be perceived by the two school communities?
■ What methods of communication should you use to enable some consensus to be reached between those making the decision and those directly affected by it?

DISCUSSION QUESTIONS

1. With what techniques for identifying risk are you familiar? What are the advantages and disadvantages of each technique?

2. What prevents an organization ranking all its risks as potentially 'high' in magnitude?
3. 'The real level of risk is the measure calculated by the relevant experts'. Discuss.
4. 'Judgements on the acceptability of risk should be made on the basis of "the greatest good" and should not be influenced by a vocal minority.' Discuss.
5. Do the media have a positive role to play in issues of risk communication? Justify your answer with reference to real-life examples of public risk issues.

REFERENCES

Adams, J. (1996) *Cars, Cholera and Cows: Virtual Risk and the Management of Uncertainty*, Manchester: Manchester Statistical Society.

Bennett, P. (1999) 'Understanding Responses to Risk: Some Basic Findings', in P. Bennett and K. Calman (eds), *Risk Communication and Public Health*, Oxford: Oxford University Press.

Bennett, P., Calman, K., Curtis, S. and Fischbacher-Smith, D. (2010) 'Understanding Public Responses to Risk: Policy and Practice', in P. Bennett, K. Calman, S. Curtis and D. Fischbacher-Smith (eds), *Risk Communication and Public Health*, Oxford: Oxford University Press, pp. 3–22.

Bradbury, J.A., Branch, K.M. and Focht, W. (1999) 'Trust and Public Participation in Risk Policy Issues', in G. Cvetkovich and R.E. Löfstedt (eds), *Social Trust and the Management of Risk*, London: Earthscan.

Coles, D. (1999) 'The Identification and Management of Risk: Opening Up the Process', in P. Bennett and K. Calman (eds), *Risk Communication and Public Health*, Oxford: Oxford University Press.

Commission of the European Communities (2000) *Communication from the Commission on the Precautionary Principle*. Available at: <http://ec.europa.eu/dgs/health_consumer/library/pub/pub07_en.pdf> (accessed 3 June 2014).

Covello, V.T. (2010) 'Strategies for Overcoming Challenges to Effective Risk Communication', in R.L. Heath and H.D. O'Hair (eds), *Handbook of Risk and Crisis Communication*, New York: Routledge, pp. 143–67.

Douglas, M. (1985) *Risk Acceptability According to the Social Sciences*, New York: Russell Sage Foundation.

Douglas, M. and Wildavsky, A. (1982) *Risk and Culture*, Berkeley: University of California Press.

Earle, T.C. and Cvetkovich, G.T. (1995) *Social Trust: Toward a Cosmopolitan Society*, Westport, CT: Praeger Press.

European Environment Agency [EEA] (2002) *Late Lessons from Early Warnings: The Precautionary Principle 1896–2000*, Copenhagen: EEA.

Fink, S. (1986) *Crisis Management: Planning for the Inevitable*, New York: American Management Association.

Fischbacher-Smith, D. (2012) 'Getting Pandas to Breed: Paradigm Blindness and the Policy Space for Risk Prevention, Mitigation and Management', *Risk Management*, 14(3): 177–201.

Fischoff, B. (2012) 'Risk Perception and Communication', in B. Fischhoff (ed.) *Risk Analysis and Human Behavior*, London: Earthscan, pp. 3–32.

Fischhoff, B., Lichtenstein, S., Slovic, P., Derby, S.L. and Keeney, R. L. (1981) *Acceptable Risk*, Cambridge: Cambridge University Press.

Fisk, D. (1999) 'Perception of Risk – is the Public Probably Right?', in P. Bennett and K. Calman (eds), *Risk Communication and Public Health*, Oxford: Oxford University Press.

Frewer, L.J. (1999) 'Public Risk Perceptions and Risk Communication', in P. Bennett and K. Calman (eds), *Risk Communication and Public Health*, Oxford: Oxford University Press.

Gupta, A. (2013) *Risk Management and Simulation*, Boca Raton, FL: CRC Press.

Health and Safety Executive [HSE] (1988) *The Tolerability of Risk from Nuclear Power Stations*, London: HMSO.

Health and Safety Executive [HSE] (2006) *ALARP 'at a Glance'*. Available at: <http://www.hse.gov.uk/risk/theory/alarpglance.htm> (accessed 1 June 2014).

Hensgen, T., Desouza, K.C. and Kraft, G.D. (2003) 'Games, Signal Detection, and Processing in the Context of Crisis Management', *Journal of Contingencies and Crisis Management*, 11(2): 67–77.

Herman, M.L., Head, G.L., Jackson, P.M. and Fogarty, T. E. (2004) *Managing Risk in Nonprofit Organizations: A Comprehensive Guide*, Hoboken, NJ: John Wiley & Sons.

Hutter, B. and Power, M. (2005) 'Organizational Encounters with Risk: An Introduction', in B. Hutter and M. Power (eds), *Organizational Encounters with Risk*, Oxford: Oxford University Press, pp. 1–32.

Institute for Risk Management [IRM] (2012) *Risk Culture Under the Microscope: Guidance for Boards*. Available at: <http://www.theirm.org/media/885907/Risk_Culture_A5_WEB15_Oct_2012.pdf> (accessed 19 May 2014).

Jaeger, C.C., Renn, O., Rosa, E.A. and Webler, T. (2001) *Risk, Uncertainty, and Rational Action*, London: Earthscan.

Langford, I.H., Marris, C. and O'Riordan, T. (1999) 'Public Reactions to Risk: Social Structures, Images of Science, and the Role of Trust', in P. Bennett and K. Calman (eds), *Risk Communication and Public Health*, Oxford: Oxford University Press.

McComas, K.A, Arval, J. and Wesley, J.C. (2010) 'Linking Public Participation and Decision through Risk Communication', in R.L. Heath and H.D. O'Hair (eds), *Handbook of Risk and Crisis Communication*, New York: Routledge, pp. 365–85.

Morgan, M.G., Fischhoff, B., Bostrom, A. and Atman, C.J. (2002) *Risk Communication: A Mental Models Approach*, Cambridge: Cambridge University Press.

National Consumer Council [NCC] (2002) *Running Risks: Summary of NCC Research into Consumers' Views on Risk*, London: National Consumer Council.

Office of Government Commerce [OGC] (2002) *Management of Risk: Guidance for Practitioners*, London: The Stationery Office.

Otway, H. (1992) 'Public Wisdom, Expert Fallibility: Toward a Contextual Theory of Risk', in S. Krimsky and D. Golding (eds), *Social Theories of Risk*, Westport, CT: Praeger Press, pp. 215–228.

Pidgeon, N., Hood, C., Jones, D., Turner, B. and Gibson, R. (1992) 'Risk Perception', in The Royal Society, *Risk: Analysis, Perception and Management*, London: Royal Society.

Rayner, S. (1992) 'Cultural Theory and Risk Analysis', in S. Krimsky and D. Golding (eds), *Social Theories of Risk*, Westport, CT: Praeger Press, pp. 83–116.

Renn, O. (2008) *Risk Governance: Coping with Uncertainty in a Complex World*, London: Earthscan.

Russell, L.D. and Babrow, A.S. (2011) 'Risk in the Making: Narrative, Problematic Integration, and the Social Construction of Risk', *Communication Theory*, 21(3): 239–60.

Slovic, P. (1992) 'Perception of Risk: Reflections on the Psychometric Paradigm', in S. Krimsky and D. Golding (eds), *Social Theories of Risk*, Westport, CT: Praeger Press, pp. 117–52.

Slovic, P. (1999) 'Perceived Risk, Trust, and Democracy', in G. Cvetkovich and R.E. Löfstedt (eds), *Social Trust and the Management of Risk*, London: Earthscan.

Slovic, P. (ed.) (2010) *The Feeling of Risk: New Perspectives on Risk Perception*, London: Earthscan.

Smith, D. and Toft, B. (1998) 'Editorial: Issues in Public Sector Risk Management', *Public Money and Management*, 18(4): 7–10.

Smith, D. and Tombs, S. (2000) 'Of Course It's Safe, Trust Me!', in E. Coles, D. Smith, and S. Tombs (eds), *Risk Management and Society*, Dordrecht: Kluwer Academic Publishers.

Standards Australia (2004) AS/NZS 4360:2004 *Australian/New Zealand Risk Management Standard*, Sydney: Standards Australia, Wellington: Standards New Zealand.

Starr, G., Langley A. and Taylor, A. (2000) *Environmental Health Risk Perception in Australia: A Research Report to the Commonwealth Department of Health and Aged Care*. Available at: <http://www.health.gov.au/internet/main/publishing.nsf/Content/5 42B32498B45834ECA257BF0001B0799/$File/envrisk.pdf> (accessed 2 June 2014).

Strydom, P. (2002) *Risk, Environment and Society*, Buckingham: Open University Press.

UK Resilience (2006) *Communicating Risk*, London: Cabinet Office.

Wiener, J.B. (2003) 'Whose Precaution After All? A Comment on the Comparison and Evolution of Risk Regulatory Systems', *Duke Journal of Comparative & International Law*, 13: 207–62.

FURTHER READING

Institute of Risk Management (2012) *Risk Culture: Under the Microscope Guidance for Boards*, London: IRM.
This publication gives a brief overview of what we mean by risk culture, why it is important to understand the risk culture in an organization and how it might be changed. As with the publication on risk appetite and tolerance, listed below, it is available to download free of charge from the IRM's website at <www.theirm.org>.

Institute of Risk Management (2011) *Risk Appetite and Tolerance*, London: IRM.
This brief executive summary promotes the view that both risk appetite and risk tolerance are inextricably linked to organizational performance over time. The authors pose a number of questions for board members to address as they consider the significance of the various risks facing the organization and decide what steps, if any, they will take to address them.

Herman, M.L., Head, G.L., Jackson, P.M. and Fogarty, T.E. (2004) *Managing Risk in Nonprofit Organizations: A Comprehensive Guide*, Hoboken, NJ: John Wiley & Sons.

There are few publications that tackle risk management from either a public service or a not-for-profit perspective. Written by four leaders from the Non-profit Risk Management Center in Washington, DC, this book examines each stage of the risk management process and highlights five key reasons why risk management should be high on the agendas of both staff and the governing bodies of non-profit organizations. These include: asset stewardship; achieving public accountability; attracting stakeholders; freeing up resources for mission and staying true to mission. The book is divided into three main sections: (1) managing risk in the non-profit sector, which explores the nature and context of risk management; (2) understanding the general risks facing non-profit organizations, which explores a range of threats including those to property, income, people and reputation, and (3) risk financing for non-profits, which explores insurance and other strategies for managing the financial impacts of risk. While some of the terminology and issues are US-oriented, this is nonetheless an excellent book for those involved in either not-for-profit, voluntary or public service organizations.

Douglas, M. and Wildavsky A. (1982) *Risk and Culture: An Essay on the Selection of Technological and Environmental Dangers,* Berkeley, CA: University of California Press.
This is a classic text that starts with the question 'Can we know the risks we face, now or in the future?' Douglas and Wildavsky's answer is 'No, we cannot: but yes, we must act as if we do.' Although focused on environmental risk assessment, the authors' questioning of alleged scientific objectivity and exploration of why people emphasize some types of risk while largely ignoring others is both provocative and significant in the field of public risk debates.

Bennett, P. and Calman K. (eds) (1999) *Risk Communication and Public Health,* Oxford: Oxford University Press.
A collection of essays from academics, professional practitioners and government officials which had its origins in a conference organized by the UK Department of Health in November 1997. Organized into four sections, Part 1 offers an introduction to risk communication as a topic for research. Part 2 consists of studies of prominent cases, including E. coli and BSE, and the lessons to be drawn from them. Part 3 offers some perspectives on institutional issues, including public perceptions and consumer concerns. Finally, Part 4 pulls the threads together and sets out some implications for those tasked with risk communication. The varied views presented make this a worthwhile addition to the library of anyone interested in public risk and particularly public health issues.

Chapter 4

Responding to risk

Strategies and methods

LEARNING OBJECTIVES

By *the end of this chapter you should:*

- be aware of the four key strategies for responding to risks;
- understand the purpose of risk treatment and its role within the overall risk management process;
- be aware of a range of methods of risk control;
- be able to distinguish between the management of financial risk, and risk financing;
- understand the concept and practices of business continuity planning; and
- be able to discuss the key steps in the business continuity management process.

KEY POINTS OF THIS CHAPTER

- Responses to risk depend on whether there is a potential for positive or negative outcomes.
- Options involve tolerating, terminating, transferring or treating the risks.
- Decisions on risk treatment are predicated on a robust risk identification and evaluation process, and on the prioritization of threats.
- Methods of risk control include physical measures, management systems, human resource strategies and financial risk controls, including risk financing (insurance and alternatives).
- Business continuity planning is part of the risk treatment stage of the risk management process.

- Government agencies are increasingly providing advice on organizational resilience to businesses and public authorities, in the face of global threats such as terrorism and pandemics.
- A significant element of the business continuity management process is the conduct of a business impact analysis, which identifies those functions that will need to be resumed as a matter of urgency.
- Risk management strategies require monitoring and reviewing at regular intervals.

KEY TERMS

- **Business continuity management** – an integral part of sound risk management; part of the risk treatment stage of the process and dependent on the outcomes of a rigorous process of identification, evaluation and analysis; designed to strengthen the resilience of the public body and enable it to recover quickly from an adverse event.
- **Business continuity planning** – the planning and drafting stage of the business continuity management process.
- **Business impact analysis** – an analysis of the critical functions or activities within the organization.
- **Insurance** – a method of financing aspects of risk; a form of risk transfer.
- **Mission critical activities** – the functions or activities that will need to be resumed as a matter of urgency should any form of interruption occur.
- **Risk treatment** – methods of controlling and reducing risk.

STRATEGIES FOR RESPONDING TO RISKS

Once current and potential risks have been identified and evaluated, decisions can be taken on how to respond and, in particular, what actions to take that will improve future outcomes. These tasks require judgements to be made about the most appropriate response – from a range of possible options – and take into account the costs and benefits of each proposed action, as well as the likely reaction to it from stakeholders and other interested parties. The definitions of risk treatment that are used in the United Kingdom and Australia/New Zealand Risk Management Standards are shown in Box 4.1.

Decisions on treatment depend on whether the risk has the potential for positive outcomes (opportunities) or negative ones (threats), and a range of responses may be appropriate in any given set of circumstances. Where there is the possibility of positive benefit being gained from pursuing an opportunity, a decision might be taken to start

101

BOX 4.1 DEFINITIONS OF RISK TREATMENT IN RISK MANAGEMENT STANDARDS

Risk treatment is the process of selecting and implementing measures to modify the risk. Risk treatment includes as its major element, risk control/mitigation, but extends further to, for example, risk avoidance, risk transfer, risk financing, etc.

(AIRMIC, ALARM, IRM 2002: 10)

[Risk treatment is a] process of selection and implementation of measures to modify risk.

(ISO/IEC Guide 2002: 73)

or continue with a particular activity, to share the opportunity with other parties through partnerships or joint ventures, or to change certain factors that will impact on the likelihood of success. Where the risks have negative outcomes (and it should be borne in mind that opportunities have the potential for loss as well as gain) the approach is similar, although a key decision might be to avoid the risk by not starting, or by discontinuing, the activity that gives rise to the risk in the first place (AS/NZS 4360:2004: 20–21).

The importance of risk culture needs to be emphasized at this point because the culture of any organization will influence its attitude to risk tolerance/risk-taking. The Institute for Risk Management (IRM) has defined a risk culture as the 'values, beliefs, knowledge and understanding of risk shared by people with a common purpose' (2012: 7). The IRM states that an appropriate risk culture 'enables and rewards individuals and groups for taking the right risks in an informed manner' (2012: 6) and, conversely, an inappropriate culture is one where risky activities will take place which are 'at odds' with the pre-existing policies and strategies of the organization. Moreover, such activities are likely to be ignored, approved of or go unseen in a problematic culture. Indeed, the moral hazard surrounding the investment banking industry pre financial crisis is a good example of an inappropriate culture that went unrecognized. Contemporary risk management thinking suggests that culture needs to be defined in terms of risk and, if problematic, changed. According to the IRM culture can initially be understood in terms of three layers:

1. *Predisposition to risk at a personal level* – some people are cautious, some are spontaneous. Some leaders will take risks if they believe there is no downside while others take risks on an estimation of gains. Risk cultures start with individual attitudes. The IRM suggests that these can be defined using personality assessment

tools such as the Risk Type Compass, which typifies an individual's risk-taking attitude.

2. *Personal ethics* – closely linked to the psychology of an individual in relation to risk is their wider ethical attitude. How do they view rule compliance? Do they have an empathy or respect for non-fiduciary stakeholders? Is their decision-making inclusive or autocratic? Such questions reveal an individual's ethical profile which is also a building block of risk culture.

3. *Organizational culture* – the IRM stresses that high levels of sociability (the coherence between organizational members) and solidarity (the focus on tasks as reflected in goal orientation and team performance) are crucial elements in establishing an effective risk culture

A more detailed model for assessing risk culture is also offered by the IRM. This has four themes: leadership, governance, decision-making and competency. In each theme, there are two areas for self-assessment. Thus under leadership the organization should reflect upon clarity of direction given by leaders vis-à-vis risk and the way in which the agency reacts to problematic events. Under governance, issues of accountability for managing risk need to be considered as does the transparency of information about risks. Under competency, assessment must be made about the organization's commitment to enhancing risk management skills and the overall investment made in risk management capacity generally (see Box 4.2 below) and, finally, under decision-making some reflection about the information behind decisions and the performance management regime surrounding those decisions must be undertaken.

Within any risk culture, individuals have a number of options for treating risk, which can be described in terms of the four 'Ts' – tolerating, terminating, transferring and treating (OGC 2002).

Tolerating risk

A decision to 'tolerate' a risk involves accepting and retaining the risk, and the threat or opportunity it presents. This tactic might be appropriate in situations where the benefits outweigh the risks/costs, or when it would be too expensive/inconvenient to change or where the alternatives appear to be 'worse'. Whatever the case, a conscious decision to tolerate a risk is one that requires regular monitoring and review, as circumstances may change and thereby shift the balance towards adopting a different strategy. Within a public service environment, the PSO may have little choice but to tolerate certain threats. For example, in the case of social welfare provision, there are rare occasions in which a case worker is attacked and injured by a mentally disturbed person whom they are visiting at home. Despite these threats, such visits are likely to continue – and the risk tolerated – as there is both a need for the home care of such individuals and little in the way of alternatives. Budgets may not stretch to enable two staff to attend each home visit, although this would provide more security for the staff involved.

BOX 4.2 CORE COMPETENCIES IN PUBLIC SECTOR RISK MANAGEMENT

Good organizational performance depends on having effective management systems in place and on employing individuals who have the right kind of skills and knowledge to do the job. The question arises: 'What skills, knowledge and attributes does a successful risk manager need to have?'

This question has prompted a number of organizations and professional institutes around the world, to identify these 'core competencies'. The key characteristics normally include a mixture of technical knowledge, business-related and interpersonal skills, and personal attributes.

Risk management core competency models have been created with both private-sector (see the example from the USA-based organization RIMS at www.rims.org) and public sector risk managers in mind. An example of the latter would be the one developed by ALARM in the United Kingdom (see www.alarm-uk.org). Indeed, the competency models share a number of features in common as many of these skills are easily transferrable from one sector to another.

Competency models can be used in a number of ways. At the strategic level, they can be used to help motivate staff to deliver the best possible services and achieve the highest levels of performance, while at the operational level, they can be used to design staff appraisal forms and create personal development plans. Normally, the competencies are expressed in terms of functions that the individual ought to be able to carry out. For example, one would expect a risk manager to be able to identify and evaluate risks. To do this, an individual would need an understanding of the internal and external threats as well as the organization's appetite for and tolerance of risk, be able to apply a range of risk identification and evaluation tools and have the skills to make the right selection of tools for the task.

Taking this further, it is possible to create a framework that more specifically outlines what might be expected of risk professionals at various stages of their careers. The competencies – both in terms of knowledge and skills – required of a new recruit to the profession will be less than that expected of a risk manager or chief risk officer.

Similarly, the requirements for technical knowledge will vary depending on the specialist area in which the individual works (legal services, HR, insurance, etc.) The benefit of working with a core competency model is that it clarifies what the key knowledge and skill requirements are, and what might be needed for more advanced roles in the future.

Should such incidents increase in number and/or severity, this approach may be further reflected upon and strategies to reduce the risk (see 'risk treatment' below), or ultimately to terminate the service, may have to be considered.

Terminating risk

This strategy involves eliminating or avoiding the risk completely. Within the PSO, decisions could be taken to terminate a risk by ceasing to offer a particular aspect of the service that has proven to be problematic, or to deliver it in a completely different way. Such a decision may, of course, neither be practical nor politically acceptable and it is worth considering whether the elimination of one set of risks might introduce a whole range of new and hitherto unforeseen problems. When it comes to what are known as 'pure' risks, such as weather-related threats, natural disasters, fire, theft and accident, it is very difficult if not impossible to eliminate these completely. The probability of occurrence can be reduced through preventative measures and, exceptionally, may result in total elimination of the threat. Examples include the passing of legislation to ban smoking in public places, conducting background checks on individuals who are working with young children and enforcing environmental, anti-pollution measures to protect health and prevent climate change. Breaches of the law may result in penalties, such as fines, imprisonment or community service orders, intended to reinforce the message that such risks are not to be tolerated. Likewise, regulations can be used in an attempt to eliminate certain health and safety risks, governance failures and negligent professional practice, with penalties again being in place to reinforce such measures.

Transferring risk

The wholesale transfer of risk is rare. However, it is possible to transfer some aspects of the risk – such as the public, employer or product liabilities – or the financial uncertainties associated with the threat to another party. The latter may be transferred through the use of insurance contracts. However, this strategy – as discussed later in the chapter – is designed to smooth the uncertainties relating to the financing of risk, rather than to transfer the risk per se. It is perhaps better to think of this in terms of risk distribution, or the sharing of risk, between interested parties. Thus, the liabilities related to a specific venture may be shared with, or transferred by contract to, a third party. This is a particular feature of outsourced or subcontracted work, where the contractors assume responsibility for injuries to (or death of) the employees working on the contract; for accidents or damage involving members of the public; and for other liabilities arising out of the work they are contracted to undertake. The increasing use of private–public partnerships (PPP) by public bodies and government-funded agencies for the construction of schools, hospitals and major infrastructure projects has brought this issue to the fore. Other examples where outsourcing has been used to carry out functions on behalf of a PSO include data processing, the management of prisons, community refuse collection and claims management. Transferring the risk is unlikely to result in complete protection in the face of an adverse event. For example, aspects of risk that are almost impossible to transfer relate to reputation and trust. As far as the general public are concerned, it is the public authority that is constructing the major infrastructure projects in their area, and it is this authority (and not their contractors) that is likely to face the wrath of the electorate if things go wrong. Furthermore, contract conditions can be open to interpretation, and lengthy civil proceedings may have to be entered into before allocations of responsibility, and costs, are settled.

Treating risk

Treating the risk involves taking some action to control or contain the threat. Risk control methods may involve physical measures, changes in management systems, human resource strategies and risk financing alternatives. These forms of risk treatment may be put in place before the risk materializes – to reduce the likelihood of the threat arising – or employed after an incident occurs – to reduce its impact. An example with regard to fire risk would involve a no-smoking ban as a preventative (before the event) measure, designed to reduce the likelihood of such a fire, while the fitting of a water sprinkler system would reduce the impact of a fire (after the event) by extinguishing it more quickly. By building in pre- and post-loss controls, both the likelihood and the magnitude of specific types of risk scenario can be considerably reduced. A further means of treating risk, post-event, is through business continuity planning (BCP) and business continuity management (BCM), which will be discussed later in this chapter.

These responses to risk may combine different categories of control, as described by the United Kingdom's Office of Government Commerce (2002) and illustrated in Table 4.1. The categories are not mutually exclusive. For example, the use of insurance could be viewed as both 'preventative' (avoiding the undesirable outcome of financial loss) and 'corrective' (providing necessary finance after the event). In comparison, the conduct of a post-loss evaluation of structural damage would involve elements that were both 'directive' (use of safety equipment) and 'detective' (learning lessons from what occurred).

The UK Risk Management Standard states that, as a minimum, a system of risk treatment should provide for:

- effective and efficient operation of the organization;
- effective internal controls; and
- compliance with laws and regulations.

(AIRMIC et al. 2002)

Decisions on risk treatment are predicated on a robust risk identification and evaluation process, and on the prioritization of threats to both the strategic and operational aspects of the organization. Selecting the most appropriate option involves balancing the cost of implementing the control mechanism with the benefit derived from it, in terms

Table 4.1 *Categories of control*

Category of control	Description
Directive	Designed to ensure that the particular outcome is achieved. Typically associated with health and safety, e.g. wearing protective clothing during performance of dangerous tasks; insisting on staff being properly trained before undertaking a project. Also includes risk sharing (e.g. insurance).
Preventative	Designed to limit the possibility of an undesirable outcome being realized. The majority of controls fall into this category. Separation of financial responsibilities in order to prevent fraud is an example.
Detective	Designed to identify occasions when undesirable outcomes have been experienced. Their effect is after the event, so they are only appropriate where loss or damage has been incurred. Examples include stock or asset checks and post-implementation reviews that identify lessons learned from projects for future application.
Corrective	Designed to correct undesirable outcomes that have happened. They provide a route to achieve some recovery against loss or damage. An example of this would be design of contract terms to allow recovery of overpayment. Insurance can be regarded as a form of corrective control.

Source: Adapted from Office of Government Commerce (2002: 26).

of the risk reduction that is achieved. This is not simply a matter of economics, as both direct and indirect costs and benefits – some of which may not be measurable in financial terms – have to be taken into account. The cost of *not* taking any action should also be considered. With issues of accountability and transparency being particularly relevant in public service organizations, there is an assumption that effective internal controls should be in place not only to protect delivery of the service itself, but also to demonstrate prudence with public funds. Compliance with laws and regulations is a requirement rather than an option and therefore measures must be in place to assist the public body to achieve the necessary compliance. Obvious examples arise in relation to health and safety, governance and professional practice.

There is no single risk treatment option that will address all potential threats to a public body, or enhance the likelihood of success when pursuing an opportunity. Instead, a range of tactics will be needed. In making choices about appropriate methods of treatment, it is essential to have an understanding not only of the obvious causes of a possible future event but also the multiple factors that may underlie and contribute to its occurrence. Unless these contributory factors are targeted, treatment strategies may be less effective, and risks are more likely to reoccur. As budgets may be constrained, this requires further decisions to be taken about priorities and the scale of the response, and these can only be made within the unique context of the individual PSO and its understanding of likely stakeholder opinion on its proposed plan of action.

Before discussing some of the techniques that can be used, it is worth remembering that risk treatments may themselves introduce new threats, or simply displace the risk elsewhere. The university that locks its library's fire exit doors in order to prevent students from stealing books creates a potentially fatal scenario were a real fire to break out. Additionally, the installation of CCTV cameras in schools, hospitals and other community facilities can displace the risk of vandalism and theft to alternative, less well-protected sites.

METHODS OF RISK CONTROL

The types of treatment available to reduce risks include physical measures/barriers, changes to management systems, human resource strategies and the use of contracts. A few examples are illustrated here.

Physical controls

Physical controls can be put in place to protect people, property, plant and valuable records. These controls may prevent the occurrence of a risk, or reduce its impact post-event. Examples include:

- *Fire* – smoke and heat detectors and alarms, sprinkler systems, fire doors, fire retardant materials and fire fighting equipment.
- *Security* – controlled entrances, identification badges, locks, window grills and shutters, use of CCTV, vehicle alarms and immobilizers.
- *Health and safety* (of employees and the public) – guards and other safety mechanisms on dangerous machinery and plant, non-slip flooring, personal protective equipment, good street lighting, well-maintained roads and pavements.
- *Environment* – filters for reducing toxic emissions into the atmosphere, ground or water systems, safe disposal of waste, decontamination of acquired land.
- *IT* – access passwords, data backup and off-site storage, firewalls, atmospheric controls for mainframes.

Management systems controls

Incidents blamed on 'human error' are often, in hindsight, found to be symptomatic of failures in management systems (Toft and Reynolds 1994). This can be improved through the implementation of:

- *Safe systems of working* – ensuring that effective systems of operation, monitoring and checking are devised and that staff apply them. In the health field, protocols are often used in relation to medical procedures and are designed to ensure the safety of the patient, and the achievement of intended outcomes; planned maintenance of buildings, machinery and equipment.

- *Customer/client service agreements* – being clear about the level of service that is expected and can be delivered.
- *Fraud prevention* – not placing the management of valuable assets, bank accounts or cash under the control of one person; ensuring that employees with financial responsibilities take at least two weeks' uninterrupted annual leave (giving more opportunity for fraudulent activity to be discovered).

Systems that involve verbal double-checking can fail when responses become automatic. This is referred to as 'automaticity', i.e. skilled actions are undertaken automatically as a result of repeated practice (Toft and Mascie-Taylor 2005). While such automaticity can be beneficial in certain circumstances, for example allowing us to drive a car without being consciously aware of every set of traffic lights yet stopping us when a red signal shows, there is also evidence that it can result in serious failures. See Box 4.3 for examples where certain verbal-challenge protocols (verbal double-checking) failed.

BOX 4.3 VERBAL CHALLENGE–RESPONSE PROTOCOLS

In sectors where the safety of employees and/or the public is paramount, such as the aviation industry or the medical profession, the verbal double-checking of instructions is a normal part of safety procedures. This is sometimes referred to as 'witnessing', where one person checks to ensure that the other has not missed some crucial activity or element of the procedure. Unfortunately, verbal witnessing does not always prevent serious errors from being made.

An investigation into four adverse events in an English National Health Service Trust found a mixture of inadvertent human error and systems failures, including double-checking protocols (Toft 2004). In one incident involving the incorrect identification of sperm samples in a reproductive medicine unit, an informal double-checking procedure had been temporarily suspended due to shortage of staff and pressure of work. Only when a member of staff became available, and a double-check was carried out, did the mistake come to light. The resultant embryos were not used.

Verbal witnessing is also used when administering certain drugs, yet it has been estimated that errors occur in more than two per 1000 doses, even where two members of staff have been involved in the checking.

> The evidence appears to suggest that where identical verbal double-checking safety protocols are repeatedly undertaken the performance of those carrying out such a task can be adversely affected without them realizing it, for the persons involved can unconsciously act in a manner that follows an expected pattern of behaviour rather than that actually required by the situation, and as a consequence form an erroneous but firm belief about the safety of the system they are operating. Once established, the erroneous belief that has been generated because of involuntary automaticity becomes 'reality' and it is that belief which then influences their conscious and deliberate actions.
>
> (Toft and Mascie-Taylor 2005: 213)

A number of remedial measures can be employed to help prevent or reduce the incidence of such errors, including more stringent concentration on the task in hand; announcing each checklist item out loud and waiting for the response before moving onto the next item; and undertaking checks completely independently of the other person and then reporting back findings. Rather than seeking to blame the individuals who make the mistake, Toft and Mascie-Taylor (2005) advocate investigating the organizational factors that appear to induce involuntary automaticity, and addressing the issues that make accidents more likely to occur and, in the health environment, put patient safety at risk.

Sources: Adapted from Department of Health (2004); Toft (2004); Toft and Mascie-Taylor (2005).

Human resource management controls

The contribution made by key organizational functions, such as human resources, to the management of risk, can be overlooked or undervalued. Since most major incidents (other than natural disasters) involve some element of human error, the role played by the HR department is critical. Employee risks encompass not only the prospect of human error, but illness or injury to the employee and a range of issues, such as gender and racial discrimination, human rights and pension entitlements, that may result in the employer being sued. Such threats can be reduced through the following measures:

- recruitment and selection of suitably qualified and experienced staff;
- a comprehensive induction programme, and ongoing staff development training;
- clarity of individual responsibilities and the boundaries of their authority;
- good systems of communications between and across all levels of the public body;
- genuine consultation with staff and their unions on issues relating to change;

- provision of occupational health and counselling services to assist staff who may be dealing with stress, ill-health, injury, or who are in need of gradual rehabilitation following a prolonged absence from work; and
- ensuring equal opportunities and compliance with employment legislation in areas such as parental rights, human rights, gender and racial discrimination, and industrial relations.

Financial risk controls

Financial risk controls take many forms but can be grouped into two main categories. First, there are accountancy and auditing procedures designed to ensure good financial decision-making, reporting and management. These involve judgements on investment, issues of cash flow, the impact of changes in bank interest, inflation or exchange rates, as well as the need for protection against theft and fraud. These procedures are necessary no matter what the size of the PSO. Of course, the greater the funds at risk, the greater the potential for a major loss. When the Bank of Credit and Commerce International (BCCI) collapsed in 1991, it was not only private individuals or companies in the private sector that suffered from the criminal actions of the firm. Western Isles Council in Scotland was one of several local government bodies that lost considerable amounts – in their case, around £24m – when the bank collapsed. This seriously affected the council's ability to operate and resulted in the UK national government having to give it a substantial loan in order to enable it to continue delivering basic services. Although he was not directly responsible for the council's investments in BCCI, the chairman resigned from his post as a matter of honour and as a gesture of sympathy to the losses suffered by the people of the Western Isles.

The second category of financial risk control relates to the financing of damage or loss that may occur as a result of an unexpected event. This is usually referred to as 'risk financing'. The risk assessment process (see Chapter 3) identifies and evaluates the threats and opportunities that attach to the public body's areas of operation. In doing so, an estimate of any potential losses has to be made. These losses may involve tangible and intangible, financial and non-financial elements. Once action has been taken to reduce the likelihood of any negative events and the severity of their impact, an element of 'residual risk' is likely to remain. As discussed previously, the PSO may decide to tolerate the risk and, in doing so, hope to absorb any financial consequences within normal budgets. A further strategy is to gain some financial protection against the impact of negative risks by transferring the financial element of the risk to another party, such as an insurance company. Transferring risk to an insurer is essentially a loss-smoothing operation, where the financial uncertainty of a potential future loss is replaced (in return for an agreed premium) with the certainty of insurance cover. A list of commonly insurable risks is shown in Box 4.4.

BOX 4.4 COMMONLY INSURABLE RISKS

1. Threats to property, such as:
    a) lightning, storm and flood;
    b) accidental fire and explosion; and
    c) deliberate acts such as vandalism, arson and fraud.
2. Potential loss of earnings as a result of industrial action, and from the consequences of some of the threats shown in (1) above.
3. Accident and injury to employees and members of the public.
4. Air, water and ground pollution.
5. Professional negligence.
6. Other liabilities, including product liabilities.

Source: Adapted from *Croner's Management of Business Risk* (2000: 3, 130–1).

This approach is not, however, comprehensive because insurance policies will restrict their cover to specified 'perils' (threats) and impose 'excesses' or 'deductibles' (similar to those on a private car or house policy) that require the policyholder to be responsible for a certain amount of the loss. In the case of a PSO, these deductibles can range from a few hundred to millions of pounds/dollars depending on its size, financial strength and willingness to bear risk (risk appetite). Furthermore, insurance can provide no protection against criminal penalties, reduced employee morale or client confidence, bad publicity in the media or damage to reputation. Insurance works on the premise that the premiums of the many will pay for the losses of the few, as well as covering the operating costs of the insurer and contributing to profits that will be distributed amongst its shareholders. The cost of insurance (the premium) is calculated on the basis of largely historical data on the likelihood and consequences of particular types of event in specific industries or sectors. In return for agreeing to provide cover, the insurance company may insist on improvement (risk control) measures being implemented, or may offer a discount for measures already in place. Insurance companies promote the security they can offer, but for corporate clients uncertainties remain, including under- and over-insurance, duplication and overlapping of covers, incorrect assessment of exposure, policy wordings being negotiated after the cover has commenced, and the threat of insurer insolvency (ALARM 2005).

While individuals and small companies depend on the regular insurance market to provide for their risk-financing needs, large PSOs – including city, regional and local government – have a range of other strategies at their disposal (see Box 4.5). An example of one of these alternative risk-financing strategies – risk pooling – is illustrated in Case Study 4.1.

BOX 4.5 SOME ALTERNATIVE RISK-FINANCING STRATEGIES

Self-insurance (unfunded) – tends to be used for low-severity/ low-frequency risks. No special budget is set aside as losses are considered to be low enough to be covered out of on-going operating costs.

Self-insurance (funded) – tends to be used for low-severity/ high-frequency risks. Because of the high frequency of these incidents, their occurrence is fairly predictable and a fund can be established that will pay for the estimated amount of losses as they arise.

Captives – a 'captive' insurance company is a limited purpose, wholly owned subsidiary of an organization that is not in the insurance business. Its purpose is to insure some aspects of the risks faced by the parent organization, without having to pay an insurer's overheads and profit. Most captives operate from offshore financial centres in 'tax havens' such as Bermuda and the Cayman Islands. Careful feasibility studies are necessary before deciding whether a captive is appropriate and beneficial for an organization, as there are obviously costs to establishing and operating a captive.

Risk pooling – this is an example of risk spreading and economies of scale amongst similar organizations, such as local government authorities. Risk financing pools have existed in Japan, the United States and the Netherlands since the 1940s. In the United Kingdom, these types of arrangement are known as 'mutuals', owned by their members who utilize their services. In mutual risk pools, it is not the risks themselves that are being shared, but their negative financial consequences. The aim is usually for a group of organizations in the same industry or sector to pool a specific risk, e.g. property or pollution. The rest of their insurance needs may still be met by the conventional insurance market, or other strategies.

Source: Adapted from ALARM (2005).

ISSUES OF PROPORTIONALITY

In selecting the appropriate risk treatment measures, it is important to ensure that the control that is put in place is proportional to the risk being presented. Apart from the most undesirable outcomes, such as loss of life, it is generally sufficient to implement controls that give a 'reasonable assurance' that losses will be confined within the risk appetite of the public body (HM Treasury 2001). The costs associated with the control

CASE STUDY 4.1 UNIVERSITIES' MUTUAL INSURANCE FUND

Although quite different from local government authorities in terms of their financing, management and regulation, universities in the United Kingdom share many of the insurable risks which authorities face and the problems associated with financing those risks. Like any public sector bodies, universities are subject to spending constraints and are therefore highly conscious of costs and value for money.

In 1992, four universities formed Universities Mutual Association Ltd (UMAL). This was set up as a discretionary mutual (DM), therefore avoiding many of the constraints and regulations placed upon other forms of insurance providers. As with any DM, payments (premiums) are paid into the common pool, with the payment of claims made against that pool being at the discretion of the UMAL board. UMAL protects its members by purchasing reinsurance from the market. Each member's contribution to the common pool is based on traditional underwriting practices, i.e. the contribution is in relation to the degree of risk which the member brings to the pool, the sums insured required and the loss history of the member.

The Association employs professional insurance managers who manage the day-to-day business, provide general risk and insurance services and guidance. Reflecting the ability of pools to be selective in the risks that they retain, UMAL will act as an intermediary between its members and the traditional insurance market for those risks which it considers to be unusual or more appropriate to the Lloyd's or insurance company market.

Source: Adapted from ALARM (2005: 46).

measure – both financial and otherwise – should therefore be balanced out by the benefits to be gained from taking the action. Box 4.6 illustrates some of the issues that may influence decisions about risk treatment. These issues highlight, once again, the wider impact of decisions on risk treatment, including political and regulatory dimensions, as well as their overall acceptability to individuals and communities.

Controlling claims

A further cost that requires consideration in the management of risk is that involved in handling any claims that might arise. Regardless of whether a particular type of risk is insured or not, management time has to be devoted to investigating the circumstances surrounding a claim and for processing the information. A PSO might need to consider the ease with which the public can report loss or damage, how such claims are investigated and their verity ascertained, how quickly valid claims can be settled and how false

BOX 4.6 A SAMPLE OF DECISION-MAKING ISSUES

- *Acceptable* – will the option be acceptable to the stakeholders? How might different stakeholders react?
- *Cost effective* – will the expenditure outweigh the benefits to be gained? Could the same effect be achieved at a lower cost?
- *Environmental* – what are the environmental implications of the decision?
- *Ethical* – are there any moral, social or ethical issues attached to the options under consideration?
- *Regulatory* – will the decision breach any regulatory requirements?
- *Unexpected impact* – will the selected course of action lead to potential new risks?

or exaggerated claims can be deterred or detected. PSOs often work closely with their insurers on such issues, as increased claims costs will subsequently be reflected in increased insurance premiums.

Claims costs have to be absorbed within budget allocations, i.e. the more money spent on handling and paying compensation claims, the less there is likely to be for frontline services. Other costs of risk treatment, such as inconvenience and aesthetics, have also to be taken into account; for example, the disadvantages of turning schools and colleges into 'fortresses' (for fear of a Dunblane or Columbine-type massacre), closing public playgrounds (for fear of children injuring themselves on the play equipment) and removing hanging flower baskets (for fear of them falling and injuring a passer-by or damaging a parked car).

AUDITING AND REVIEWING

Where publicly funded entities are concerned, issues of accountability and value for money are paramount. In order to gain assurance that effective control measures are in place, the PSO will need a reporting structure that allows management to feed information upwards about how risk management is operating. This process may be supplemented by internal audits. The function of internal audit in the risk management process has stimulated some debate in recent years. In a number of organizations, internal auditors have been used as expert internal consultants, assisting and advising on the risk management strategy. In some cases, the risk management function has been subsumed within internal audit, raising questions over the extent to which internal auditors are able to give 'independent' assurance about the way in which the public body's risks are being managed. One significant issue identified by the chartered

Institute for Internal Auditors (IIA) relates to the 'maturity' of risk management policy. The IIA states that:

> Internal audit's role in risk management is dependent on the maturity and future direction of the organisation's risk management process. In principle, the more risk mature the organisation is the more internal audit can give the board a realistic picture of how well risks to their strategic objectives are being managed, highlighting key areas of risk, and giving depth and focus to its work.
>
> (IIA 2013: 1)

It would seem therefore that audits have the most to offer those organizations that have had risk management strategies embedded for some time. In those organizations where risk activities are emerging or deemed tangential, internal audits have little traction. Nevertheless, in their annual survey the IIA consistently found that the internal audits of risk management processes tended to focus on three priority areas: data security, IT issues and regulatory compliance. Regardless of maturity, these would seem to be three core areas where internal audit can provide reassurance that risk management activities are working well.

BENCHMARKING RISK MANAGEMENT PERFORMANCE

Closely linked to the issue of auditing is the process of benchmarking. That is, comparing organizational performance internally and externally against standardized measurements. The United Kingdom's Chartered Institute of Public Finance and Accountancy (CIPFA) has long experience in local government benchmarking across a large number of corporate services, including accountancy, insurance and legal services (www.cipfa.org). The premise of the benchmarking exercise is to answer key questions such as:

- How are you performing?
- Are you performing better year on year?
- How does your performance compare with peer organizations?
- Are you providing value for money?

All organizations hold data that allow them to compare a variety of key performance indicators from year to year, including data relating to their risk management performance. However, solely relying on internal data does not provide any sense of how the PSO is performing compared with other similar organizations in their sector or geographical area. Is the risk management performance of a city council, for example, better or worse than that of a neighbouring city? Are their risk management activities at an early stage of implementation or fairly mature and embedded throughout the organization? And, in any case, do we know what 'good' risk management looks like in a public service organization?

The Alarm National Performance Model for Risk Management in the Public Services, published in 2009, was designed to answer the latter question. The Alarm model breaks down risk management activity into seven strands and tests the extent to which such activities are having a positive effect on the organization by assessing the level of risk management maturity on a five-point scale, as shown below:

- Level 1 risk management is engaging with the organization.
- Level 2 risk management is happening within the organization.
- Level 3 risk management is working for the organization.
- Level 4 risk management is embedded and integrated within the organization.
- Level 5 risk management is driving the organization.

What is significant is that the fifth and final level takes risk management beyond the 'embedding' stage – a stage that many PSOs still strive to reach – and positions it at the forefront of strategic decision-making, i.e. as 'driving' the organization. The model does however rely on a process of self-assessment in making judgements about the maturity of current risk management performance and, in that respect, is vulnerable to any lack of honesty or poor judgement on the part of those completing the question-naire.

Benchmarking clubs also enable PSOs to learn from other member organizations and discover how they might improve performance in future. The Alarm model outlined above has been used as the basis for collaboration between Alarm and CIPFA, which subsequently led to the launch, in 2010, of the first Risk Management Benchmarking Club in the United Kingdom (www.alarm-uk.org).

The club enables organizations to assess their progress against a recognized national standard in risk management, track changes in performance – both improvements and weaknesses – from the previous year and compare themselves with a range of organizations that are members. Members also have access to details on how other organizations solved key risk management challenges. In a period in which public funding has been decreasing, such information sharing can be vital in assisting the PSO to find better ways of managing resources effectively through the introduction of innovative, cost-effective solutions that have already been tried and tested elsewhere.

BUSINESS CONTINUITY PLANNING AND MANAGEMENT

Since risk can never be reduced to absolute zero, plans need to be developed, resourced and tested in order to ensure continuity of service provision when a major disruptive event occurs. This is known as business continuity planning (BCP) and is part of the broader risk management process, requiring the identification, evaluation and control of potential threats to have been carried out before business continuity plans are created (Wallace and Weber 2011). BCP can be distinguished from contingency planning as the latter deals with putting plans in place for coping and recovering from a crisis or disaster, not only for the organization itself but also for the wider community (see Chapter 5). Public bodies may, of course, take the view that 'it will never happen here', 'we would cope if anything bad occurred', or 'our insurance would pay for all that'. All of these views could prove to be short-sighted, ill-informed or, particularly with regard to the latter statement, hopelessly naïve. Experience shows that organizations which are ill-prepared for unexpected events, suffer greater losses and take longer to recover – if at all – compared to those which have addressed their business continuity needs in advance. As for insurance, it is considerably more difficult in the wake of disasters such as 9/11 and Hurricane Katrina for PSOs to get insurance for terrorist attacks, but there remains an insurance incentive for organizations to have BCPs in place as part of a holistic approach to minimizing disruption in the event of disaster. For example, based on research undertaken for the UK Cabinet Office and the British Insurance Brokers' Association, 83 per cent of the insurers surveyed stated that they would offer a discount to premium or improved terms and conditions if an organization had a business continuity plan in place (Friel 2012).

Business continuity planning has been defined as 'planning which identifies an organization's exposure to internal and external threats and synthesizes hard and soft assets to provide effective prevention and recovery for the organization, whilst maintaining competitive advantage and value system integrity' (Herbane et al. 1997, cited in Elliott et al. 2002: 2). This definition is rooted in a crisis management approach that takes a broad view of business continuity management and acknowledges that the process is shaped by new challenges arising from legislation, regulation and the stakeholders of individual organizations (Elliott et al. 2002). Additional detail on this crisis management approach can be found in Box 4.7. The process is further shaped by the historical legacy of previous continuity practice, as well as the strategic importance that is given to BCM both within the organization, and externally.

Historically, much of business continuity management has its roots in the 1970s, and in particular protection of computer systems and facilities, with the idea of data backup and recovery sites, in the event of an IT failure, gradually extending to other aspects of businesses (Herbane 2010). Many organizations that did not have any plans for business continuity were prompted to address this issue when the 'Millennium Bug', otherwise known as 'Y2K', became a major area of concern in the late 1990s. Fear of complete systems failure drove many organizations to establish business continuity task forces and adopt strategies that would both reduce the likelihood of their experiencing significant losses, and enable them to respond to a crisis, should it occur. Having gone through this process, many organizations came to realize that non-IT failures also needed to be addressed and that the principles of BCP that had been utilized for Y2K could easily be adapted for other types of risk.

BOX 4.7 A CRISIS MANAGEMENT APPROACH TO BUSINESS CONTINUITY MANAGEMENT

A crisis management approach may be defined as one that:

- recognizes the social and technical characteristics of business interruptions (organizations are socio-technical systems);
- emphasizes the contribution that managers may make to the resolution of interruptions (importance of the human response element);
- assumes that managers may build resilience to business interruptions through processes and changes to operating norms and practices (need to manage the risk);
- assumes that organizations themselves play a major role in 'incubating the potential for failure' (early detection vital);
- recognizes that, if managed properly, interruptions do not inevitably result in crises (importance of preventative measures);
- acknowledge the impact, potential or realized, of interruptions upon a wide range of stakeholders (think beyond the impact on the organization itself).

Source: Adapted from Elliott et al. (2002: 2).

A further driver for BCM has come through the corporate governance agenda and the need for chief executives and senior management to demonstrate that they have fully addressed the risks facing their organization. This involves ensuring that potential threats have been systematically identified, evaluated and treated and that continuity plans have been developed to deal with any adverse incidents. Where this is undertaken merely to ensure compliance with existing legislation and regulation, BCM is likely to be viewed as yet another 'cost' for the organization, and routes sought to minimize this cost by addressing selected aspects of the operation only and outsourcing specialist tasks to disaster recovery specialists. This approach can limit the value to be gained from undertaking a programme of BCM.

Elliott et al. (2002) identify a further approach, which they describe as 'value-based'. This perspective is less concerned with issues of regulation, compliance or technological failure than it is with the potential for BCM to add value to the organization. As with the enterprise-wide approach to risk management, the value-based approach to BCM is viewed as one which encompasses the entire organization and is integrated into every aspect of the operation, including decision-making on new developments. By considering risk management and BCM issues at an early stage, the likelihood of the public service organization experiencing positive outcomes in service delivery and increased client satisfaction is heightened. In addition, a more rapid response to potential problems can be assured through careful pre-planning at the BCP stage.

RISK MANAGEMENT VERSUS BUSINESS CONTINUITY MANAGEMENT

The relationship of risk management to business continuity management has been the subject of some debate, along the lines of 'Which came first, the chicken or the egg?' In other words, is risk management a part of the BCM process or vice versa? It can be argued that business continuity planning is a complementary function to that of risk management, with the latter's findings from risk assessments acting as input for the business continuity development process (*Croner's Management of Business Risk* 2000).

The Australian Business Continuity Standard AS/NZS 5050:2010 was released after the International Risk Management Standard ISO 31000 was adopted by both Australia and New Zealand, and follows the same three-part model – principles, framework and process – but with a BCM focus. AS/NZS 5050 clearly establishes the link between enterprise risk management and business continuity management. In other words, it places BCM within a holistic approach to the management of risk, one that integrates business continuity management practices with the existing corporate governance infrastructure.

BCM is generally accepted as arising within the 'risk treatment' stage of the risk management process. For it to be fully effective, there needs therefore to be a robust approach to the identification and evaluation of the threats facing the organization, followed by the implementation of appropriate treatment measures. The 'risk-based' approach of AS/NZS 5050 is not without its critics in the wider BCM community. Others take the view that although they are complementary disciplines, the focus and methods of business continuity differ significantly from that of risk management.

In a similar vein to the Australian and New Zealand agencies, the BCI views business continuity management as requiring an integrated, organization-wide approach, adopting the ISO definition of BCM as:

> a holistic management process that identifies potential threats to an organisation and the impacts to business operations those threats, if realised, might cause, and which provides a framework for building organisational resilience with the capability of an effective response that safeguards the interests of its key stakeholders, reputation, brand and value-creating activities.
>
> (ISO 22301:2012)

There appears to be general agreement that BCM includes the concept of organizational resilience and that by addressing areas where significant losses of resources – including staff, equipment and finance – might occur, the organization can benefit both before a

120

major disruption and after such an event. A significant issue for most PSOs is the potential for damage to reputation and loss of trust, resulting from an incident that might have been prevented by good risk management or where the consequences appear to have been mismanaged. In contrast, effective business continuity management can provide reassurance to stakeholders and enhance the reputation of the organization and its senior management.

THE RESILIENT ORGANIZATION

The issue of organizational resilience has been given greater prominence following the 9/11 terrorist attacks in the United States, and the Madrid and London bombings. Given the threat that such attacks could take place almost anywhere and at any time, and involve not only conventional weapons but also nuclear, radiological, chemical or biological agents, governments have sought to heighten awareness of the need for continuity planning. In the United Kingdom, the *Civil Contingencies Act 2004* not only provides a single framework for civil protection but places responsibility on key authorities and services to ensure that they are prepared to deal with a full range of emergencies – from local incidents to catastrophic events. The expectation is that local authorities, the emergency services and the health sector, along with other key service providers, will be able to provide normal services in abnormal circumstances, so far as is reasonably practicable. This duty relates to all their functions and not simply those that are required for an emergency response. The Act divides local responders into two categories:

- *Category 1 responders* are the emergency services, local authorities, the Marine and Coastguard Agency and the Environment Agency.
- *Category 2 responders* are the utilities, telecommunications, harbour authorities, rail operators and the Health and Safety Executive.

Significantly, local authorities have been given statutory responsibility not only for developing emergency and business continuity plans for their own organizations – to ensure that education, welfare, housing and other services continue to be delivered – but also for providing advice and assistance to local businesses and voluntary organizations about their business continuity management needs. These duties go far beyond previous practice. Moreover, the definition of an emergency has been widened to include disruption to the political and economic stability of a particular region, security threats and other localized emergencies such as an outbreak of foot and mouth disease, avian flu or a natural disaster such as a flood or storm.

Similar messages have come from the Ministry of Civil Defence and Emergency Management in New Zealand (www.civildefence.govt.nz) which advises businesses that

121

prior to initiating or reviewing their continuity planning arrangements, they should understand that:

1. It is not an option to be unprepared. Disasters do happen, but you can 'make the mess less' and hasten a return to normalcy through prior planning and committing to mitigation and preparedness activity. This can save time and money in the long term.

2. Risk assessment must consider risks posed by external factors, particularly inter-dependencies or outsourced services/arrangements.

3. Business continuity must protect business assets – staff, equipment, facilities, IT systems, reputation, market share, liquidity, etc.

4. Business continuity must protect both internal and external service capability, particularly in support of CDEM* critical activity (such as emergency services and medical facilities) – forecast and prioritize external demand before the event

5. Planning can only be effective if developed cooperatively with all business stake-holders so that responsibilities and roles are clearly understood and assumptions validated.

6. Risk, asset and emergency management or continuity planning processes must develop across an entire organization, from hazard assessment through to exercising, audit, review and feedback.

Specifically, the New Zealand *Civil Defence and Emergency Management Act* 2002 requires organizations to assess the risks posed by the hazards they face, both natural and man-made, then prioritize and plan across the '4Rs' of risk reduction, readiness, response and recovery. The expectation is that such planning can be done utilizing the principles of the risk management standard and within current guidelines on corporate govern-ance. Once again, the message appears to be that time and money spent on BCM should be viewed as an investment, rather than a cost, since preparation before a disaster will minimize loss of life and revenue, and enable speedier recovery after the event.

Where major threats – such as that posed by the avian flu pandemic – could poten-tially affect widespread geographical areas, national governments have produced their own advice to organizations on how to minimize the impact of such an outbreak on their operations, and reduce the risk to their employees' health. In 2006, the timing, likeli-hood and magnitude of an influenza pandemic were still uncertain. Nonetheless, this was considered a sufficiently serious global threat for the World Health Organization to advise countries that they should plan and prepare for a pandemic. With medium to large businesses in mind, the UK government published specific advice on contingency planning for a possible influenza pandemic and produced a checklist that organizations

* Note: CDEM refers to Civil Defence and Emergency Management

could use as a starting point in their own planning process. The checklist covered the following aspects:

1. Planning for the impact of a pandemic on the business.
2. Planning for the impact of a pandemic on employees and customers.
3. Establishing policies to be implemented during a pandemic.
4. Allocating resources to protect employees and customers during a pandemic.
5. Communicating to and educating employees.
6. Coordinating with external organizations and helping the community.

A selection of questions relating to Section 2 of the checklist is shown in Table 4.2.

THE BUSINESS CONTINUITY MANAGEMENT PROCESS

For BCM to be effective, it should be an integral part of the risk management process, driven from the top of the organization and set out in a policy that is fully endorsed and promoted by the executive. This policy forms the framework around which the business continuity plan is created and against which it can be monitored and audited. As with other aspects of risk management, BCM requires the participation of every function and every level within the organization – managerial, operational, administrative and technical – as well as liaison with external agencies.

The Business Continuity Institute's (2013) *Good Practice Guidelines* and the Australian/New Zealand Standard for Business Continuity Management AS/NZS 5050:2010 *Business Continuity – Managing Disruption-Related Risk* both describe the BCM process in terms of a number of steps or stages. While the number of steps might vary and be articulated slightly differently, they both include the elements outlined below.

Conducting a risk assessment and a business impact analysis

A risk assessment is part of the overall risk management process and enables the organization to gain an understanding of the threats and opportunities it may face. Risk assessment should also help identify the critical success factors and resources necessary for the organization to achieve its objectives. A business impact analysis (BIA), on the other hand, helps determine the functions that will need to be resumed, as a matter of urgency, should any form of interruption occur. These functions are often referred to as 'mission critical activities' and, for each, the maximum acceptable outage time (MAOT) needs to be estimated. The MAOT is the time after which any stoppage of the service delivery will have an unacceptable impact. The aim is therefore to establish the shortest MAOT in which 'business as usual' can be resumed. Examples include the time taken to resume power when a major cable has been accidentally cut during construction work, or the provision of meals for the elderly in the face of a strike by

123

Table 4.2 *Extract from a pandemic influenza checklist for businesses*

Plan for the impact of a pandemic on your employees and customers

Complete	In progress	Not started	
☐	☐	☐	Guided by advice issued by the government, forecast and plan for employees' absences during a pandemic (could be the result of a number of factors including personal illness, family member illness, bereavement, possible disruption to other sectors, for example closures of nurseries and schools or reduced public transport).
☐	☐	☐	As a general approach to reducing the spread of the infection across the country, assess your business needs for continued face-to-face contact with your customers/suppliers and consider plans to modify the frequency and/or type of face-to-face contact (e.g. video or teleconferencing instead of traveling to meetings) among employees and between employees and customers. Government is likely to advise against non-essential travel and this should be taken into account in planning.
☐	☐	☐	Plan for a likely increase in demand for employees' welfare services, if they are available, during a pandemic.
☐	☐	☐	Identify employees and key customers with special needs and incorporate the requirements of such persons into your preparedness plan.
☐	☐	☐	Consider your customers' needs during a pandemic and review your business model and arrangements to ensure that you can continue to meet those needs (e.g. enhance mail ordering and Internet shopping capacities).

Source: Adapted from the Civil Contingencies Secretariat (2006).

catering staff, or the payment of benefits and salaries when the finance information system is shut down. As part of the BIA process, interviews are conducted with key staff and management in each department or function of the organization. This highlights the critical functions, relationships and dependencies between functions, and the 'single points of failure' that would have multiple impacts if destroyed or disrupted, such as a location through which both telephone and computer communications pass. BIA interviews use prepared questionnaires on which the findings are recorded and

BOX 4.8 SAMPLE BIA QUESTIONS

- What are the main functions or operations carried out? What does each of these functions do? What is its purpose?
- How does the function achieve its purpose? Briefly describe.
- Does the function depend on anything supplied externally?
- Does the function depend on anything supplied from within the organization?
- What is the impact of non-performance of the function?
- After how long will the impact become unacceptable?
- What are the minimum resources that would be needed to restart this function after a disaster?

Source: Adapted from *Croner's Management of Business Risk* (2000: 6–96).

from which comparisons can be made between respondents to enable any discrepancies or inconsistencies to be examined and resolved. Examples of some BIA questions are shown in Box 4.8.

Deciding on appropriate response strategies

Having identified the mission critical activities, and considered the range of scenarios that might impact on the ability of the organization to function normally, strategies have to be developed to deal with such events. These strategies will need to address three key stages: the immediate emergency, continuity of the service operation during the crisis and the staged return to normality. Through BCM, a team can be identified and developed to provide a lead during any incident that might occur. Because of the leadership skills required during the incident response, the composition of such a team is critical and it may be that those who developed the plans are not the best individuals in such circumstances. For example, a major disruption caused by an IT failure will require considerable technical input, while the affect on the organization's reputation may necessitate the attention of externally sourced PR consultants.

Determining resource requirements and developing continuity plans

Once the overall business continuity strategies have been determined, consideration can be given to the detailed resource requirements at each stage. Questions of which staff may be needed, what records and equipment, where offices can be relocated, and what telecommunications support will be necessary are just a few of the issues that will need to be addressed. Moreover, relationships with clients, suppliers, partners,

125

contractors and regulators will have to be considered during the planning process. A well-developed communication strategy will be necessary so that staff, stakeholders and the general public get the right information at the right time, direct from the organization itself, utilizing a variety of internal and external media.

Training, testing and maintaining plans

A continuity plan will not work effectively unless the staff, who will be involved in responding to a particular type of incident, are adequately trained to do so. Basic training is needed by every individual who has a role to carry out in the event of the plan being activated. Additionally, all staff should be made aware of the existence of the organization's continuity plans and participate in testing the plans. This testing can take a number of forms including desktop reviews, 'live' scenarios and business recovery exercises, where access to a critical part of the infrastructure or key resource is withdrawn, and the planned recovery measures are tested for their effectiveness. Lessons learned from such testing should be incorporated into revised continuity plans (see also Chapter 5 on the role of crisis training and simulation). Finally, as organizations experience constant change – in personnel, technology and processes – the BCM programme needs to adapt to deal with such changes. This is better achieved if BCM is embedded within the normal management processes of the organization, rather than being viewed as something that is 'stand-alone' and only revisited periodically.

A RISK MANAGEMENT IMPLEMENTATION STRATEGY

In some public bodies, responsibility for governing the delivery of services rests with the board. In the case of local, municipal or regional government, it is elected members who are accountable to their communities, and failure to deliver services efficiently or to prevent a high-level incident from occurring can result in the public questioning the competence of those in charge (Audit Commission 2001). While there is no expectation that individual board or council members will personally manage all of the risks that their authority faces, they do have overall responsibility to ensure that such risks are being managed effectively. This is part of their stewardship role and it has been suggested that they do this by:

- seeking implementation of a strategic risk management process as soon as practicable;
- agreeing on member and officer structures for planning and monitoring the risk management process across the authority;
- correctly positioning risk management as a strategic and operational tool, rather than treating it as a compliance exercise;

- promoting the correct mindset and attitude that will ensure successful implementation and robust, ongoing risk management processes;
- committing the right level of resources to implementation and training over the medium term;
- taking a top-down approach, focusing on issues of corporate significance, leaving officers to summarize and communicate the main messages arising from the operational risk assessments; and
- aiming for continual improvement over the longer term.

(Adapted from Audit Commission 2001: 21)

The implementation of a risk management strategy requires a good understanding of the human and cultural dimensions of the workplace and awareness that there may be resistance to change. To overcome such barriers, good communication is essential with a clear explanation being given as to why and over what period of time the risk management process will be implemented. Staff may view such measures as yet another 'administrative' burden – essentially, a 'tick-box' exercise to show compliance, rather than actions that will effect real change. This can be overcome by identifying change champions who can communicate the purpose of the changes, assure staff and set achievable milestones that will act as visible success stories and motivate further action and change.

EXERCISE 4.1 STRATEGIES FOR RESPONDING TO RISK

Select a public organization with which you are familiar and provide at least one example of a risk that has been:
a) tolerated;
b) terminated;
c) transferred; or
d) treated.

DISCUSSION QUESTIONS

1. Why should it make a difference, when deciding on risk treatment options, as to whether a risk has the potential for positive or negative outcomes?
2. Can risk be eliminated entirely and, if so, by what means?
3. How can a public body protect itself against the risks inherent in a private–public partnership?

4. What methods can be used to reduce the risk of human error?
5. What are the advantages and disadvantages of utilizing insurance as a means of controlling the financial aspects of risk?
6. What is the role of internal audit in the risk management process?
7. What are the key drivers for business continuity management in public service organizations?
8. Is risk management part of business continuity management or vice versa?

REFERENCES

AIRMIC, ALARM, IRM (2002) *A Risk Management Standard*. Available at: <http://www.oat.ethz.ch/education/Autumn_term_09/Material_on_Psychological_Aspects/AIRMIC_Risk-Management-Standard_1_.pdf f> (accessed 11 June 2014).

ALARM (2005) *Alternative Risk Financing: Guidance on Alternatives to Traditional Insurance Market Products*, Online. Available at: <http://www.alarm-uk.com>.

Audit Commission (2001) *Worth the Risk: Improving Risk Management in Local Government*, London: Audit Commission.

Business Continuity Institute (2013) *Good Practice Guidelines: A Framework for Business Continuity Management*. Available at: <http://www.thebci.org>.

Chartered Institute of Internal Auditors [IIA] (2013) *Governance and Risk Report 2013 – The IIA's Annual Survey*. Available at: <http://www.iia.org.uk/policy/governance-and-risk-report-2013/> (accessed 19 May 2014).

Civil Contingencies Secretariat (2006) *Contingency Planning for a Possible Influenza Pandemic*, London: UK Cabinet Office.

Croner's Management of Business Risk (2000), London: Wolters Kluwer (UK) Ltd.

Department of Health (2004) *The Department of Health's Response to Professor Brian Toft's Report: Independent Review of the Circumstances Surrounding Four Adverse Events that Occurred in the Reproductive Medicine Units at The Leeds Teaching Hospitals NHS Trust, West Yorkshire*, London: Department of Health.

Elliott, D., Swartz, E. and Herbane, B. (2002) *Business Continuity Management: A Crisis Management Approach*, London: Routledge.

Friel, M. (2012) 'Business Continuity Plans Likely to Reduce Premiums', *Insurance Age*, 15 February. Available at: <http://www.insuranceage.co.uk/insurance-age/news/2152647/business-continuity-plans-reduce-premiums> (accessed 10 June 2014).

Herbane, B., Elliott, D. and Swartz, E. (1997) 'Contingency and Continua: Achieving Excellence through Business Continuity Planning', *Business Horizons*, 40(6): 19–25.

Herbane, B. (2010) 'The Evolution of Business Continuity Management: A Historical Review of Practices and Drivers', *Business History*, 52(6): 978–1002.

HM Treasury (2001) *Management of Risk – A Strategic Overview*, London: HMSO.

Institute for Risk Management [IRM] (2012) *Risk Culture under the Microscope: Guidance for Boards*: Available at: <http://www.theirm.org/media/885907/Risk_Culture_A5_WEB15_Oct_2012.pdf> (accessed 19 May 2014).

International Organization for Standardization [ISO] (2009) ISO 31000 *Risk Management – Principles and Guidelines*, Geneva: ISO.

International Organization for Standardization [ISO] (2012) ISO *22301 Societal Security – Business Continuity Management Systems,* Geneva: ISO.

International Organization for Standardization [ISO], International Electrotechnical Commission [IEC] (2002) *Guide 73: Risk Management Vocabulary – Guidelines for Use in Standards,* Geneva: ISO.

Office of Government Commerce (2002) *Management of Risk: Guidance for Practitioners,* London: The Stationery Office.

Standards Australia (2009) AS/NZS ISO 31000:2009 *Risk Management,* Sydney: Standards Australia.

Standards Australia (2009) AS/NZS 5050:2010 *Business Continuity – Managing Disruption-Related Risk,* Sydney: Standards Australia.

Toft, B. (2004) *Independent Review of the Circumstances Surrounding Four Adverse Events that Occurred in the Reproductive Medicine Units at The Leeds Teaching Hospitals NHS Trust, West Yorkshire,* London: Department of Health.

Toft, B. and Mascie-Taylor, H. (2005) 'Involuntary Automaticity: A Work-System Induced Risk to Safe Health Care', *Health Services Management Research,* 18: 211–16.

Toft, B. and Reynolds, S. (1994) *Learning from Disasters: A Management Approach,* 1st edition, Oxford: Butterworth-Heinemann.

Wallace, M. and Weber, L. (2011) *The Disaster Recovery Handbook: A Step-by-Step Guide to Business Continuity and Protect Vital Operations, Facilities, and Assets,* 2nd edition, New York: Amacom.

FURTHER READING

Risk assessment and risk control

Jeynes, J. (2002) *Risk Management: 10 Principles,* Oxford: Butterworth Heinemann. This book identifies ten elements of operation that present risk to a business, yet are equally to be found in public service organizations. Divided into three parts, the second section is particularly relevant as background reading to Chapters 3 and 4 of this book as it deals with both the risk assessment process and various methods of risk control.

Croner's Management of Business Risk (2000), London: Wolters Kluwer (UK) Ltd. This is a comprehensive text, written by a number of senior risk management practitioners, consultants and solicitors, which addresses the legal, compliance and practical issues of risk management. Risk control and treatment are dealt with in section 3 of the book, while risk financing mechanisms and business continuity planning are discussed in sections 4 and 6, respectively. This book is the core text for the Institute of Risk Management's Certificate in Risk Management.

Business continuity management

Detailed guidance on the business continuity management process can be gained from the Standards Australia/Standards New Zealand handbook on BCM (HB 221:2003). Similarly, the *Good Practice Guidelines* (2005) of the Business Continuity Institute provide a framework that can be followed in the development, exercising, maintenance auditing of plans. The BCI guidelines can be downloaded from <http://www.thebci.org>.

129

Elliott, D., Swartz, E. and Herbane, B. (2002) *Business Continuity Management: A Crisis Management Approach*, London: Routledge.
This book provides both a historical perspective on the development of business continuity management and detailed consideration of the regulatory and legislative issues that surround it. Chapters 3 to 6 develop BCM from the initiation and planning stage to the testing and handling of incidents. The book is supplemented with extensive references, suggestions for further reading and student exercises.

Wallace, M. and Weber, L. (2011) *The Disaster Recovery Handbook: A Step-by-Step Guide to Ensure Business Continuity and Protect Vital Operations, Facilities, and Assets*, 2nd edition, New York: Amacom.
This is a clearly written 'how to' book, which also addresses the relationship between BCM and contingency planning.

Chapter 5

Contingency planning and crisis preparedness

LEARNING OBJECTIVES

By *the end of this chapter you should:*

- be aware of the general importance, and the distinctions between, planning and preparing for crisis;
- have developed a solid understanding of the principles and practices that constitute 'good practice' in contingency planning and preparedness;
- have developed an understanding of the concept of resilience as a preparatory tool; and
- have a clear understanding of the multiple reasons why the ideals of pre-crisis preparedness are less easy to realize in practice.

KEY POINTS OF THIS CHAPTER

- Preparing and planning in advance for crisis is essential for public sector organizations.
- The most robust organizations are those whose crisis preparedness is embedded in organizational culture and practices, rather than being an 'add-on'.
- Contingency plans are vital for successful preparations.
- Contingency plans must be seen as one element of a larger preparedness cycle, which also includes capabilities assessment, scenario development and plan testing.
- The concept of resilience can be used as part of a reform process that expands the scope of preparedness activity.
- There is a tension between the ideals of pre-crisis management and the realities of political and organizational life.

KEY TERMS

- ▦ **Contingency** – a threat that may arise, but will not necessarily do so.
- ▦ **Contingency plan** – a written document which specifies roles, responsibilities, lines of communication and provides guidance in the event of a crisis.
- ▦ **Scenarios** – estimates of impacts caused by probable threats. These are then used to prepare contingency plans.
- ▦ **Capabilities assessment** – an ongoing audit of pre-existing and required crisis management capacities.
- ▦ **Preparedness cycle** – a series of activities including audit, threat assessment, plan development and plan testing.
- ▦ **Resilience** – a concept being used to reform crisis management practice that emphasizes adaptation, integration and shared responsibility for crisis management.

PLANNING AND PREPAREDNESS: A PRIMER

Normal planning processes and everyday decision-making procedures are unlikely to be sufficient in the face of a crisis. Public organizations cannot hope to manage through a crisis effectively unless specific attention is given to preparing for low-probability/ high-impact issues in advance. It is little wonder, therefore, that the crisis management literature emphasizes the importance of 'being prepared' for these events as a vital part of the crisis management cycle (see Chapter 1).

Typically, organizations tend to engage in this process via the formalization of contingency plans. A contingency plan is a document that sets out the roles, procedures and objectives for an organization in relation to potential threats and how to manage these threats in the event that they materialize. Documents of this nature are absolutely crucial to the successful management of a crisis. For most PSOs, contingency plans represent the foundations upon which their crisis responses will be made because, as an absolute minimum, they should stipulate clear guidance about decision-making authority. Knowing *who* can take decisions in a crisis and *what* the nature of those decisions can be – legally, ethically or organizationally – is absolutely essential knowledge which must exist before a crisis arrives. This is what makes the creation of a contingency plan a 'must do' for all would-be crisis managers.

However, contingency plans are more than just strategic documents. As crisis management knowledge develops, we are beginning to appreciate how important contingency plans can be in other areas. From a psychological perspective, plans can be seen as a mechanism to avoid individual paralysis. In periods when crisis managers could be stunned by the enormity of events or unable to think through the fog of uncertainty caused by a crisis, the existence of a plan can ensure that some form of remedial action initially takes place.

■ **132**

Contingency plans are also political documents. The cardinal sin for any public organization is not to have a plan in place for a specific threat, especially if that danger is clearly apparent in their immediate environment. The mere existence of a contingency plan, therefore, can show those seeking to apportion blame post-crisis that some degree of thought had gone into preparing for the worst. For this reason alone, public managers should create clear plans for multiple threats.

It is also crucial that public managers understand that planning does not always create preparedness and that the existence of a contingency plan does not guarantee crisis management success. There are many examples, provided in this chapter and elsewhere, of crisis management failures even though sophisticated contingency plans were in existence (see also Boin and McConnell 2007; McConnell and Eriksson 2011). Planning documents can be created relatively easily but, just like all strategic and operational guides, to be effective they must be more than documents – they must be 'alive' within an organization. This means that plans have to be rehearsed, evaluated, updated and, most importantly, absorbed into an organization's culture. Plans which gather dust on a public manager's shelf will affect nothing. Consider, as a simple example, the standard emergency fire drill. There is a documented plan underpinning all fire drills but that plan is of little practical use unless (1) the basic principles of fire safety are communicated and imbued in the workforce and (2) the plan is rehearsed repeatedly over time. Only once the plan is institutionalized in this way can it be truly effective. That the principles and practices of the simple fire drill are so well known in organizational life highlights how planning documentation can develop into meaningful preparedness.

The distinction between having planned for a crisis and being properly prepared for a crisis, helps us structure this chapter. We first provide a series of lessons about 'good practice' vis-à-vis planning, which are based around a cycle of activities. We then introduce the concept of resilience as a means of broadening out preparedness measures. Finally, we discuss a number of issues surrounding planning and preparedness which emerge from tensions between the ideal of planning and the messy reality of crises. Public managers need to navigate around these issues if they wish to turn planning documents into prepared organizations.

A CYCLE OF PREPAREDNESS

We cannot provide a universal checklist that, once completed, means that a PSO will be fully prepared for a crisis. Public managers must be aware from the outset that, by their very definition, crises will present unforseen challenges. We must always remember that during any actual crisis, therefore, there will be a need to adapt preparations to real-world contingencies as they unfold. Nevertheless, there are a series of lessons, principles and procedures that have been developed by crisis management analysts which can be considered 'good practice' in a general sense. The first of these has already been outlined above in our statement that preparations for a crisis must go beyond the

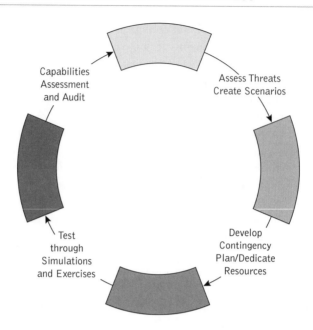

Figure 5.1 *Main stages in pre-crisis contingency planning*

creation of a contingency planning document. As Choularton (2007: 4) argues, the starting point for understanding this stage of the crisis management process requires us to see contingency planning as one piece in the preparedness puzzle. This simple but important point is emphasized in Figure 5.1, which displays a very basic preparedness cycle. This shows that the preparation of a plan is only one stage of a larger framework.

The stage at which a public manager might begin the cycle depends on the history of their organization in terms of its risk and crisis management practice. If a PSO has given some consideration to risk and crisis management in the past, the first step towards greater levels of preparedness is to begin an audit of the extant crisis management arrangements to determine if they are robust enough to meet known threats. However, public managers who are beginning to plan for the first time, such as those in newly created PSOs, should begin by assessing threats and developing scenarios. This means creating estimates of the probable impacts that will be brought about by potential crises.

Regardless of starting point, it is crucial to understand that these stages are two sides of the same coin. Crisis management capabilities can only be evaluated in the light of anticipated threats and, conversely, understanding the nature of organizational capabilities provides a fine-grained view about how vulnerable an organization is to a specific scenario. Each stage must therefore be continuously returned to as an organization learns more about the threats it faces and the capacities it has to respond to them. Let us now turn to each stage of the preparedness cycle.

Stage one: assessing capabilities

Any audit of current arrangements should ideally encapsulate a full capabilities assessment. These assessments not only audit the finances and equipment available for crisis management but should also cover, amongst other things, governance structures and networks, decision-making mechanisms, strategic documents and caches of expertise. The key question in any capabilities assessment is quite simple; do we have adequate resources to respond to probable threats?

One of the most comprehensive capabilities assessments in the world is conducted by the Civil Contingencies Secretariat in the United Kingdom. This continuous, large-scale assessment of national crisis management capacities crosses twenty-two work streams based around four themes. These themes are relevant to any organization looking to conduct a thorough capabilities assessment:

1. *A functional theme* – what systems are in place to respond to the most probable threats? Work streams here relate to specific threats that have been identified in risk assessments, designated as high priority and subsequently documented in risk registers. In the United Kingdom eight specific threats, from flooding to animal disease, have been identified, and capacities to respond to each are continually monitored. The message here for all PSOs is that if threats are probable, specific response capabilities need to be audited.

2. *An essential services theme* – what are the core elements of the organization required for its continuity? These essential aspects must be protected and then those protections must be audited. The Civil Contingencies Secretariat defines essential services in terms of national infrastructure (such as the National Health Service) but at the individual PSO level, telecommunications or supply chain inputs might be crucial to survival. Determining if these are protected and the strength of those protections is a crucial element in a capabilities assessment.

3. *A structural theme* – are frameworks for coordinating a crisis response in place? Are there specific structures and mechanisms for crisis decision-making? Have these been well communicated in clear plans? This assessment requires that structures are in place to manage crises and that everyone knows about them. Moreover, these mechanisms should be flexible enough to deal with different threats that are unforseen (more of this later).

4. *A support systems theme* – these work streams relate to generic aspects of administrative support that can come in handy during any kind of crisis. Audits should examine whether organizational aspects, such as public relations or secretarial units, for example, will be able to function in a crisis and are cognizant of their crisis management responsibilities.

A key element in any self-assessment relates to understanding the crisis management network within which the PSO operates. Crisis managers must establish their location,

135

in crisis management terms, within the larger political/administrative system in which they reside. This is an element that differentiates public and private sectors. While private companies tend to be 'standalone' entities that may have to 'go it alone' during a crisis, in the public sector roles, responsibilities and resources will have been distributed out across a system of agencies. What this means is that the burden for managing any large-scale crises will always be shared across a larger network. Some bodies will coordinate and strategize, some will implement policy, others may only perform communicative roles while others will exist purely to scrutinize actions and hold decision-makers to account. Understanding the specific crisis management network that envelops a PSO therefore represents a crucial part of a self-assessment. It forces the PSO to consider the tasks that it will be responsible for during a crisis, what it can expect in terms of assistance from elsewhere and, most importantly, it provides an early indication of the kinds of resources that will be needed to perform crisis management duties. Most crisis management systems now operate around the principles of decentralization and subsidiarity. This means that local government represents the front-line of most emergency responses and that higher tiers of government perform more strategic functions (Boin et al. 2005). Underneath this broad framework, however, will be a system and a set of organizations that are unique to a region or policy area. Capabilities assessments must map out these idiosyncrasies and identify who does what as part of their audit.

Small PSOs working under severe resource constraints and those that operate in less threatening environments obviously have to 'cut their own cloth' accordingly when it comes to resourcing capabilities assessments. However, all PSOs should conduct some form of initial self-assessment as part of their preparedness programme in order to determine whether they have the capacities to produce a crisis response.

Stage two: creating probable scenarios

As we have already discussed in previous chapters, there are a number of managerial processes, particularly relating to risk management, which can assist the identification of potential threats. The creation of scenarios must draw on as much information about risks as possible so that a PSO can estimate what kinds of crisis are likely and, more importantly, what their organizational impacts could be. A scenario can be defined simply as 'an account or synopsis of a possible course of events that could occur, which forms the basis for planning assumptions' (IASC 2001: 22). Scenarios then lead to the creation of plans that cater towards a range of 'what ifs'.

Sometimes scenarios can be based on previous events, which are scaled up or down. If an organization repeatedly has to deal with animal disease outbreaks, for example, scenarios might be based around the impacts of a small, localized outbreak affecting a handful of farms; or a series of outbreaks involving different diseases; or a national epidemic involving thousands of farms. Scenarios can also be built around timelines. What to do in the first hours, days, weeks and so on, or what to do as a crisis escalates (called the augmentation approach). At other times, scenarios might be based on

136

Table 5.1 *Strengths and weaknesses of different scenario approaches*

Approach	Advantages	Best Use
Best, most likely and worst-case approach (classic scenario planning default)	Provides a basis for planning around different scales Easy to understand Enhances flexibility by considering different demands	Planning for a single situation When scenario development involves many actors
Augmentation approach (focuses on next level of escalation and the dynamic response needed)	Good for planning for situations that are likely to be dynamics (transboundary crises for example) Will facilitate good understanding of ramping up/ changes in operations	Allows for scenarios about scale but not necessarily unforeseen contingencies What happens when a crisis completely changes character?
Timeline approach (setting out timelines and responses required at each point)	Allows planners to adapt operations as a crisis evolves Can lead to the inclusion and withdrawal of human resources at appropriate points in the crisis	Predicting the chronology of a crisis is problematic There is no template for specific periods in a crisis Resources traditionally used in recovery stages might be required for emergency response
Representative approach (viewing a scenario as having similar needs to another scenario that has already been planned for)	Allows for a greater focus on operations Can develop more flexible plans Can be used to identify all hazards preparedness measures for multiple threats	Problems of prediction Can be too vague

Source: Adapted from Choularton (2007: 17).

scientific evidence about probable risks. These often relate to natural disasters where forecasts form the basis for impact assessments. Scenarios can also be based upon a trifecta of visions about the 'best', 'most likely' and 'worst-case' crisis or, finally, they can be developed around generalized representations of a threat that is less scenario-specific and more indicative of broad crisis characteristics (representative approach).

The problem of accurate prediction plagues all efforts to create scenarios. We know that using historical analogy to prepare for future events can open up the possibility of 'fighting a former war' that will not correspond to the next event (Brändström et al. 2004). We also know that scientific modelling and prediction, particularly in relation to weather events, involve a liberal dose of guesswork and interpretation alongside the hard maths. And anticipating a worst-case scenario requires some degree of imagination about what the one in one million crisis might look like. Moreover, categorizing from best to worst is an exercise that can easily fall victim to overly optimistic views about what the 'worst' could actually be.

These issues with prediction mean that multiple scenarios should be created so that crisis managers can get a feel for different impacts and the requirements for each vis-à-vis management tools. Hopefully, experience of multiple scenarios will then allow crisis managers to assess impacts and tailor capacities when the real thing occurs, which, in turn, will enhance the flexibility of a crisis response.

Like capability assessments, there are resource costs attached to the creation of scenarios and each PSO must decide the level of resources that can be ascribed to their development. It is important, however, to understand that detailed and complicated scenarios can actually be unhelpful. They can mean that crisis managers prepare around very specific scenarios that are unlikely to occur and they can also obscure learning about generic crisis management skills. Large resource inputs are not necessarily the key to creating an effective scenario. Simple designs that are realistic can be extremely effective. Most importantly, scenario designers need to remember that their estimates are a means to an end. Their purpose is to lead to the development of an effective contingency plan, not to create an alternate universe.

Stage three: the development of the plan

The next stage requires the creation of the specific plan itself. The immediate question that has to be answered here is numerical: how many plans do you require? Contemporary opinion on this tends to stress that unnecessary confusion, duplication and procedural determinism can be avoided by creating the smallest number of plans possible. Ideally, this would be one simple plan with the capacity to be adapted to the range of potential scenarios identified. This idea sits at the heart of the now-fashionable 'all-hazards' approach to crisis management, which encourages a single preparedness framework and (optimally) a single plan to deal with every threat.

However, despite its popularity, an all-hazards approach does not, and sometimes cannot, lead to one single planning document. While most agree that multiple threats can be catered for under a single preparedness framework, organizations often draw together multiple plans under an all-hazards rubric. The capabilities assessment of the Civil Contingencies Secretariat described above, for example, funnels into a series of plans about eight core threats defined via the National Risk Assessment. In this context, crisis managers can take something of a 'pick and mix' approach to crisis responses by using elements of different plans to tailor a specific strategy to a unique event. Even in this context, however, it is imperative that plans are kept to a minimum and that they balance respect for specific scenarios with a degree of generality to achieve that all important flexibility.

There are no universal rules for pre-crisis planning and preparedness. Nevertheless, many academics and practitioners have developed a broad and quite flexible set of principles which can be seen as good practice both in terms of the creation of specific plans and enhancing preparedness more widely (Perry and Lindell 2003; Alexander 2005; Choularton 2007). In an excellent briefing paper for the Humanitarian Practice

138

Network, Richard Choularton (2007: 4) sets out a series of planning principles, which, like a good contingency plan itself, are both unambiguous and pragmatic. These are outlined in Box 5.1.

With these principles in mind, and the knowledge they have gained from capabilities assessments and scenario building, public managers can begin to build their plans. The key question at this point is obvious: what should be included? There are no hard and fast rules about what is in and what is out in this regard but contingency plans do tend to share some common features.

BOX 5.1 NINE PRINCIPLES OF CONTINGENCY PLANNING

1. Contingency planning should be practical. In other words, it should be based on realistic parameters and should not be a bureaucratic exercise undertaken for its own sake. This starts with a scenario that is detailed enough to allow equally detailed planning and preparedness – but not overly detailed. It also requires enough flexibility to adapt plans in the likely event that real life differs from the assumptions made in the scenario.
2. Contingency planning should be simple and easy to do. Contingency planning should not be a complex task undertaken only by specialists; rather, all staff – and indeed community members – should be able to participate.
3. Contingency plans should be realistic enough that they can be implemented when needed. Plans that are not grounded in reality run the risk of failure and may create a false sense of security.
4. Contingency plans should allow for efficient, effective and equitable use of resources to meet humanitarian needs appropriately.
5. Contingency planning should be process driven. Although written plans are important, without a good process contingency planning can be ineffective, resulting in plans being left on the shelf or in the filing cabinet.
6. Contingency planning should be participatory, in order to maximize the benefits of the planning process.
7. Contingency planning exercises should be followed up. Preparedness actions that are identified as a result of contingency planning should, where possible, be taken up, and further planning should be done if necessary.
8. Contingency planning processes should be regularly tested through exercises, such as table-top exercises. This helps improve planning and increases staff members' familiarity with the plan.
9. Contingency planning processes should include regular updates.

Source: Choularton (2007: 4).

- *Activation* – contingency plans should be quite clear about when a crisis response should be triggered in the first instance. Activations of a plan tend to relate to the seriousness of a potential threat or actual impacts. Regardless, a good contingency plan should contain a clear sense of how, when and by whom they should be activated.

- *Objectives* – this would seem self-evident. It is essential to have a clear sense of purpose in any plan and the resolution of the crisis would seem to be the most obvious. More careful consideration, however, reveals that a range of objectives can exist in a crisis. Objectives can be differentiated on a number of scales. First, they depend on who is affected. Humanitarian organizations, for example, create plans to provide relief to communities in developing nations. In this regard, priorities often relate to respecting democratic values, human rights and providing accountability to the suffering. These objectives could be contrasted with the plans of a domestic PSO in a developed nation, where aims may relate to avoiding political censure, ensuring efficiency and organizational survival. Objectives can also be delineated chronologically. What are the goals for the first twenty-four hours or the first year of a crisis response? Each will be quite different. Finally, objectives may be also be differentiated across the specific stages of crisis management, across the larger crisis management network or, most commonly, by predetermined scenarios created previously.

- *Response processes* – response processes must be linked to specific objectives and subsequently matched with decision-makers (see below). These processes are often constituted through a combination of different means. The delineation of response strategies should link scenarios to broad objectives and from there to specific policy measures. Implementation plans can then be detailed. These provide the fine-grained details of implementation such as the logistics of achieving a response strategy. The next level down is operational support plans, which document the ancillary aspects of a crisis response, such as media relations or the coordination of volunteers, which can become critical to any successful crisis response. An absolute must in terms of operational support, which is now being seen as a crisis management prerequisite, relates to media communications. The symbolism and politics of crisis management mean that media strategies should be planned for in advance, ideally in relation to specific scenarios. The importance given to response strategies, implementation plans and operational support plans will depend on the contingencies being faced and it is important to view them as flexible components, which could be used fully or partially depending on the scenario.

- *Decision-making authority* – as was noted above, at the heart of a contingency plan are clear instructions about who is taking what decisions. Typically, allocations of responsibility for decisions tend to be distributed across strategic, operational and ancillary levels. A good example here comes from the UK emergency services which coordinate around a 'bronze', 'silver' and 'gold' hierarchy in any emergency: bronze commanders take operational decisions on the front-line, silver

140

leaders take tactical decisions from a removed coordinating position and gold decision-makers occupy strategic decision-making roles, often at more centralized sites. Decision-making authority should also be parcelled out in a contingency plan in accordance with the specific processes that are required to deal with a scenario. Alongside this, there may also be a requirement to create unique decision-making forums or mechanisms. Such mechanisms can be unique to crises and should seek to bring together network players while ensuring the sanctity of the decision-maker's authority.

■ *Resources* – it is important that resources are allocated to specific response strategies. Increasingly, contingency plans contain specific budget projections linked to scenarios and, perhaps more importantly, details of where assistance can be sought in the event of maximum capacity being exceeded. These sources of assistance can often be created through mutual aid arrangements. Threats can be universal, which means that multiple agencies may have stockpiled resources to deal with the same crisis. If they are unaffected then these agencies can provide aid to their peers who are embroiled in a crisis. For example, the European Union's Civil Protection Mechanism exists as a means through which national governments can request additional crisis management resources from any of the twenty-eight member states that constitute the Union.

Once a document is created, all of those involved in the implementation of the plan must be informed of its contents and their relevant roles. Thereafter, the plan must be tested.

Stage four: testing plans

A number of activities are at the disposal of public authorities in the quest to ensure adequate training and testing of plans (see Flin 1996; 't Hart 1997; Perry 2004 for an overview). Four are particularly pertinent:

1. *Tabletop exercises* – involving case study and/or role-play situations. Such exercises are typically cost effective and can be useful as an initial introduction of personnel to crisis situations, as well as a means of thinking about new and emerging threats.
2. *Simulations* ('hot-seat' exercises) – involving simulation of crises through various means, including simulated control rooms, virtual reality simulators and computer-based simulations. These have the added advantage of introducing elements of stress and realism for participants.
3. *On-site function exercises* – involving one or more agencies and usually focusing on testing one aspect of a response plan, such as emergency medical services in the event of a terrorist attack or police in the event of a riot. A distinct benefit of such approaches is that they are 'hands on', in real time and involve scenarios that can be highly realistic.

141

4. *Full-scale exercises* – involving testing all major functions and responders in a situation as close as possible to a real crisis situation. Contingency planning can be trialled and weaknesses identified. Staff from responder groups and organizations can develop working relations. In addition, the public and other stakeholders can be made aware that government is vigilant and has a plan to deal with all potential threats.

Such activities are the very essence of crisis preparedness, and some guidelines for 'good practice' in simulations and exercises can be found in Box 5.2. Learning occurs in a 'safe' environment and hence mistakes can be rectified and lessons can be learnt as part of personal and organizational education in preparation for the 'real thing'. However, like all aspects of crisis preparedness, there is a tension between the need for planning and the realities of crisis management. This is not to suggest that we should reject the need for active planning through training and exercises. Such activities are vital.

BOX 5.2 SOME GUIDELINES FOR EFFECTIVE CRISIS SIMULATIONS/ FULL-SCALE EXERCISES

1. Developing the simulation/exercise

- Where possible, obtain the agreement of senior officials/political decision-makers that they will participate.
- Ensure that an appropriate simulation/exercise has been chosen, consistent with the goals, priorities and resources of the organization.
- Ensure that all relevant locations (simulated control rooms, on-site locations) and resources are available.
- Ensure that the broad development of the crisis and the specific sequence of events has been carefully staged in advance. This should promote a progressive crisis atmosphere, provide key decision-making challenges, be underpinned by an intent to mimic the uncertainty, chaos and time constraints of a crisis, and induce particular types of behaviour such as groupthink and inter-organizational conflicts.

2. Prior to the simulation/exercise

- Assign individuals to roles.
- Brief individuals on their responsibilities.
- Allocate pre-crisis reading (if considered relevant).
- Provide relevant equipment (for full-scale exercises).

3. Conduct of simulation/exercise

- Introduce a crisis situation or notification of an impending crisis.
- In most cases, record activities on video.
- Adhere to the plan for development of the 'crisis', and resist temptation to improvise and make it easier/more difficult for the participants. This may have unforeseen effects later on and undermine the integrity of the whole exercise.

4. After the simulation/exercise

- Allow time for a short break to ensure that trainers/observers are able to develop a debriefing strategy.
- Explore and discuss key decision points and themes (using video playback where relevant), examining the feasibility of different strategies/tactics/ decisions.
- Ensure that participants learn from their errors and their successes.
- Conduct a post-exercise evaluation in order to identify further training needs and/or necessary organizational reforms.

Source: Adapted from Rosenthal and Pijnenburg (1991); Flin (1996); Hermann (1997); 't Hart (1997); Borodzicz and van Haperen (2002).

However, we should be aware that use of a range of exercises is neither inevitable nor necessarily equated with highly robust preparedness for crisis. Three main reasons can be identified.

First, pre-crisis exercises can be expensive, and the nearer the simulation to reality, the greater the expense. In the United Kingdom in 2004, Exercise Triton 04 simulated a large flood scenario, involving more than sixty organizations and almost a thousand participants at a cost of £1.5m (Younge 2005). In the US in 2005, TOPOFF 3, a major terrorism exercise sponsored by the Department of Homeland Security, involved 10,000 individuals and 275 organizations and cost $16m. Such high costs constrain pre-crisis preparedness and ensure that use of exercises (especially full-scale exercises) is not inevitable. For example, a report by the United Kingdom's National Audit Office (HC 36 2002–3) on National Health Service preparedness found that:

- One-third of health authorities had not tested plans for chemical, biological and mass causality incidents.
- Four-fifths had not tested plans for radiological or nuclear incidents.

143

The usefulness of simulated and full-scale exercises is almost universally lauded. The other side of the coin, however, is that such exercises cannot be conducted in every public institution for every possible scenario.

Second, even when exercises are conducted, adjustments in policies, practices and behaviours are by no means inevitable. In essence, such fine-tuning can be constrained by the forces mentioned earlier which are protective of the status quo. In the aforementioned NHS example, one quarter of health authorities who had tested their incident plans still considered themselves not to be well prepared for radiological/nuclear incidents (HC 36 2002–3). A high-profile example of the failure of lesson-drawing lies with the Hurricane Pam exercise for New Orleans in 2004. Levees continued to be considered suitable, even though they could only withstand a Category Three hurricane (Katrina would prove to be Category Four). Follow-up planning activities such as how to provide shelter for thousands of displaced individuals, suffered because of lack of funds.

Third and finally, crises do not respect organizational training and planning. By their very nature, crises are chaotic, unpredictable, threatening and do not provide crisis managers with the time or the information they would ideally like before making deci-sions. Indeed, the nature of modern crises is becoming increasingly inconceivable in a world of globalization, hyper-terrorism, mutating viruses, etc. (Lagadec and Carli 2005). Indeed, the nature of crises may be changing to the point that unstable, blurred and hyper-complex states are already beyond our 'out-of-the-box thinking' (Topper and Lagadec 2013). Nevertheless, we certainly should not reject pre-crisis training and exercises, but as students of crisis management we should be aware of their limitations. For public institutions, giving the impression of crisis readiness is vital if they are to avoid charges of complacency. However, the symbolism of high-level 'readiness' that comes with pre-crisis exercises shouldn't necessarily be equated with the same level of operational preparedness.

Understanding preparatory efforts as a cycle of activities highlights how this stage of crisis management involves more than the creation of a plan. Contextualizing planning as one component in a larger, interdependent process of preparing and responding to crises takes us to the concept of resilience, which is now being promoted as a means of enhancing preparedness further.

 EXERCISE 5.1 A CONTINGENCY PLANNING PROBLEM

Pick any public organization, infrastructure or building with which you are familiar, and identify (a) probable crisis scenarios it might face; (b) the main components of a contingency plan in response; and (c) how the plan can realistically be taken forward through training and testing.

THE CONCEPT OF RESILIENCE

The concept of resilience was introduced in Chapter 4 as a means of exploring the relationship between business continuity and civil protection. Resilience has become very popular as a motif under which preparations for crises are now being managed. The term, however, still remains rather ambiguous and it has been used for very different purposes by crisis analysts and practitioners. What we can say initially is that resilience emerged within crisis management thinking as an antidote to the view that crises could be easily prevented (Wildavsky 1988). For some, therefore, 'the concept of resilience holds the promise of an answer' to a general pessimism about the 'shortcomings' of conventional prevention and preparedness policy-making (Comfort et al. 2010: 1). But what does resilience actually mean? A number of views exist and are summarized below. Each has a different set of implications for the design of a preparedness framework.

Resilience as 'bouncing back'

In studies of engineering, resilience is observed in systems that can adapt to pressure in a way that will quickly return them to a normal equilibrium (Fiksel 2003: 5330). Tensile plastics, for example, have resilience: they bend and then return to their original shape. When applied to crisis management, this definition translates into the idea of an organization, system or community having the capacity to 'bounce back' from a crisis so as to return to stable normality. If this view of resilience is promoted in crisis preparations, plans and frameworks will tend to focus upon putting in place reconstruction efforts that will ensure a speedy recovery after an event. This view dictates that 'resilience is the last line of defence' (Comfort et al. 2010: 8).

Resilience as adaptation

In studies of ecology, resilient systems are not necessarily those that 'bounce back' efficiently but rather those that can continuously adapt to unremitting environmental fluctuations (Gunderson 2003: 35). If this definition of resilience is adopted in preparedness terms, more planning will be done before a crisis arrives around threat recognition and organizational adaptation (Comfort et al. 2010). Achieving this state of readiness is something of a holy grail for any organization as the truly resilient organization will be able to 'roll with the punches' and 'negotiate flux without succumbing to it' (Boin et al. 2010: 8). For this to take place, crisis managers must go beyond plans which start and end with each new crisis and move their organization into a space where the accommodation of environmental threats is simply part of everyday routine.

145

Resilience as community participation

Community resilience is now a cornerstone of many crisis preparations. At its simplest, community resilience is an idea that stresses the value of local, non-state resources which allow citizens to perform crisis management roles in ways that complement the official aspects of a crisis response (CCS 2013). The extent to which community resilience has diffused into crisis management strategies over the past decade is quite astounding. It can now be found in the policies of international humanitarian organizations, such as the United Nations, at the centre of national government policy in places like Australia, the United Kingdom, Canada and the United States, amongst others, and across inter-institutional crisis management forums populated by policy officials, such as the Multi-National Resilience Policy Group.

The community resilience literature stresses the benefits of non-governmental responses to crisis in two ways. First, it emphasizes how community networks can deliver a level of spontaneity, adaptive capacity and humanity to a crisis response which government agencies cannot hope to replicate (Murphy 2007; Norris et al. 2008). Second, in the aftermath of a crisis, the social capital and solidarity of a community are said to mean that communities can rebuild in a more profound and personal manner than anything that could be achieved by government agencies (Aldrich 2011). In preparatory terms, adoption of this definition of resilience means that affected communities and even individual citizens need to be given a significant voice in the planning process and incorporated into response strategies in meaningful ways.

Resilience as integration

In countries like the United Kingdom and Australia, resilience has become a compass for internal government reform. It became part of a remedy, alongside other concepts such as integrated emergency management, for changing a cold-war template for crisis management that had come to be seen as too centralized, hierarchical and 'silo-driven' (Bach et al. 2010). In these countries resilience has become a banner under which policy officials have sought to make crisis management policy more integrated across organizations. Australia's National Strategy for Disaster Resilience, for example, is indicative of a view that resilience is about integration and interdependence. Alongside a focus upon community resilience, this national plan is driven by the need to make preparations for disaster a shared responsibility that threads across private, public and community groups (COAG 2009).

Looking across the academic work which has analysed the concept of resilience, and the specific public sector reforms that have been conducted under its banner, we can say that resilience is a metaphor through which a broader form of preparedness can be realized. For planning purposes, adopting a resilience strategy means new activities; greater respect for the relevance of government and non-government actors; more

146

attention to the citizen as a potential crisis manager; consequentially, more attention on joining up policy networks; and, crucially, privileging adaptation (in the form of bounce back or constant change) as a key planning principle.

It would be remiss, however, to conclude that the adoption of a resilience strategy is unproblematic. As Brassett et al. (2013: 224–5) emphasize, there is a tacit acceptance that it somehow 'works' and is a 'good thing' in itself. This assumption exists despite the fact that 'there is still relatively little grounded academic commentary on the extent to which resilience should be accepted as an organizing principle to be inculcated, invested in and striven-for throughout society'. And on the few occasions when questions have been asked, critical responses have answered. Most criticisms relate to the concept's ambiguity or apparently contradictory character. For example, Boin et al. (2010: 7–8) point to the contradiction between resilience as post-crisis recovery and pre-crisis preparedness as a potential problem for policy designers. Others have questioned whether the fundamental values of public sector organizations complement a concept that leans heavily towards adaptation (Stark 2014). Finally, the value of community as a benign and unproblematic public good has also been raised in relation to community resilience (Bulley 2013). Most notable in this regard are a small handful of scholars who have been concerned to show how community resilience is often built upon 'an outdated, romantic, united and "unitary" conception of community' (Bulley 2013: 271) which fails to acknowledge deeper issues around religion, gender and socio-economics. Resilience may be a fashionable buzzword but policy designers must tread cautiously and be very sure what they mean when they seek to reform policy around it.

IDEAL PLANNING VERSUS PUBLIC SECTOR REALITY

At various points in our discussion above we have suggested that despite good planning and preparedness, successful crisis management outcomes are not guaranteed. Despite the 'best-laid plans', communities may not be vehicles for resilience, simulations may not lead to meaningful policy changes and contingency plans may simply be left on shelves rather than permeated through organizations. What these instances alluded to was the fact that the 'real world' does not often lend itself to the ideals of crisis planning. More commonly, crisis analysts observe varying processes and levels of planning/preparedness which stand in contrast to the broad portrayal of 'good practice' we outlined above.

In terms of these organizations, Table 5.2 indicates three broad types and their basic characteristics. Those least prepared would tend to be dismissive of threats and have little or no contingency planning. The mid-range type would give fairly serious consideration to threats and the need for plans, although institutional preparedness would tend to be an 'add-on' to existing practices and values. In contrast, high-preparedness organizations would give high priority to threats and the need for contingency planning.

Table 5.2 A typology of organizational preparedness for crisis

	Low preparedness	Medium/mixed preparedness	High preparedness
Importance of contingency planning on the organizational agenda	Little or no importance. Not an item for serious consideration. Main focus is 'routine' survival and growth	Fairly important on occasion, but normally of much less priority than 'routine' organization goals	Very high. Crisis preparedness becomes part of the core goals of the organization
Attitude to threats	Dismissive. 'It couldn't happen here' mentality	Fairly serious consideration. A range of threats should be recognized and planned for	Very serious consideration. Organization must give high priority to planning for a range of threats
Extent of contingency plans	None at all, or at best a plan tucked away with little or no awareness by staff or stakeholders	Fairly detailed and extensive contingency plans as an 'add-on' to existing organizational structure and practice	Very detailed and extensive contingency plans, permeating the structures, practices and culture of the organization and its interactions with stakeholders
Extent of active readiness through trials and simulation	Non-existent	None or patchy. Plans on paper are considered adequate	Highly active readiness through regular crisis training and exercises
Organizational psyche	Major limits on emotional and cognitive capacities. Constant quest for existence/ego satisfaction. Unable to cope with anxiety. Self-inflated or self-defeatist outlook	Reasonably open (within limits) to emotional and cognitive change. Some ability to balance core drivers with the need to address problems. Some but limited toleration and capacity to cope with anxiety. Reasonably strong self-image, although prone to over-regarding or under-regarding itself	Openness to emotional and cognitive change. Major concern with addressing problems. Is able to tolerate and cope with anxiety. Positive self-image

Source: Original table, but drawing on Pauchant and Mitroff (1992: 146).

Furthermore, pre-crisis planning would be embedded in all aspects of organizational structures, practices and culture.

Reasons for this disparity are not absolute, but the following discussion attempts to go some way towards greater explanation. It identifies and fleshes out a fundamental tension between (1) the 'ideals' of crisis preparedness and (2) the unpredictability of crisis and the realities of organizational and political life. In doing so, it identifies some key pressure points for those seeking to develop robust contingency planning.

High potential impact of crisis versus low priority of crisis management

Chapter 2 documented just how hard it can be to get crisis management onto the agenda of public sector organizations. The low probability of crises, combined with the lack of discernible output from good preventative measures, means that public managers cannot always push forward a proactive preparedness agenda.

A key concern in the design of public policy is whether the policy domain is with or without a definable public (May 1991, 2003). For May (1991: 194), the formulation of preparedness policy for low-probability/high-impact events is a public good that rarely attracts support from interest groups or politicians once the furore caused by a crisis has calmed. If you have been in a crisis you will care about crisis preparedness but the vast majority of citizens have never experienced a meaningful disaster or crisis. Those who bang the drum for crisis management, therefore, tend to be a minority, and once the media spotlight moves on from the latest catastrophe they can be easily forgotten about. This situation can be contrasted with social and economic policies, for example, which can be clearly associated with our everyday circumstances. As a consequence, interest groups develop around these policy areas, citizens become concerned and the politics of decision-making around these policies become important. This is not necessarily the case for crisis management, which means it can easily sink below competing public sector priorities.

Moreover, while contingency planning may bring longer-term and less tangible benefits of security for powerful political and economic interests, it does not provide them with a day-to-day stream of the revenues/benefits/rewards needed for survival. For example, mining companies in Australia rely on state legislation to enable them to mine for iron, gold and bauxite. Farmers in the EU rely on the Common Agricultural Policy (CAP) to provide subsidies and guaranteed prices. For interests such as these, public sector contingency planning is akin to a low-profile 'public good' which is desirable but secondary to the primary benefits from subsidies, legal rights and so on. Indeed, other public goods such as the army and defence are more politically and economically salient than contingency planning. For example, a huge industry of arms manufacturers and defence contractors obtains direct financial benefit from states performing their traditional role as defender of the nation.

149

The outcome of this tension between the destructive potential of crisis and the low priority afforded to crisis management is that organizations often struggle to find a sympathetic political ear. They are acutely aware of the need to place contingency planning high on agendas, but they confront political power, institutional inertia, budgetary constraints and more powerful priorities. Paradoxically, their best hope is for a crisis to destabilize existing institutions and practices, hence producing 'open windows' (Keeler 1993; Kingdon 2003; Birkland 2007) to their views. For example, the two monumental crises that bookended the last decade – 9/11 at the start and the financial crisis at the end – galvanized many countries into reforming their crisis planning operations.

The low priority that is given to contingency planning during quiet periods of an organization's existence are one reason why contingency preparations can be little more than 'fantasy documents' (Clarke 1999). Such plans cannot act as blueprints for coordination and action in times of crisis because they are 'hollow' in the sense that they are created to satisfy minimum requirements instead of facilitating preparedness. As a result, contingency plans can be reduced to symbolics – a form of reassurance both internal and external to the organization. They reassure us, for example, that the mail will still be delivered after a nuclear attack, that regulators and oil companies can clean up after massive oil spillages. For many organizations, it is easier to produce 'fantasy' documents than to continue to fight for contingency planning to move up the agenda. The consequences of this neglect can, however, be disastrous.

Need for planning and order versus uncertainty and disorder of crisis

Attempts to engage in pre-crisis planning are complex. Planning in general requires a maximalist approach, involving a considerable amount of detail in the allocation of roles, responsibilities, resources and the specification of targets. However, decision-making under crisis circumstances typically lacks the type of evidence base that would normally be available for routine decision-making. Indeed, a paradox exists whereby the more elaborate a contingency plan is, the less likely it is that it will be of use in a crisis ('t Hart 1997). Therefore, significant aspects of crisis responses need to be improvised based on immediate circumstances and time constraints. It is not possible, for example, to give *detailed* guidance in advance in terms of:

- the timing of the use of force when hostage negotiations have broken down;
- the level of aid allocated to a region devastated by a hurricane;
- what to tell the media at a press conference when there is conflicting evidence of contamination in domestic water supplies; or
- what one agency should do in a disaster situation if another agency has not adhered to an agreed protocol for cooperation.

150

CASE STUDY 5.1 FANTASY DOCUMENTS AND THE QUEENSLAND FLOODS

The Lockyer Valley Regional Council area covers 2,272 km^2 of the Australian state of Queensland and contains a population of just under 37,000 people. This arithmetic adds up to a sparsely populated region. From late December through to early January 2010–11, parts of the Lockyer Valley were flood affected. However, a major flash flood event occurred on 10 January 2011, the scale and severity of which far exceeded earlier events. What was described by one Queensland Police Commissioner as an 'inland instant tsunami' tore through the Lockyer Valley, destroying hundreds of homes and claiming nineteen lives – 'ground zero' being the town of Grantham, which was almost entirely demolished.

In the wake of the disaster, the official flood inquiry criticized the preparations of the Lockyer Valley Council. While the council officially adopted its disaster management plan in 2009, it had failed to perform its statutory obligations by doing little to establish, review and improve its capabilities over time. The extent to which preparedness policy had been disregarded was made quite apparent through the official flood inquiry. It noted:

- There had been no disaster management meetings for twelve months.
- The disaster management plan required updating.
- There were no sub-plans for different scenarios.
- The council had not established a dedicated disaster response command centre.
- There was no contingency planning for the possibility that key staff would be away on leave or physically unable to attend in the event of a disaster.

The details of these criticisms reveal that the council's plans were 'fantasy documents' – symbolic documents that gave the impression of preparedness rather than any meaningful guidance. A perfect description of this state of affairs was provided by the flood inquiry's description of the council's flood evacuation plan as a mere 'pro forma document into which some inconsequential details had been inserted; but no information of substance'. These problems were exacerbated by the lack of resources applied to disaster management preparations in the region. It is telling that from a 2010/11 council budget of $69 million, there was no funding specifically allocated for flood management, with a mere $5,000 set aside for bush fire preparedness (only half of which was spent). Given this pretext, it is unsurprising that the council's response to the disaster represents a typical case of paralysis.

The Lockyer Valley floods were unavoidable and the community would have been devastated regardless. However, the existence of these fantasy documents, rather than properly resourced plans, exacerbated the crisis in the crucial hours and days after the flood.

Source: Stark and Taylor (2014).

Crisis, therefore, pulls planning in a minimalist direction, because it requires considerable room for individual autonomy in responding to extraordinary and unpredictable circumstances as they arise. The consequence is that contingency planning needs to straddle the tension between maximalist and minimalist approaches. It needs to find a way to ensure that strategies are robust enough to produce good effects but not overly prescriptive as this can put crisis managers into procedural straightjackets. The most common pathway is a contingency plan that identifies lines of authority, roles and responsibilities and means of coordination, leaving key individuals with considerable autonomy to carry out their roles and respond as they feel appropriate. However, alternative planning processes are now beginning to recognize that plans and procedures can be coordinated around values. Stark (2014), for example, documents how crisis managers are slimming down their planning guidance and encouraging inter-operability between agencies by training around core values. This requires training that is based less around providing overly detailed instructions (if X happens you do Y + Z) and more around encouraging crisis managers to think creatively about how they can respond to a threat with a clear idea of appropriate behaviour (if X happens act accordingly with key response principles in mind).

Giving respect to leadership in this way is absolutely crucial in planning terms but, as McConnell and Eriksson (2011) stress, poor leadership qualities can also be one reason why plans fail in the reality of crisis. Variations in personality, ability to handle stress, management styles, ability to use expert advice and ability to take collective decisions are factors of a leader's style that can preclude the effective plan from becoming an effective reality. What this draws our attention towards is the importance of training and simulation; there is no point in having the best plan if you have the most inexperienced or unreliable leader at the forefront of a crisis.

Need for an integrated approach versus realities of institutional fragmentation

The norm among crisis management theorists and practitioners is to recommend coordinated pre-planning for crisis. The result is that relations within and between institutions are united through common goals, strategies, plans and allocation of responsibilities throughout shared networks. Such an approach can allow for a diversity of views in terms of the preparation of plans, but diverse interests then give way to a 'common good' plan.

Such an approach is not so easy to realize in practice. Political systems are vertically and horizontally fragmented. Whether vertical fragmentation is constitutionally entrenched (in federal systems such as the United States, Australia and Canada), or created though laws and convention (in unitary systems such as the United Kingdom and New Zealand), a common feature of all modern liberal democracies is the spread of political decision-making authority over national, sub-national and local levels. Most of such authorities are directly elected, but there is an increasing trend towards non-elected governance in the form of agencies, quangos, non-departmental boards and so on (as well also to private companies who have primary responsibility for many forms of critical infrastructure – from energy systems to toll roads). Horizontal fragmentation, by contrast, refers to the dispersal of policy and administrative functions across the same levels of governance – for example, between local councils and between health authorities. This vertical/ horizontal/ political/ administrative fragmentation is replicated in contingency planning. Crisis management needs to draw on multiple expertise across a range of networks (Hillyard 2000).

Dispersal of power and authority can pose a number of difficulties for the integration of crisis preparedness. First, layers or levels of government or governance are often subject to different political control. Therefore, there is the potential for conflict between different political agendas and priorities. Second, layers or levels of non-elected governance have their own individual bureaucratic specialisms and interests in health, defence, policing, education and so on. This is a breeding ground for bureaucratic politics, where a major priority of each organization is the defence of its own interests.

Third, public authorities may need to coordinate with non-governmental organizations (NGOs). This is an exceptionally common practice in pre-crisis plans, because there is a widespread acceptance that engaging with the expertise and local knowledge of volunteers can be an efficient and cost-effective method of contingency planning. For example, social services, medical units and police services can be supported by voluntary groups. Volunteers can perform roles such as staffing family centres, befriending victims, providing first aid and giving information and advice. However, potential difficulties include:

- volunteers not being involved in the planning process and not feeling ownership of the plan;
- conflicts between the outlooks of part-time 'amateurs' and full time professional specialists;
- volunteers overstepping their assigned responsibilities; and
- volunteers lacking resources and not receiving appropriate training.

Fourth and finally, local communities need to be brought into the contingency planning process. In practice, such rationales are less easily achieved. As we have already discussed in terms of community resilience, there are no guarantees that a 'community' will be a unified whole.

Overall, the foregoing issues highlight the tension between the integrated logic of contingency planning, and the disaggregated nature of the public, private, voluntary and community bodies. Potential solutions are offered by Donald Moynihan who has examined the Incident Command System (ICS) in the United States, which is the primary means of coordinating crisis responses in that country. Moynihan (2008, 2009) provides evidence of how the ICS, which is essentially a hierarchical command and

153

control framework, encounters difficulties when faced with unique inter-organizational networks that materialize during a crisis. However, Moynihan's research also points to a number of factors that can overcome fragmentation. The creation of standard operating procedures, the development of trust between potential network actors and the existence of shared models of understanding (around crisis management values) are all aspects that can enhance coordination (Moynihan 2008). These should be considered as part of a preparedness strategy.

The need for solidarity versus crisis interests

The assumption in most preparedness strategies is that everyone in the planning process, and those who could potentially be involved in a crisis, will share the objectives documented in the contingency plan. For example, plans may assume that those who have an economic interest in a sector affected by a crisis will naturally be on board when it comes to contingency planning implementation. However, the arrival of a crisis may galvanize interests that are threatened by crisis responses. Hence response strategies and implementation plans decided at the comfort of the planning table may be ignored or reinterpreted by powerful interests (McConnell and Eriksson 2011: 95).

Moreover, contingency planning processes themselves are not devoid of powerful interests. We can see their influence, for example, in the efforts of powerful finance and banking institutions to affect the nature of pre-crisis regulation after the Global Financial Crisis. We can also see the influence of the insurance industry in preparedness terms, as brokers increasingly expect public and private institutions to develop business continuity/contingency plans.

Citizens need to be considered here as well. During the United Kingdom's 2001 foot and mouth epidemic, farmers wishing to prevent their livestock from being culled barricaded their farms and threatened violence towards officials who attempted to enter their land. In 2004, during the Beslan school hostage crisis, traumatized parents breached security perimeters in a desperate attempt to save their children from terrorists. And in 2013, the police response to a small local protest about land use in Turkey sparked national political protests involving over 3.5 million citizens across 5,000 locations. What these incidents show is that plans can easily backfire if the interests of citizens are not taken into account or the public mood is ignored. More specifically, these crises show the need to enhance the legitimacy of contingency plans amongst those who will be affected by their outcomes. In the absence of popular support for crisis management actions, everyday citizens can react in ways that can render good crisis planning meaningless.

CONCLUSION

Preparing for a crisis is both an art and a science. Assessing potential threats requires an objective eye and the ability to determine probabilities from more or less scientific data. Yet designing realistic scenarios demands creative skill so that plans can be representative of real threats. Developing a plan requires public managers to have a working knowledge of how to formulate strategies and implementation channels and how to align appropriate resources. But judgement is needed to leave enough room in a plan for decision-makers to act in a flexible and autonomous way during uncertain times. Simulating, testing and auditing plans may require sophisticated managerial practices, but political and administrative will is also needed to ensure that plans are transformed from documents into prepared organizational cultures.

In these specific ways, a preparedness strategy can be seen as a balancing act that combines managerial expertise with intuition, judgement and creativity. In all of these efforts, public managers need to be aware that preparedness is a cycle. This means preparations can never stop. There is no end point when an organization can relax and rest easy in the knowledge that it is ready for a crisis. The cycle is iterative and continual, and being truly prepared represents a moving target. As our understanding of preparedness grows through concepts like resilience, we are beginning to see that good crisis management at this stage is something more than a mere managerial activity. It should become a way of organizational life.

DISCUSSION QUESTIONS

1. Why should public sector organizations plan in advance for a crisis?
2. What are the main elements of good practice in preparing for a crisis?
3. For a public sector organization you are familiar with, map out the key components of: (a) a contingency plan for a potential crisis; (b) a preparedness framework for a potential crisis.
4. In relation to the above, what were the main planning difficulties you encountered?
5. How feasible is an 'all-hazards' approach to contingency planning?
6. Why does contingency planning struggle to get to the top of the political agendas?

REFERENCES

Alexander, D. (2005) 'Towards the Development of a Standard in Emergency Planning', *Disaster Prevention and Management*, 14(2): 158–75.
Aldrich, D.P. (2011) 'The Power of People: Social Capital's Role in Recovery from the 1995 Kobe Earthquake', *Natural Hazards*, 56: 595–611.

Bach, R., Doran, R., Gibb, L., Kaufman, D. and Settle, K. (2010). 'Policy Challenges in Supporting Community Resilience'. Paper presented to the Multinational Community Resilience Policy Group. Available at: <http://dev.naccho.org/topics/HPDP/health-disa/upload/Policy-Challenges-in-Supporting-Community-Resilience.pdf> (accessed 0 May 2014).

Birkland, T.A. (1997) *After Disaster: Agenda Setting, Public Policy, and Focusing Events,* Washington DC: Georgetown University Press.

Birkland, T.A. (2007) *Lessons of Disaster: Policy Change after Catastrophic Events.* Washington, DC: Georgetown University Press.

Brassett, J., Croft, A. and Vaughan-Williams, N. (2013) 'Introduction: An Agenda for Resilience Research in Politics and International Relations', *Politics,* 33(4): 221–8.

Boin, A., Comfort, L.K. and Demchack. C.C. (2010) 'The Rise of Resilience', in L.K. Comfort, A. Boin and C.C. Demchack (eds), *Designing Resilience: Preparing for Extreme Events,* Pittsburgh: Pittsburgh University Press, pp. 13–32.

Boin, A. and McConnell, A. (2007) 'Preparing for Critical Infrastructure Breakdowns: The Limits of Crisis Management and the Need for Resilience', *Journal of Contingencies and Crisis Management,* 15(1): 50–59.

Boin, A., 't Hart, P., Stern, E. and Sundelius, B. (2005) *The Politics of Crisis Management: Understanding Public Leadership when it Matters Most,* Cambridge: Cambridge University Press.

Borodzicz, E.P. and van Haperen, K. (2002) 'Individual and Group Learning in Crisis Simulations', *Journal of Contingencies and Crisis Management,* 10(3): 139–47.

Brändström, A., Bynander, F. and 't Hart, P. (2004) 'Governing by Looking Back: Historical Analogies and Crisis Management', *Public Administration,* 81(1): 191–210.

Bulley, D. (2013) 'Producing and Governing Community (through) Resilience', *Politics,* 33(4): 265–75.

Choularton, R. (2007) *Contingency Planning and Humanitarian Action – A Review of Practice,* No. 59, Humanitarian Practice Network, London: Overseas Development Institute.

Clarke, L.B. (1999) *Mission Improbable: Using Fantasy Documents to Tame Disasters,* Chicago: University of Chicago Press.

Comfort, L.K., Boin, A. and Demchack, C.C. (2010) *Designing Resilience: Preparing for Extreme Events,* Pittsburgh: Pittsburgh University Press.

Council of Australian Governments [COAG] (2009) *National Strategy for Disaster Resilience: Building our Nation's Resilience to Disasters.* Available at: <http://www.coag.gov.au/node/81> (accessed 10 September 2013).

Civil Contingencies Secretariat (2013) *Lexicon of UK Civil Protection Terminology.* Available at: <https://www.gov.uk/government/publications/emergency-responder-interoperability-lexicon> (accessed 1 August 2014).

Fiksel, J. 2003. 'Designing Resilient, Sustainable Systems', *Environmental Science and Technology,* 37(23): 5330–9.

Flin, R. (1996) *Sitting in the Hot Seat: Leaders and Teams for Critical Incident Management,* Oxford: Oxford University Press.

Gunderson, L.H. (2003) 'Adaptive Dancing: Interactions between Social Resilience and Ecological Crises', in F. Berkes, J. Colding and C. Folke (eds), *Navigating Social-Ecological Systems: Building Resilience for Complexity,* Cambridge: Cambridge University Press, pp. 33–52.

156

't Hart, P. (1997) 'Preparing Policy Makers for Crisis Management: The Role of Simulations', *Journal of Contingencies and Crisis Management*, 5(4): 207–15.

HC 36 (2003), House of Commons Health Committee, *The Victoria Climbié Inquiry Report*, Session 2002–3, London: The Stationery Office.

Hermann, M.G. (1997) 'In conclusion: The Multiple Pay-Offs of Crisis Simulations', *Journal of Contingencies and Crisis Management*, 5(4): 241–3.

Hillyard, M.J. (2000) *Public Crisis Management: How and Why Organizations Work Together to Solve Society's Most Threatening Problems*, Lincoln, NE: Writers Club Press.

Inter-Agency Standing Committee Reference Group on Contingency Planning and Preparedness [IASC] (2001) *Inter-Agency Contingency Planning Guidelines for Humanitarian Assistance*, IASC Working Group.

Keeler, J.T.S. (1993) 'Opening the Window for Reform: Mandates, Crises and Extraordinary Policymaking', *Comparative Political Studies*, 25(4): 433–86.

Kingdon, J. (2003) *Agendas, Alternatives and Public Policies*, 2nd edition, New York: Longman.

Lagadec, P. and Carli, P. (2005) 'Crossing the Rubicon', *Crisis Response*, 1(3): 39–41.

McConnell, A. and Eriksson, K. (2011) 'Contingency Planning for Crisis Management: Recipe for Success or Political Fantasy?' *Policy and Society*, 30(2): 89–99.

May, P.J. (1991) 'Reconsidering Policy Design: Policies and Publics', *Journal of Public Policy*, 11: 187–206.

May, P.J. (2003) 'Policy Design and Implementation', in B.G. Peters and J. Pierre (eds), *Handbook of Public Administration*, London: Sage, pp. 223–33.

Moynihan, D.P. (2008) 'Combining Structural Forms in the Search for Policy Tools: Incident Command Systems in US Crisis Management', *Governance*, 21(2): 205–29.

Moynihan, D. P. (2009) 'The Network Governance of Crisis Response: Case Studies of Incident Command Systems', *Journal of Public Administration Research and Theory*, 19(4): 895–915.

Murphy, B.L. (2007) 'Locating Social Capital in Resilient Community-Level Emergency Management', *Natural Hazards*, 41: 297–315.

National Audit Office (2002–3) *Facing the Challenge: NHS Emergency Planning in England*, London: The Stationery Office.

Norris, F. H., Stevens, S. P., Pfefferbaum, B., Wyche, K. F. and Pfefferbaum, R. L. (2008) 'Community Resilience as a Metaphor, Theory, Set of Capacities, and Strategy for Disaster Readiness', *American Journal of Community Psychology*, 41: 127–150.

Pauchant, T.C. and Mitroff, I. (1992) *Transforming the Crisis-Prone Organization: Preventing Individual, Organizational and Environmental Tragedies*, San Francisco: Jossey-Bass.

Perry, R.W. (2004) 'Disaster Exercise Outcomes for Professional Emergency Personnel and Citizen Volunteers', *Journal of Contingencies and Crisis Management*, 12(2): 64–75.

Perry, R.W. and Lindell, M.K. (2003) 'Preparedness for Emergency Response: Guidelines for the Emergency Planning Process', *Disasters*, 27(4): 336–50.

Rosenthal, U. and Pijnenburg, B. (eds) (1991) *Crisis Management and Decision Making: Simulation Oriented Scenarios*, Dordrecht: Kluwer.

Stark, A. (2014) 'Bureaucratic Values and Resilience: An Exploration of Crisis Management Adaptation', *Public Administration*, DOI: 10.1111/padm.1208510.1111/padm.12085.

Topper, B. and Lagadec, P. (2013) 'Fractal Crises: A New Path for Crisis Theory and Management', *Journal of Contingencies and Crisis Management*, 21(1): 4–16.

Wildavsky, A. (1988) *Searching for Safety*, New Brunswick: Transaction.

Younge, P. (2005) 'Exercise Triton 04 – Lessons from the UK's Largest Flood Scenario', *Blueprint: The Magazine of the Emergency Planning Society*, Autumn: 10–11.

FURTHER READING

Two of the most worthwhile sources for articles on the topics of contingency planning and crisis preparedness are the *Journal of Contingencies and Crisis Management* (*JCCM*) and *Disaster Prevention and Management* (*DPM*). Several articles are particularly useful. Eriksson, K. and McConnell, A. (2011) 'Contingency Planning for Crisis Management: Recipe for Success or Political Fantasy?', *Policy & Society*, 32(2): 89–99 address the complex relationship between crisis plans and crisis management outcomes, arguing that the former do not guarantee the latter. Alexander, D. (2005) 'Towards the Development of a Standard in Emergency Planning', *DPM*, 14(2): 158–75 has a highly practical application and does what its title suggests. Perry, R. and Lindell, M. (2003) 'Preparedness for Emergency Response: Guidelines for the Emergency Planning Process', *Disasters*, 27(4): 336–50 is similar, but puts particular emphasis on preparedness as a process rather than simply being about 'having a plan'. Boin, A. and Lagadec, P. (2000) 'Preparing for the Future: Critical Challenges in Crisis Management', *JCCM*, 8(4): 185–91 is a particularly useful reminder that 'crisis' is always confronting us with new and unexpected challenges, so we should be wary of complacency. In Topper, B. and Lagadec, P. (2013) 'Fractal Crises: A New Path for Crisis Theory and Management', *Journal of Contingencies and Crisis Management*, 21(1): 4–16, the argument is advanced further with a plea to rethink all our assumptions about crisis and its challenges. In an earlier article, 't Hart, P. (1997) 'Preparing Policy Makers for Crisis Management: The Role of Simulations', *Journal of Contingencies and Crisis Management*, 5(4): 207–15, there is a different focus again on a wide-ranging exploration of the conduct, opportunities and pitfalls of crisis simulations.

Very few books deal with crisis preparations alone. The most useful sources are those which deal with planning and preparedness in a wider context. Flin, R. (1996) *Sitting in the Hot Seat*, New York: John Wiley & Sons is an authoritative examination of a range of issues surrounding the training and leadership of incident commanders. Many other books locate crisis preparedness (public and private sector) within wider processes of crisis mitigation, resolution and recovery. These include Nudell, M. and Antokol, N. (1988) *The Handbook for Effective Emergency and Crisis Management*, Lexington: Lexington Books; Seymour, M. and Moore, S. (2000) *Effective Crisis Management: Worldwide Principles and* Practice, London: Continuum; and Mitroff, I. (2004) *Crisis Leadership: Planning for the Unthinkable*, Hoboken, NJ: John Wiley & Sons. A highly stimulating book which focuses on the limitations of 'plans' is Clarke, L. (1999) *Mission Improbable: Using Fantasy Documents to Tame Disaster*, Chicago: University of Chicago Press. A step-by-step guide for business continuity is Wallace, M. and Webber, L. (2004) *The Disaster Recovery Handbook*, New York: American Management Association. Schwartz, P. (2003) *Inevitable Surprises: Thinking Ahead in a Time of Turbulence*, New York: Gotham suggests that many of tomorrow's crises are in fact inevitable and quite predictable.

158

Many government agencies and departments now have websites which provide easy access to a wide range of publications – including disaster plans. The main site for the United Kingdom is through the Cabinet Office (https://www.gov.uk/government/topics/public-safety-and-emergencies). In the United States, the Federal Emergency Management Agency can be found at (http://www.fema.gov). In Australia, the relevant agency is Emergency Management Australia at (http://www.ema.gov.au). This also provides links to a very useful (free) publication, the *Australian Journal of Emergency Management*.

Chapter 6

Managing the acute phase of crisis

From politics to technology

LEARNING OBJECTIVES

By the end of this chapter you should:

- have a realistic understanding of what the acute stage of crisis management entails and how response efforts should be evaluated;
- be aware of the five most important functions to be performed during the acute phase – establishing and adapting response structure; gathering and assessing information; facilitating communications; managing networks; providing meaning to events;
- have developed an appreciation that certain aspects of these functions will have to be adapted contingently mid-crisis;
- understand the key contextual issues that can confound a crisis response – crisis type; leadership quality; ability to improvise; capacity to determine when to act; and
- appreciate that managing a crisis involves not only an operational element, but also a political-symbolic element.

KEY POINTS OF THIS CHAPTER

- Acute-stage management is often about 'coping through' rather than successfully 'managing' a crisis.
- The arrival of a crisis situation does not mean that all relevant actors and institutions automatically give up their self-interest in order to resolve that crisis. In particular, crisis response structures can be undermined by bureau politics.

- Emerging forms of technology and social media can assist information gathering in this phase but there are a number of issues that must be considered if these mediums are to add value to crisis managers.
- Crisis management responses must give adequate consideration to crisis communications and a key part of this relates to symbolic forms of communication.
- The management of networks is an essential crisis management task in the face of highly dynamic crises.
- We need to understand the informal and the psychological aspects which underpin crisis responses if we are to improve leadership decisions.

KEY TERMS

- **Centralized response** – a response framework in which a majority of operational and strategic decisions are taken by a central group of high-level decision-makers. Effective when a crisis response needs additional authority and resources.
- **Decentralized response** – a response framework, based around the principle of subsidiarity, in which as many decisions as possible are taken at the lowest possible level. Effective when a crisis response needs to be tailored to local circumstance.
- **Bureau politics** – dissent and conflict between individuals and within/between organizations during a crisis. Often based upon a perceived need to protect an organization's jurisdiction or protect it from blaming.
- **CRIP** – a commonly recognized information picture shared across the agencies involved in a crisis response. Essential for strategy, coordination and avoiding criticism.
- **Framing** – a process through which an agency or actor presents a specific interpretation of events or crisis management actions (required or under way). Framing language is a means through which actors can give meaning to crisis phenomena.

ACUTE CRISIS MANAGEMENT: ELEMENTARY ISSUES

This chapter focuses upon the acute stage of crisis management, which is the point at which pre-crisis planning will be put to the test by the 'real thing'. When acute-stage policies are activated it means that the emergency has arrived: the earthquake has struck, the flood has broken through, the scandal or policy failure has gone public or, worse still, a truly inconceivable event has catapulted onto the agenda. Working at the sharp end of a crisis response, regardless of whether the challenges are political or policy oriented, represents the hardest of managerial trials. The emergency response stage is an occasion where pre-planned implementation strategies must be blended with decisive leadership and improvisation under conditions of severe stress. This is a hard task in itself but, unfortunately, many case studies also show how the uncertainty and fluidity of a crisis can place the decision-maker in a 'no-win' situation where the best possible outcome may simply mean damage limitation (Rosenthal et al. 2001).

However, crisis managers anticipating such periods should not despair. Three reasons exist for some optimism. First, as we argued in the previous chapter, the creation of a robust, well-rehearsed preparedness framework, which anticipates the need for adaptation, can result in an effective crisis response even if the arriving threat does not perfectly match planning protocols. Second, success stories do exist. Within twenty-four hours of the Madrid terrorist attacks in 2004, for example, an effective crisis response had returned the city to 'normal' (Cornall 2005). Third, crisis managers should take comfort from the fact that this stage of the management cycle has attracted a significant amount of attention from different commentators (Weick 1993; Flin 2001; Boin and 't Hart 2003; Lodge and Wegrich 2012; Rose et al. 2013). This means that there is a wealth of theoretical and practical knowledge which can be used to enhance our understanding of the managerial functions required in the heat of a crisis and the issues that may arise to confound a crisis response. These two areas – the functions and issues of acute-stage management – structure this chapter.

We first outline a rather modest definition of acute-stage management, which emphasizes 'coping through' rather than preventing a crisis before it hits. We then outline five crucial functions of emergency management that must be considered on an ongoing and contingent basis mid-crisis:

- establishing and adapting response structure;
- gathering and assessing information;
- facilitating communications;
- network management; and
- providing 'meaning' to events and actions.

Finally, we outline the four key issues which 'matter most' in terms of shaping the outcomes of an acute-stage crisis response: context, leadership, improvisation and action versus inaction.

Once again, however, we attach the now familiar proviso to the points we make in this chapter. Crises will always confound and surprise and, therefore, good practice in the acute phase is very hard to identify because what may work for one acute situation may not work for another. Nevertheless, amid the crisis management literature and the evidence from an endless array of case studies, we can discern certain tools, practices and strategies that are commonly undertaken and may prove beneficial.

162

FUNCTIONS AND RESPONSE PATTERNS

In this section, we are concerned with providing public managers with an understanding of acute-stage crisis management that is both realistic and functional. Being realistic about how we define crisis management in this stage means being aware that the measurements of success in an emergency do not correspond with those that are used in 'normal' times. In crisis management terms, for example, a successful crisis response may relate to a situation in which a crisis cannot be prevented and wreaks havoc for some time, yet is recovered from with relative speed. Applying conventional understandings of policy success in this context would almost inevitably lead to negative evaluations. However, we must understand that the job of the crisis manager at this stage will not be about prevention; that horse has already bolted. We also have to understand that, at times, crisis managers will be powerless to change the nature and impact of a crisis initially. In this regard, crisis managers, like citizens, can be spectators merely observing the sudden impact of a threat. Finally, we need also to be aware that the odds of being seen as a heroic figure and a worthy leader during a crisis episode are not high (although some high-profile examples do exist, such as the case of Mayor Rudolph Giuliani post 9/11 and Australian Premier Anna Bligh during the 2010–11 Queensland floods). The key question then becomes, what is the role of the crisis manager in this period?

The core acute-stage challenge relates to the point after immediate impact. In this sense, crisis management means reacting in a way that stops a bad situation from getting worse; alternatively, it may mean simply 'coping through' a crisis and getting to the other side as unscathed as possible. Hence we need to view acute-stage crisis management as a process of *moderating* the escalation of pre-existing threats. From this realistic view, policy success and failure can be judged more in terms of the actions that allow an organization, community or population to withstand and recover from shocks rather than in terms of avoiding them entirely. This means that acute-stage crisis management is often about the promotion of resilience in the face of the inevitable. It is on these grounds that we need to define and then analyse crisis response efforts.

Taking a functional approach to the acute stage means defining the key managerial processes that can help moderate a crisis. Five functions of acute-stage management are outlined below.

Establishing and adapting the response structure

The previous chapter discussed the importance of designing a response structure as part of the pre-crisis planning process. We also noted that the tendency amongst most public sectors is to orientate around a decentralized model which is shaped by the principle of subsidiarity. However, response structures need to be constantly assessed for efficacy in the acute stage and, if seen to be failing, need to be adapted contingently. One of the clearest examples of such adaptation took place during the 2001 foot and mouth crisis in the United Kingdom. As the crisis response lurched, the largest strategic decisions

163

were centralized to Downing Street. This centralization of authority subsequently meant that a more robust and better-resourced decentralization could take place in terms of the operational dimensions of the crisis response. The key lesson to be taken from such adaptations is that sticking to the plan as the ship sinks around you is almost as negligible as having no plan in the first place. Knowledge of the pros and cons of decentralization and centralization can facilitate changes based on contingency. Here we discuss these issues in detail.

Centralization

This is the 'classic' response to crisis (Williams 1989; 't Hart et al. 1993). In the face of extreme threats to an organization or society, people turn to leaders to deal with the situation. Many a Hollywood film or pulp fiction novel presents an image of a lonely and tormented political figure, glass of alcohol in hand, struggling late at night with a 'life or death' decision in the face of a previously unthinkable crisis situation. Such scenarios are plausible and do occur. Overwhelmingly, however, centralized crisis decisions are taken by small groups of political and administrative elites. Sometimes they will meet in forums that have already been established for this purpose. The United Kingdom, for example, has COBR, the acronym for the Cabinet Office Briefing Rooms where a civil contingencies committee sits, comprising the prime minister and home secretary, as well as senior officials from a number of departments and agencies depending on the specific threat faced. At other times, such elite crisis groups will be ad hoc, put together quickly as a direct response to the given situation. Indeed, we need to recognize that formal and informal crisis groups can spring up throughout different layers and levels of governance (central executives, assemblies, local councils, arms-length agencies) in response to broadly the same threat.

In crisis situations, the benefits of elite 'group' decision-making in central institutions are many (Williams 1998; 't Hart et al. 1993). First, there is an inbuilt system of checks and balances to ensure that no particular individual view prevails without others having had the opportunity to spot weaknesses. Second, the existence of several decision-makers can encourage a wider range of views and 'outside of the box' thinking. Third, bargaining and trade-offs are confined to one small forum, without the need to delay decisions by involving outside actors. Fourth, elite groups will demand high-quality information and are more liable to get it than lower-level groups who may be disempowered by their status and lack of access to sensitive information. Fifth, many (if not all) members of the group will be involved in putting decisions into practice. This may involve anything from making vital telephone calls, to activating emergency powers. Sixth, relatedly, groups involving key elites will ensure that any decisions carry a strong degree of legitimacy. Finally, as the foot and mouth example above shows, decisions that emanate from such groups are authoritative. They command attention and bring with them a commitment in terms of resources, which may not be present in lower-level forums.

164

Centralization may also generate weakness. It can create bottlenecks at the top by placing unrealistic demands on a few shoulders, as was arguably the case with the disappearance of Malaysian flight MH370 and the handful of officials who bore public responsibility for key decisions. Filtering information upwards to a select few can mean overload, and vital information available at lower levels may not make it to the table. It may also result in slow decision-making and can exclude important stakeholders from crucial decisions. Finally, centralizing upwards to the top of the chain of command means that decision-makers are ultimately politicians who may not be able to divorce the consequences of decisions from wider issues relating to public opinion and electoral success.

Decentralization

Most crises require some form of front-line response from the emergency services (police, fire, ambulance) as well as other workers depending on the particular circumstances (health-care workers, vets, laboratory testers and so on). Some decentralization can be an ad hoc response to particular circumstances, but decentralization is typically undertaken on the basis of prior contingency planning rather than a situational usurping of higher-level powers. The core advantage of decentralization is that it allows for 'local' responses that need urgent decisions which cannot wait for approval further up the chain of command. 'Local' has various meanings. It can be municipal level but also state, region or province level. The Australian experience is fairly typical of reliance on 'local' responses. A review of disaster management for the Council of Australian Governments (2002: 61) stated that: 'Commonwealth involvement in disaster response occurs only when events are of national significance, or when a State or Territory requests Commonwealth assistance in an event where State or Territory resources are insufficient or exhausted, or specialist resources owned by the Commonwealth are required.'

This common-sense rationale may be supported by previous harsh experiences where a lack of devolved authority to act has had major consequences. However, decentralization is not guaranteed to be effective, especially when power is devolved to particular individuals and/or units. Individuals need to be clear about their powers and authority, otherwise they may be reluctant to take decisions which make operational sense but which may leave them exposed to subsequent censure or job loss.

Another serious issue relates to the lack of attention given in such response frameworks to geographical scale. Stark and Taylor (2014), for example, have argued that decentralization to local government agencies can be problematic when there is an assumption that local governments are capable of reaching every community in their region. In large, sparsely populated nations, such as Australia, local governments often have to provide disaster management services across geographical areas that are larger than many European countries. In these situations, decentralized systems that devolve authority down to local governments are often incapable of meeting all local needs in the event of a large crisis. Stark and Taylor (2014) have therefore argued that decentralized systems in these localities need to take an additional step whereby crisis management resources are devolved 'down' (to local governments) and then 'out' into local communities. Effectively this means the creation of local disaster management sub-units which engage, and are supported by, local citizens. This second stage of decentralization is absolutely crucial in terms of the development of community resilience in countries such as Australia.

Bureau politics

To varying degrees, all crises will exhibit elements of bureau politics (Rosenthal et al. 1991) and these can compromise a response structure. In other words, power and decision-making will be spread across different departments, agencies and other organizations such as NGOs. There are many benefits of such fragmentation in crisis responses. Diversity creates multiple venues for crisis containment, harnesses differing areas of expertise, puts agencies to the test and promotes a plurality of views. There can, however, be negative consequences. A crisis often throws together organizations that are not used to working together and which may have long histories of rivalry. A number of problems may result. Their response may, in part, be focused on protecting their own organization, and so there may be a reluctance to cooperate and share information with others. For example, an Australian House of Representatives inquiry into the 2003 bushfires in Canberra found that the response was hampered by inter-agency confusion and conflict between fire fighters and land managers from different jurisdictions.

Over the past few years and especially since the post-9/11 reviews conducted by western governments, there has been a move to eradicate or at lease minimize bureau politics through 'whole of government' responses. Some cases such as Australia's response to the Bali bombings and the Asian tsunami were well coordinated as a consequence of extensive and prior 'joined up' planning (Paul 2005; Shergold 2005), although other responses have not been quite so effective. Hillyard (2000) argues that a minimization of bureau politics can be developed at the planning stage by:

- identifying and securing common purpose across networks;
- identifying proper divisions of authority between administrative and operational networks;
- offering incentives (e.g. time, money, equipment) for participation in inter-organization relationships;
- promoting a public safety macroculture; and
- establishing clear and effective inter-organizational structures.

By following these guidelines, suggests Hillyard, organizations can work together in response to crisis, rather than against each other. However, we should be aware that such 'off-the-shelf' ideas are admirable in theory but are not always so easy to put into practice. Pursuing an approach aimed at minimizing bureau politics requires a strong leadership willing to promote inclusive resilience strategies in the crisis preparedness phase.

Information gathering and assessment

Decision-makers typically cannot make decisions unless they have some piece of relevant information at their disposal. However, in a crisis situation, they may know very little in the early stages. Therefore, leaders confront an immediate dilemma. On the one hand, there is the instinct to seek out additional information before acting. On the other hand, the need for swift action may negate waiting on additional information.

This problem is compounded in two ways. First, crises are always media intensive occasions and stoke high levels of public interest. In other words, they get people talking and subsequently create 'explosions' of information. Those with an interest in political survival, reputation and blame cannot afford to ignore these wider expressions of public mood. However, public commentary can, at times, be unhelpful. It can constitute 'background noise' which distracts decision-makers and fails to provide the objective data that they need to make good policy choices.

The second issue relates to the dramatic changes that have occurred over the past decade in terms of media outlets. We now live in a twenty-first-century world of continuous news cycles, blogospheres, multimedia platforms and ever-changing forms of social media that allow citizens to communicate their experiences directly to a public audience as a crisis unfolds. In some respects, these advances are beneficial. They mean that the gathering of information in real time is easier in certain respects. For example, during the 2008 terrorist attacks in Mumbai, Twitter and Flickr were used by Indian citizens to locate loved ones, pool information about the attack sites and to share on-scene photographs with news agencies (Goolsby 2009). Indeed, Facebook and Twitter are now a regular feature in the management of natural hazards around the world, and are used by governments to identify local threats, provide official communications, tell survivor stories and make appeals for assistance. The utility of social media platforms of this nature is also being harnessed in exciting new ways via new software packages that can create 'public access maps' which citizens update by documenting the threats they have encountered (Goolsby 2010). The potential of social media in this regard certainly sits well with the concept of community resilience raised in Chapter 5, and public service organizations should not discount the use of social media as an information source. These channels are easy to create, they are a fast way to communicate and they can draw potentially useful information from affected people quickly (see Box 6.1).

We must be careful, however, not to eulogize social media. This type of information gathering is reflexive (Preston 2012), meaning that citizens observe official communications, listen to the media and each other's views and then make their own commentary. As such, overlapping, complex stories about crises can develop which have a life of their own and may not necessarily reflect 'fact'. Situations can change quickly in a crisis, and

BOX 6.1 FROM FACEBOOK TO PUBLIC-ACCESS MAPS

The 'Virginia Tech' massacre of 2007 was a tragic crisis in which thirty-two students and teachers lost their lives at the hands of a student turned gunman. In the aftermath of the crisis, the Virginian college struggled to communicate anything other than the total number of casualties. Students, however, took to Facebook immediately to share stories and determine who was and wasn't affected by the shooting. As Winerman (2009: 376) states, 'by the time the university released the names one day later, it was old news to the online community: they had identified all 32 of the deceased already'. The Virginia Tech story shows how valuable social media can be for citizens but the fundamental issue for crisis managers remains: can information posted on social media sites be trusted? Historically, first responders and crisis managers have been reluctant to engage with social media outlets. Information that is not authoritative and immediately verifiable can cost lives. However, public-access crisis maps can provide valuable information in realtime for crisis managers. One such system is the Ushahidi Platform, which was originally created to document instances of election fraud in Kenya. The system accepts texts, photographs and videos from mobile communication devices and places them on an electronic map. An instance in which a threat or issue has been identified by a member of the public is represented on the map by a flag and if multiple public communications confirm the existence of the issue, the flag grows bigger as information is added. The Ushahidi Platform was used with some success during recent elections in Afghanistan and in the response to the 2010 Haiti earthquake. In that disaster, volunteers translated messages for assistance onto the map and these requests were accessed and addressed by volunteers working in the area. Public-access maps therefore offer a wealth of verifiable public information that can be used by crisis managers to deal with contingencies as they develop.

Source: Winerman (2009); Goolsby (2010).

experiences from an hour, a day or a week in the past may not reflect the reality on the ground. Subsequently, 'myths' can develop about crisis responses, which cannot be controlled. Social media also creates a world of bloggers, tweeters and commentators who may appear knowledgeable but may not necessarily have the expertise to make crisis management recommendations. We must also bear in mind that social media can be used by those seeking to exacerbate crises. In the current civil war in Syria, in the G20 protests in Pittsburgh and in the London riots of 2011, protestors, rioters and security forces all attempted to exploit social media for their own purposes in ways which do not necessarily promote the rule of law or human rights.

Nevertheless, decision-makers need to conduct some form of information assessment as part of a broader situational assessment. Two specific tools are helpful for this process and should be considered very relevant to a crisis response. The first is the standard Situation Report (SitRep), which can be defined simply as a 'report produced by an officer or body, outlining the current state and potential development of an incident and the response to it' (CCS 2013). The second, less well-known tool is the commonly recognized information picture (CRIP), which is defined as 'a single, authoritative strategic overview of an emergency or crisis that is developed according to a standard template and is intended for briefing and decision-support purposes' (UK Cabinet Office 2013). Both of these communication tools should be built into contingency planning so that designated resources are applied to establishing their regular use in a crisis. Through the SitRep, the operational dimensions of a crisis are communicated. This is essentially the view from the 'front-line': How many casualties? What damage has been done? Were the causes accidental? Were the causes intentional? Is there the possibility of further or escalating threats? If such information is impossible to obtain, an alternative is to try to ascertain what is not impacted by the phenomenon, what is still intact (Lagadec 1993). This can be the beginnings of information gathering to verify what still works.

The CRIP, however, is assembled from the mosaic of agencies involved in a crisis response at all levels. It represents an attempt to ensure that all crisis actors, no matter how important or seemingly tangential, are operating around a shared view of events and a basic understanding of the strategies for resolution. In this regard, the challenge is about coordinating communication lines across a network. The danger for the decision-maker in terms of the CRIP primarily relates to information overload as every organization communicates their view, their interests and their stance. As such, the strategy for assembling a CRIP certainly cannot be 'we need as much information as we can get'. The process needs to be more selective, agreed upon before the crisis hits and very specific about the types of information that have to be requested, digested and then disseminated. Most of all, brevity is required so that a single crisis picture emerges. In this sense, it is crucial that actors in the crisis management network act as 'gatekeepers' or 'sorting mechanisms' by preventing unnecessary information from entering the system and ensuring that the correct information goes to the appropriate decision-maker (Stark 2010). This is a difficult process for sure but one which pays dividends in terms of preventing criticism of a crisis response. In situations where multiple agencies present different views of the same crisis, a picture of disorganization and chaos is painted and negative criticisms are sure to follow.

A final point in terms of crisis communication relates to reflection. That is, how do decision-makers interpret and think about the information that they receive during

169

a crisis? An interesting new mechanism in this area, developed by Patrick Lagadec and trialled in the French public sector, is the Rapid Reflection Force (RFF). An RFF is a cell of 'thinkers' – academics, senior personnel, crisis management analysts – who operate as an unconventional crisis management think-tank during an event. The purpose of the RFF is twofold: (1) to free up key decision-makers by absorbing and streamlining the mass of technical-tactical information generated by a crisis; and (2) to act as a mechanism through which decision-makers can receive (and be challenged by) unorthodox advice and recommendations which may not necessarily be considered when 'standard' crisis management tools are used. The RFF represents the cutting edge of crisis management information assessment (see Box 6.2).

BOX 6.2 RAPID REFLECTION AND ÉLECTRICITÉ DE FRANCE

Électricité de France (EDF) is a French utility company and is the world's largest producer of electricity. It primarily generates its electricity through nuclear power plants, which means it has a clear interest in crisis and risk management. In 2006, EDF implemented the Rapid Reflection Force (RFF) concept into its crisis management frameworks. Initially, this meant the creation of a twelve-person crisis management cell who were 'selected on their capacity to remain creative under intense pressure' (Béroux et al. 2008: 39). During two scenario exercises that year, the RFF performed well, proving that it had the capacity to streamline information, free up decision-makers from time-consuming information assessment and propose creative solutions to crises. In the following year, however, the RFF was tested in a series of real crises. Across 2006 and 2007, for example, a spate of worker suicides created a potential reputation crisis for EDF. Rather than adopt a traditional crisis response characterized by legalistic/technical discourse and hierarchical commands, the RFF encouraged EDF risk managers to see the crisis response as something which had to be attitudinal in nature. Consequentially, the company initiated a process of inclusive 'listening' to the workforce by encouraging them to open up about traditionally 'taboo' subjects. This attitudinal response was successful in the sense that it was publicly endorsed by members of EDF at multiple levels. The case shows how a different voice in the boardroom can result in novel and effective modes of crisis resolution and ultimately led to the EDF management declaring that there would be 'no crisis management without the RRF' (Lagadec et al. 2008: 38).

Source: Béroux et al. (2008).

Facilitating communications

External communications in a crisis situation are vital for operational as well as symbolic purposes. In particular, liaison with the media and ordinary citizens is likely to be needed. In terms of the former, public warning systems can be pre-planned using a range of tools such as social media, mobile phone networks, TV, radio, websites, sirens, loudspeakers and even door-to-door visits by uniformed officers. Difficulties encountered may seem avoidable in hindsight, but can prove remarkably easy to produce in the rush to 'get out a message'. Problems include:

- uneven distribution across different social groups;
- multiple messages containing different emphases/information;
- information applicable to one area may be received by another but not be applicable;
- inappropriate communication methods because of failure to anticipate how a particular social group will react.

(Tierney et al. 2001)

Communications with the media and other stakeholders can take a number of different forms. W. Timothy Coombs (2007) provides an insightful summary of communication 'postures', which is replicated in Table 6.1.

Regardless of the posture taken, there are a number of straightforward 'dos and don'ts' when it comes to communicating with stakeholders outside the crisis response. First, ensure that all messages are clear and straightforward. Coombs (2007: 127) reports that the ability to process information under stress can reduce by up to 80 per cent, which means that the short, sharp communication is essential. Second, be as quick as possible in terms of getting information out as the media will not wait on you to fill the vacuum. In the absence of some form of statement, rumours and innuendo will replace fact. Third, ensure that all statements, but particularly the all-important first communication, are as accurate as possible. Initial impressions matter and a rush to say something that is not properly verified will cast a shadow over the credibility of all other statements. Coombs (2007: 130), for example, provides a number of examples of misrepresenting statistics in relation to industrial accidents in the United States in which the wrong numbers of casualties and injured were reported. Credibility will not be restored after such mistakes. On one occasion, the relatives of miners were told that their loved ones had survived when in fact they were casualties of a workplace accident. Organizational reputations crumble in the face of such errors. A simple way around the tension between speed and accuracy is to make a very basic statement – we are aware of the problem, we are working to fix it and we will let you know more details as soon as we have them. Such straightforward statements may seem vacuous but they give journalists and stakeholders something, which can then satisfy their editors and communities. Fourth, silence reflects a 'we are not in

171

Table 6.1 *Crisis communication 'postures'*

Posture	Process
Denial posture	
Attacking the accuser:	The spokesperson denies the attacks of the person/group that made the claim. This often involves threatening legal proceedings.
Denial:	The spokesperson explains why there is no crisis.
Scapegoating:	The spokesperson blames an external entity for the crisis.
Diminishment posture	
Excusing:	The spokesperson attempts to minimize the agency's responsibility for the crisis. This can include emphasizing how events were outside of their control or their lack of intention to cause harm.
Justification:	The spokesperson minimizes the perception of damage and drama surrounding the crisis. This involves downplaying the severity of the crisis impacts and emphasizing a quick return to normality.
Rebuilding posture	
Compensation:	The spokesperson emphasizes how victims and those affected are being taken care of and the steps that will/are being taken to help them recover. Ideally, the emphasis should be on those steps being taken by the organization itself, which are most generous and extraordinary.
Apology:	The spokesperson publicly apologizes, taking full responsibility for events and asking for clemency.
Bolstering posture	
Reminding:	The spokesperson reminds stakeholders about past good works and track record vis-à-vis crisis and risk management.
Ingratiation:	The spokesperson praises stakeholders and asks for forbearance.
Victimage:	The spokesperson defines the organization as a victim of the crisis, appealing for solidarity with other victims.

Source: Adapted from Coombs (2007: 140).

control' mood. However, equally dangerous is the 'we are in control' statement. This type of communication should only be used in absolute certainty as the media will return to it if a crisis escalates. Finally, avoid 'no comment' as it projects a guilty image of an organization with something to hide, but do not be afraid to confess that information doesn't exist and that when it does come to light it will be communicated immediately. In all endeavours, crisis messaging must reflect a consistency (which is why the CRIP is so important), and an honesty as lies will come back to haunt an organization at the post-crisis stage. (See Box 6.3.)

172

BOX 6.3 SOME GUIDELINES FOR EXTERNAL COMMUNICATION IN A CRISIS

- Empathize with those affected by the crisis. Failure to do so can result in allegations of insensitivity and neglect.
- Demonstrate the will to resolve the crisis, even if you do not know precisely how you will do so.
- All spokespersons should relay the same message(s). Inconsistency will give the impression of incompetence.
- Make sure that the message 'adds up'. Do not send out contradictory signals.
- Use clear, simple language and avoid jargon.
- Stick to the facts and provide essential and accurate information.
- Tell the truth. Every piece of information you might want to hold will somehow find its way into the public domain at a later time. Lies will come back to haunt you.
- Do not speculate about causes or consequences. Events and/facts may prove speculation to have been wrong, hence undermining the legitimacy of the crisis response.
- Avoid 'No comment'. Doing so can give the impression of having something to hide and can lead to speculation and rumour – about the crisis itself but also about the effectiveness of the crisis response.

The efficacy of all crisis communications will benefit from a degree of centralized responsibility. In the pre-crisis stage, a public information officer must develop the communications strategy and in the acute stage the dissemination of information via the officer can ensure coordination across the different communication mediums that are now used in crisis management. Thus crisis warning systems, media liaison, community consultation and social media management can all be synthesized in ways which reduce any danger of contradiction. A key part of this officer's mandate should be the development of contacts amongst the stakeholder network so that the organization enjoys some credibility and legitimacy amongst its audiences before a crisis begins. Any public sector organization that enters into a crisis without credibility is a sitting duck for blame and scapegoating. A good liaison officer will know the key stakeholders and will have created a store of goodwill amongst them prior to a crisis. It is also essential to ensure that there is one primary spokesperson (or small unit of spokespeople) in front of the media in order to generate trust, familiarity and consistency (Fearn-Banks 2007: 19). This need not be the public liaison officer. If there is a need for a public show of repentance or a call for solidarity, for example, such communications may have to be made by the most senior member of the organization. Regardless, this person should then continue

173

to be the public face of the organization throughout the crisis. Information officers and spokespersons should work towards a prearranged series of principles that not only reflect good communication practice but also the mission and values of the agency they are representing.

Network management

We have made the case repeatedly in our earlier chapters that crisis management must be viewed as a collective effort which spans across a network of public sector actors. There is nothing to suggest that the acute-stage period is any different and this means that decision-makers, particularly those at senior levels, will have to devote attention to enabling others to respond to the crisis. Ideally, any external actors who are pertinent to the crisis response will already have been incorporated in preparedness measures. However, when this is not the case, mechanisms will have to be incorporated into response structures to accommodate them. This often means that traditional command and control forms of hierarchy have to be amended to cater for different organizations and interests (Moynihan 2009). This brings us to the concept of network management, which is a means by which a central authority can steer a network of different government and non-government actors towards a common purpose. There are a number of mechanisms available to the public manager for steering networks in a crisis.

- *The coordination centre* – the simplest and most widely used form of network coordination is the coordination centre, which should act as a network hub. Here, decision-makers and information converge in order to ensure a coordinated response. Inside the centre, stakeholders can be brought together around the table and incorporated into the crisis response through a range of means. Within coordination centres in the United Kingdom, for example, the so-called 'bird-table' meeting has proved a popular means of stakeholder inclusion. The format is informal: non-government stakeholders with an interest in crisis resolution stand around a small table, listen to a short briefing from government actors, are then invited to contribute and, most importantly, are given specific tasks which can assist the official crisis response. These tasks tend to relate to communication roles – briefing members of their organizations, persuading them of the need for action, assuring consent etc.
- *Horizontal coordination mechanisms* – these mechanisms span across and unite organizations. They include liaison officers, integrated leadership roles shared by more than one body, jointly created task forces and cross-functional team working (Jordan and Schout 2006: 47; Howlett 2011: 76). Such mechanisms certainly look good on paper as they tend to reflect the principles of joined-up working, but the reality is that they often need a lot of hierarchical direction and authority to secure agreement across bodies (Jordan and Schout 2006: 47).

174

- *'Concertative' bodies* – these are organizations that are designed specifically for negotiation and consultation. As the label implies, they can help public bodies work in concert with each other (Bouckeart et al. 2010). Such agencies, which often revolve around industrial relations agreements, can be very important mediators in certain crises. Michael Howlett (2011: 93), for example, discusses advisory councils as network management tools that can act as a 'listening post' for actors to hear each other and a conflict resolution tool through which group agreement can be facilitated. For those crises characterized by political conflict, such bodies can be crucial.

- *Contracts and performance indicators* – contractual obligations are commonplace within public sector contingency plans and they can be a network management tool. The relations that form around contracts can create routinized forms of coordination that strengthen trust, solidify partnerships and minimize transaction costs for all concerned. Performance indicators are also a means through which a central body can 'meta-govern' a network. For example, a central crisis management agency may insist that a number of specific plans, containing specific elements, are created and then summarized as a measurement of performance. Obviously, such measurements may ensure that some crisis management activity is ongoing in a network but they cannot necessarily ensure that it is effective in reality.

Aside from modes of network management, a number of authoritative decisions can be taken to assist the capacities of others to respond. First, there is authorizing the actions of others. Societies turn to leaders in times of crisis. They look for strength, reassurance and firm action from their elected representatives and the officials who advise them. However, leaders simply do not have the capacity to take all crisis decisions and even when contingency plans are activated, leaders may still have to authorize particular features of the crisis response. Most Western countries, for example, allow presidents/ prime ministers/premiers to declare a 'state of emergency' in order to invoke emergency powers. When such powers are involved, they may be heavily prescriptive but they may also smooth the pathway for lower levels of government to exercise extraordinary powers in designated 'disaster zones'. At times, however, leadership authorization may be ad hoc, that is, a direct response to critical circumstances without reliance on any legal precedent.

A second type of enabling decision is the approval of funding, i.e. emergency aid. Not only can such actions assist operational activities, but they carry strong symbolic messages of caring and compassionate government. Indeed, there can often be substantial political benefit in doing so. For example, when German Chancellor Gerhard Schröder had to contend with major flooding of the River Elbe in 2002, his financial aid package went down so well with voters that it helped turn around his electoral fortunes, despite the fact that primary disaster management responsibilities lay elsewhere in the German political system with the Länder (Bytzek 2008).

A third type is enabling others to respond by seeking outside help. Obtaining support, notably from other countries and NGOs such as the Red Cross and Oxfam, can be highly practical in supporting a national response. However, seeking help can also be portrayed as a sign of weakness and an inability to cope. In the European Union, for example, a relatively new Civil Protection Mechanism has emerged which allows countries to request assistance in times of crisis. Traditionally Eurosceptic countries such as the United Kingdom, however, have been reluctant to engage with the mechanism or request assistance because of concerns about sovereignty. Nevertheless, reluctance to seek help (or a decision to turn down help, as George W. Bush did initially in relation to Hurricane Katrina) can backfire. It can leave political decision-makers vulnerable to the criticism that 'politics' is placed before saving lives.

A fourth type is bringing in experts for advice. This strategy can prove immensely valuable. The handling of the 1998 Sydney Water contamination crisis was helped greatly by drawing on the expertise of international authorities on cryptosporidium. However, expert advice can often illustrate the inexactness of science, leaving political figures and officials to interpret the advice in a variety of different ways. In addition, advice can be taken on board when it suits a political message, or rejected when it does not (the British government's reaction to conflicting scientific messages on the threat from BSE in the 1980s is a case in point). Bringing in experts does not mean a value-free crisis response

Providing meaning to events and actions

As indicated in Chapter 1, a useful reference point to aid our understanding of responses to crisis is the distinction between operational and political-symbolic responses ('t Hart 1993). Operational responses involve front-line responders who are concerned with matters such as rescue operations and repairing damage. Correspondingly, political-symbolic responses are primarily the concern of political (and at times) bureaucratic elites who are more concerned with longer-term issues relating to public perceptions, legitimacy and credibility. It would be a mistake, however, to think of operational and symbolic matters as entirely separate. Action 'on the ground' can have symbolic repercussions – especially because it creates impressions (and media-worthy stories) regarding government's ability to cope. In addition, the wider political presentation of rescue efforts (promises of more resources, praise for emergency services and so on) can help give momentum to operations.

In this area, crisis analysts often discuss 'crisis framing', 'crisis narratives' and 'meaning making'. The basic concept of a 'frame' refers to an argument or an exposition of events that both explains and simplifies a crisis through the presentation of a specific interpretation. Those involved in crises seek to frame events in ways which are sympathetic to their needs and this typically involves 'the selective exploitation of data, arguments, and historical analogies' and the formation of 'discourse coalitions' in order to promote a particular interpretation. Such interpretations may then be used to propose a remedy to a crisis, to settle the question of who is to blame, or to escalate policy failures into political crises (Boin et al. 2005: 82;

176

Olmeda 2008: 64). From this point of view, acute-stage crisis management is essentially an exercise in providing meaning to others about events and strategies ('t Hart 1993; Boin et al. 2005).

In practical terms, this means that crisis leaders need to communicate across a range of stages ('t Hart 1993). They must visit the 'front-line' as soon as it is feasible to do so without damaging the crisis response. They must be seen communicating with those affected with empathy. They must present themselves as a competent leader at the helm of operations. They must be seen protecting the democratic process during a crisis by briefing parliaments and citizens and, most importantly, each of these symbolic moments needs to be seen as a point at which a consistent framing message is to be communicated.

Meaning making is an essential task in terms of acute-stage crisis management but performing it effectively is not so easy. Lack of concrete information and ambiguous signals aside, there will always be others in liberal-democratic societies who wish to put forward counter-frames: citizens, political parties and especially the media. Political leaders are expected to know what's going on, and to be firm and decisive. If they do not, they can be accused of being out of touch, uncaring or even incompetent. The archetypal example is George W. Bush's infamous flyover photograph during Hurricane Katrina. After receiving some criticism for not immediately cutting short his holiday due to the disaster, the president ordered Airforce One to fly over the affected zone. A picture was taken of the president peering out his plane window at the devastation. Instead of projecting an image of a leader in charge it conveyed the frame of a leader operating at some distance from those who were suffering. A white, privileged man returning from a holiday, flying high above the disaster while ethnic minorities and disadvantaged groups struggled on the ground. This simple photograph went on to became a symbol at the centre of a very negative framing process that damaged the president's standing as a crisis manager (Preston 2008). However, even if leaders adopt a proactive meaning making strategy, they can be accused of excessive partisanship and not accepting responsibility. For example, in response to failures in Sweden's capacity to act quickly in helping its citizens caught up in the 2004 Boxing Day tsunami, Prime Minister Persson was heavily criticized for his blaming of lower-level officials – and his public support suffered as a consequence (Brändström et al. 2008). There is no ideal solution to this dilemma of blaming others versus accepting responsibility. Political leaders can do little more than weigh up the varying options and then stick firmly to their adopted perspective in the hope of success, or until the credibility of the approach becomes unsustainable and a 'backflip' is the only feasible way of avoiding further damage.

INFLUENCES ON THE ACUTE STAGE OF CRISIS MANAGEMENT

Having set out some of the most important functions to be performed during the acute crisis management stage, we now turn to a series of factors that can impinge on performance. These can be understood as issues that must be considered contingently on a crisis-by-crisis basis. While each of the functions described above needs to be performed, consideration of the issues below indicates that every function also needs to be tailored to the specific circumstances in which a public sector organization finds itself during a crisis. In this sense, 'what matters' most is an appreciation on behalf of the public manager about the need to evaluate and adapt functions in the midst of an emergency.

Context matters: the properties of the crisis shape the response

An important factor in helping shape the crisis response is the particular characteristics of each crisis. There are four main dimensions of 'crisis' which we identify as being of particular importance.

First, some crises may be more familiar than others. At one end of the spectrum are 'incomprehensible crises' (Boin et al. 2005) such as 9/11, which are so sudden and devastating that political leaders and crisis managers can be at a loss in terms of how to intervene. Operational workers will muddle through and political leaders will struggle to fill the vacuum and frame the crisis in terms of causes and consequences. In general, therefore, such crises will see a high level of improvisation and departure from crisis contingency plans (where they exist). By contrast, some crises may be periodic threats, such as hijackings and kidnappings. Therefore, there is more time for planned responses based on learning from previous incidents.

Second, some crises are more complex and 'coupled' than others (Perrow 1999). The more complex the crisis, the more it will reflect threats which are multi-faceted and unpredictable, in contrast to others which produce simple, predictable and linear sequences. When a crisis is 'coupled' it means that it emerges from and affects many different systems. A simple comparison can be used to elucidate the challenge here. When a driver falls asleep at the controls of a train and causes a tragedy, the acute stage is likely to follow a predictable pattern. The operational response will be oriented around the emergency first responders, and the primary communication role will be to reassure transport users that this was an isolated incident and that changes will be put in place to ensure that it does not happen again. Hence the crisis is well understood, contained within narrow parameters and is geographically limited. All things being equal, therefore, it requires a straightforward process of crisis containment. This can be contrasted against a crisis, like BSE in the United Kingdom, where crisis managers were uncertain of the threat they faced – where it began, how it could be prevented, how to determine when the crisis it was at an end. Moreover, in this second case the crisis response impacted on farming, food, public health and even tourist sectors, and response policies existed in a range of elected levels of government (from the EU to local authorities), covering different territories within the United Kingdom, and including public and private organizations. Such crises are harder to manage because they require effective crisis response on the part of institutional policy systems and sub-systems.

178

Third, some crises raise deeper questions about the nature of a society, its institutions and its policies. These deeper issues are not always apparent as the emergency unfolds but can certainly be a factor that can hamper acute-stage management efforts. The manner in which racial divisions and poverty impacted on the response to Hurricane Katrina is one notable example. A second can be seen in the shock and national soul-searching that took place in the wake of the tragic killing of seventy-seven citizens at the hand of Anders Breivik in Norway in 2011. The kind of crisis response required here is something quite different as it is almost wholly about symbolic measures. It is exceptionally difficult for political leaders to manage the symbolic aspects of such traumatic events, however, because they are deeply rooted in society and cannot be easily influenced. Nevertheless, the Norwegian national response to the heinous acts performed by Breivik shows how important symbolism can be to crisis management and, more importantly, provides evidence of how national solidarity can emerge from tragedy (see Box 6.4).

Fourth, the timing of a crisis is crucial – especially in terms of electoral cycles, leadership career paths and the rhythms of political life. We must remember that crises pose

BOX 6.4 NATIONAL REAFFIRMATION AS A RESPONSE TO TRAGEDY

On 22 July 2011, a car bomb exploded outside a government building in the city of Oslo killing eight people. In itself, this act of terrorism would have been a traumatic experience for Norwegian citizens to come to terms with given that nation's peaceful post-war history. Such an event was inconceivable in a country defined by its progressive culture of openness, tolerance and non-violence. However, the Oslo bomb was only a prelude to a far more shocking crime. As the bomb detonated in Oslo, its perpetrator entered a summer camp of the Workers Youth League – an association affiliated with the national Labour Party – and shot dead sixty-nine Norwegians. Many of the deceased were teenagers. The trauma that followed the worst atrocity on Norwegian soil since the Second World War was made all the harder to accept by the fact that the murderer – Anders Breivik – was a Norwegian citizen who profiled as a cold, calculated killer with a far-right militant agenda. Breivik's status forced the Norwegian population to look at itself introspectively and question its cultural values. Surely this monster was a sign that the country was less tolerant than previously believed? The answer from the Norwegian people and their political and social institutions was unequivocal. As the *New York Times* reported, 'the sense that Mr Breivik's hateful beliefs should not be allowed to fill Norway with hate too was part of the country's response to the attacks from the beginning'. Symbolic messages emanated from the national political institutions reaffirming the Norwegian identity as that of a tolerant nation, and the relatives of victims publicly reaffirmed their belief that Breivik should not be subjected to corporal punishment and should be released if the prison system rehabilitated him. Tens of thousands took to the streets to sing 'children of the rainbow', a multicultural anthem that Breivik had derided publicly. These acts, both widespread and spontaneous, can be understood as a highly symbolic crisis response through which a country sought to heal the psychological scars created by tragedy.

major challenges for political leaders. They may end up rejuvenated by the crisis (like Mayor Giuliani after 9/11 or German Chancellor Gerhard Schröder after the flooding of the River Elbe) but many will be damaged because of their apparent inability to restore order or at least give the impression of doing so (FEMA Director Michael Brown after Hurricane Katrina, Icelandic Prime Minister Geir Haarde after the global financial crisis). Therefore, if a crisis hits just before national elections (the 2003 Madrid Bombings, the 1999 dioxin contamination in Belgium), we are more liable to see a crisis response that attempts to exploit the crisis for electoral advantage (claiming credit for apparent successes in the response) and/or minimizing the potential damage to electoral prospects. By contrast, political leaders tend to be at their strongest during the honeymoon period of their initial term in office. A crisis in this period will still present leadership challenges but it can be a chance to capitalize on inbuilt public sympathies for a new government, consolidate support, draw a clear line separating the current regime from its predecessor, allow leaders to make their mark and so on. All things being equal, new leaders are more likely to rise to the challenge and accept responsibility for the problem, as opposed to blaming others for failings.

Leadership qualities matter: personality can shape outcomes

Managing crises is not simply a matter of opening up a policy toolkit and applying 'rational' responses to whatever threat is looming or has already hit hard. Crisis decision-making does not operate on the basis of traditional 'policy cycle' norms, where decision-makers identify problems, generate and assess options, and then make considered choices from a range of alternatives. Crisis decision-making under conditions of acute threat is more likely to accord with models of:

■ *Naturalistic decision-making* – involving quickly changing real-time conditions, where goals and tasks are ill-structured and there is a rapid interweaving of thinking and acting. Decisions are the product of an action-feedback loop (continual situational assessment in response to changing conditions) (Flin 1996).

180

■ *Recognition-primed decision-making* – where decision-making is based much more on instinctive 'first thinking' and the focus is much more on elaborating and improving upon this option (Flin 1996).

These 'non-conventional' aspects of crisis decision-making show how crucial leadership is in terms of the variability of crisis response performance. We can aid our understanding of leadership by looking at psychological studies of crisis. For example, Janis and Mann (1977) typified the coping patterns of leaders during crisis, linking each pattern to a form of action or inaction. They identified five patterns:

1. *Unconflicted inertia* – complacency, dismissive of threats, no action taken.
2. *Unconflicted change* – threats treated seriously, memory searched for possible protective action and a preparedness to act accordingly.
3. *Defensive avoidance* – lack of interest because the consequences of threats are too difficult to bear, or 'passing the buck' to someone else, or clinging to an unrealistic solution.
4. *Hypervigilance* – panic, fear of entrapment, tendency towards snap decisions.
5. *Vigilance* – high-quality seeking out of appropriate decisions based on thorough information searching and unbiased judgements.

In effect, some of us may thrive on extreme challenges, some of us may try and block them out, or some of us may muddle through them in some way. Such variation tells us something about how individuals have differing capacities to face up to threats (see Table 6.2).

Interacting with these various coping patterns are leadership personalities and how they relate to crisis decision-making. There is an extensive range of political psychology literature that examines the role of personality and leadership traits of politicians ('t Hart 2010; Cottam et al. 2004; Post 2004) although very few pieces of research have been specifically applied to studies of crisis management. One notable exception, however, can be found in the work of Preston (2008), who argued that 'the leadership style of any national leader, whether president or prime minister, plays an important role in shaping how a given administration will respond to or manage a crisis' (Preston 2008: 35). Preston (2008) discusses the presidential leadership style of George W. Bush in relation to the crisis response that followed Katrina. The former president has been described by political psychologists as having a passive-positive leadership personality (Cottam et al. 2004: 27), which means that he was less personally engaged in the minutiae of policy-making, keen to delegate tasks to a trusted coterie of appointees and eager for reaffirmation and support from that circle. Most importantly, however, is that passive-positive leaders show 'a tendency for policy drift, especially during times of crisis, in which you expect to see confusion, delay and impulsiveness on their parts' (Cottam et al. 2004: 27). Preston examines the president's need for control and his sensitivity to context as crucial aspects of leadership style, making the case that a low

181

Table 6.2 Personality types and crisis responses

	Compulsive personality	Narcissistic personality	Paranoid personality
Core character traits	Good organizational skills, attention to detail, rational approach to problem-solving	Extremely self-confident, tendency to be surrounded by sycophants, not good at listening to constructive criticism	Always suspicious of others. Will tend to interpret events as plots and betrayals
Typical individuals	Scientists, engineers, chief executives	Senior politicians and senior officials	From all walks of political life and officialdom. Especially common among leaders in 'closed' societies
Thoughts when confronted by crisis	Tendency to panic. Out of their comfort zone	Not afraid to take tough decisions. May even relish the prospect of doing so and becoming 'heroized' by the crisis	Paranoia becomes exaggerated. The crisis is seen as part of a deeper and long-standing conspiracy
Advantages for crisis decision-making	Can be good as 'reality checkers' regarding the details of pursuing a particular response	Prepared to act quickly	None
Disadvantages for crisis decision-making	Procrastinators. Prone to too much weighing up of pros and cons. Slow to act. Lacking a 'big picture' perspective. May eventually produce impractical strategies but will defend them vigorously	Liable to rush to judgement without thinking through the consequences or listening to alternatives. Will equate their own judgements with the 'national interest'	Tendency to gross overreaction

Source: Adapted from Post (2004: 105–13).

need for control and an insensitivity to context created a number of crisis management pathologies during the Katrina response. Preston concludes that (2008: 56):

> as expected for a less controlling, insensitive leader, Bush's lack of personal engagement and substantial delegation to subordinates, coupled with his lack of attention to the surrounding policy environment, greatly slowed his personal response to the crisis . . . Bush's political response to the crisis was often out of step with the views (and perceptions) of those outside of his inner circle. This led to the clear disconnect between those events being widely covered by the media (and viewed by the public) and White House pronouncements on the subject.

Improvisation matters

Where contingency plans exist, they are liable to be activated in a crisis, and they are liable to involve role parameters, but leave some room for improvised responses based on situational contexts. In the first instance, individuals need to know whether to cope with a new threat using 'routine procedures' or to activate a contingency plan. Doing so is not always easy, because individuals must interpret the often complex and ambiguous signals that can present themselves. Is there really a crisis? Could I be exaggerating? What if I activate a crisis plan and it's not a crisis after all? What if I don't activate the plan and it really is a crisis?

If and when a plan is activated, there are immense pressures to stick with prior agreements. Otherwise, individuals may feel they will damage the crisis response and/ or face repercussions. Equally, however, crisis responses *do* require improvisation and decision-makers need to know how far to exercise their autonomy. At its most extreme, rule books get 'torn up' and the response is an overwhelming situational dominance. A classic example is the fall of the Berlin Wall, where checkpoint guards were besieged by thousands of people (jubilant at an announcement concerning the liberalization of travel laws from East to West). The response of guards, against orders but under overwhelming pressure, was simply to let everyone through. In other more tragic circumstances, there seems to be no plan at all and the crisis response is shambolic and ad hoc. The Beslan school siege of 2004, where over 300 people died (mostly children), is an example in which public authorities where at a loss in terms of what to do, while families and the media were allowed to roam freely around the site.

As Figure 6.1 indicates, the relationship between situational assessment and decision-making strategy is a crucial factor in shaping the crisis response. When risks are fairly low and there is time to act, there is the opportunity for creative and analytical responses which accord more with 'routine' decision-making. When risks are substantial and time is at a premium, there is a tendency to turn to the 'rules', i.e. contingency plans. However, when risks are extraordinarily high and there is little or no time to act, the use of cognitive resources (or 'thinking power') is limited, and

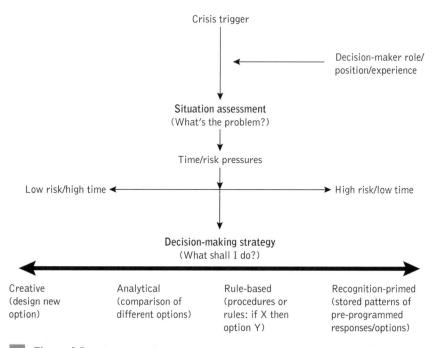

Figure 6.1 *Relationship between situation assessment and decision-making*

Source: Adapted from Crichton and Flin (2002: 209).

the response is 'recognition primed'. In other words, there is a reliance on instinct or 'gut feel' rather than a plan.

Knowing when to act matters: inaction can resolve crises too

Public policy involves decisions to act, as well as decisions not to act. Crisis management is no different, involving authoritative action on the part of leaders and managers, as well as inaction. Inactivity may vary from deliberate restraint, to paralysis in the face of extreme threats. Choosing between a range of options is difficult. As Janis and Mann (1977: 6) suggest: '[a] decision maker under pressure to make a vital decision affecting his future welfare will typically find it painful to commit himself, because there are some excepted costs and risks no matter which course of action he chooses'. We deal with each below.

The benefits of intervention have already been outlined. Crisis decision-makers may step in and authorize others to take decisions, or release funds, or make public pronouncements about the wider repercussions of the crisis. We cannot predict what would happen were such interventions not to occur. We can note, however, that criticism levelled at proactive crisis intervention is generally that it is too authoritarian, too soft, too little, or too late.

By contrast, there may be benefits from inactivity. A tactic of judicious restraint may avoid inflaming a situation or ensuring that decisions are taken by other authorities that are better placed to do so. The 1985 Heisel Stadium disaster is a good example. On-the-spot arrests were avoided because of the perceived risks of arresting individuals in an already aggressive crowd situation. In addition, the Belgian minister of internal affairs decided not to go the stadium and make a decision on whether the match should continue. Instead, he left the matter to local officials ('t Hart et al. 1993). However, such inactivity has the potential to rebound. There are strong societal expectations that authoritative decision-makers will act in a crisis situation. To not do so leaves them vulnerable to accusations of incompetence, carelessness and lack of compassion. In the Heisel example, criticism of the internal affairs minister was considerable. In the 1991 Los Angeles riots after the beating of Rodney King, Police Chief Darryl Gates' decision not to get involved in the critical early stages (he went to a fundraising event and argued that the situation would soon be under control) were described subsequently as 'mystifying' by a commission of investigation (Miller 2001). Gates never recovered from the damage to his reputation and resigned in 1992.

Inactivity is not, however, just a deliberate strategy (for better or worse). It may be a dysfunctional response to an imminent threat or one that has already caused damage (this equates with 'unconflicted inertia' as identified by Janis and Mann 1977). A form of paralysis may set in. For example, there are many different accounts of when on 11 September 2001 George W. Bush was first told of the terrorist strike. However, two things seems reasonably clear: he was told of the first attacks before entering a classroom, and then continued reading to schoolchildren for at least five minutes (accounts vary) after being interrupted by an aide who told him that a second plane had struck. Whether we sympathize with the president (after all, no-one had ever been faced with this once-in-a-lifetime situation) or are critical (he is one of the most senior of politicians, paid and expected to be decisive in difficult circumstances), 'paralysis' is not something widely researched or made available for public consumption. Bush's temporary inactivity seems to be the most striking example of political paralysis available to us in the modern world.

A different type of dysfunctional inactivity is not paralysis as such, but refusal to recognize that a crisis exists. The French heatwave of 2003, in which 15,000 people died, is one such example. The bureaucratic and segmented culture of the French public administration was not conducive to recognizing disparate signals indicating an increase in heat-related deaths. Indeed, later on the day the prime minister finally ordered a general mobilization of hospital resources, one week after initial problems emerged, the heatwave subsided (Lagadec 2002).

ACUTE-STAGE MANAGEMENT: A HIGH-WIRE BALANCING ACT

The balancing acts involved in this stage of crisis management are delicate to say the least. Response structures have to be implemented in robust ways, yet they need to be malleable enough to adapt to context. Part of this balancing act involves careful assessment of how the politics of the crisis impacts on operational aspects. Information gathering needs to be comprehensive enough to ensure that no crucial data is lost in the decision-making process, yet information has to be sorted, sifted and reflected upon selectively so that crisis managers are not overwhelmed. Networks must be well managed and well coordinated but also diverse and multi-faceted. And this balance must be struck in the pressure cooker of a crisis under the glare of a media spotlight that is moving increasingly faster, and becoming more global and diverse. Public expectations are high and tolerance of failure is low. It seems that societies' crisis managers are becoming less like heroes and more like villains ('t Hart et al. 2001).

There are also a series of unknowns in the management mix at this stage, which have the potential to influence effectiveness. We *do* know that context, leadership, improvisation and avoiding paralysis can be crucial to success or failure at this stage but what we *cannot* anticipate is how, where and when these issues will arise. What we are absolutely sure about, however, is that crisis managers can have an accurate compass for navigating uncertainty if they have a clear sense of organizational values, a clear awareness of good crisis management principles, and a willingness to evaluate and adapt practices to contingency. These are an absolute must for acute-stage crisis management

DISCUSSION QUESTIONS

1. Choose any crisis with which you are familiar and map out the network of actors that were involved in the crisis response. How, if at all, were they coordinated?
2. Provide some examples of bureau politics in action. Were these episodes helpful to the resolution of the crises?
3. Why does 'symbolism' matter in the crisis management response?
4. To what extent is centralization a necessary but not sufficient condition for an effective crisis response?
5. Can you think of any examples of crises where policies have to be adapted in the height of the emergency? Was leadership important in these episodes?

REFERENCES

Béroux, P., Guilhou, X. and Lagadec, P. (2008) 'Rapid Reflection Force Put to the Reality Test', *Crisis Response*, 4 (2): 39–40.
Boin, A. and 't Hart, P. (2003) 'Public Leadership in Times of Crisis: Mission Impossible?' *Public Administration Review*, 63: 544–53.
Boin, A., 't Hart, P., Stern, E. and Sundelius, B. (2005) *The Politics of Crisis Management: Public Leadership under Pressure*, New York: Cambridge University Press.

Bouckeart, G., Peters, B.G. and Verhoerst, K. (2010) *The Coordination of Public Sector Organizations: Shifting Patterns of Public Management,* Basingstoke: Palgrave Macmillan.

Bytzek, E. (2008) 'Flood Response and Political Survival: Gerhard Schröeder and the 2002 Elbe Flood in Germany', in A. Boin, A. McConnell and P. 't Hart (eds), *Governing after Crisis,* New York: Cambridge University Press, pp. 85–113.

Civil Contingencies Secretariat. (2013) *Lexicon of UK Civil Protection Terminology.* Available at: <https://www.gov.uk/government/ . . . /LEXICON_v2_1_1-Feb-2013. xls> (accessed 22 May 2014).

Coombs, T. (2007) *Ongoing Crisis Communication: Planning, Managing, and Responding,* Los Angeles: Sage.

Cornall, R. (2005) 'New Levels of Government Responsiveness for "All Hazards": The Public Management of Natural Disasters and Emergencies', *Australian Journal of Public Administration,* 64(2): 27–30.

Cottam, M.B., Dieter-Uhler, E., Mastors, E. and Preston, T. (2004) *Introduction to Political Psychology,* Mahwah, NJ: Lawrence Erlbaum Associates.

Council of Australian Governments [COAG] (2002) *Natural Disasters in Australia: Reforming Mitigation, Relief and Recovery Arrangements,* Canberra: Commonwealth of Australia. Online. Available at: <http://www.dotars.gov.au/disasters/publications/ pdf/natural_naturaldis.pdf> (accessed 14 August 2006).

Crichton, M. and Flin, R. (2002) 'Command Decision Making', in R. Flin and K. Arbuthnot (eds), *Incident Command: Tales from the Hot Seat,* Aldershot: Ashgate, pp. 201–38.

Fearn-Banks, K. (2007) *Crisis Communication: A Casebook Approach,* 3rd edition, New York: Taylor & Francis.

Flin, R. (1996) *Sitting in the Hot Seat: Leaders and Teams for Critical Incident Management,* Oxford: Oxford University Press.

Flin, R. (2001). 'Decision Making in Crises: The Piper Alpha Disaster', in U. Rosenthal, A. Boin and L.K. Comfort (eds), *Managing Crises: Threats, Dilemmas and Opportunities,* Springfield, IL: Charles C. Thomas.

Goolsby, R. (2009) 'Lifting Elephants: Twitter and Blogging in Global Perspective', in L. Huan, J.J. Salerno and M.J. Young (eds), *Social Computing and Behavioural Modeling,* New York: Springer, pp. 2–7.

Goolsby, R. (2010) 'Social Media as Crisis Platform: The Future of Community Maps/ Crisis Maps', *ACM Transactions on Intelligent Systems and Technology,* 1(1): 1–11.

't Hart, P. (1993) 'Symbols, Rituals and Power: The Lost Dimension in Crisis Management', *Journal of Contingencies and Crisis Management,* 1(1): 36–50.

't Hart, P. (2010) 'Political Psychology', in D. Marsh and G. Stoker (eds), *Theory and Methods in Political Science,* 3rd edition, Basingstoke: Palgrave.

't Hart, P. Heyse, L. and Boin, A. (2001) 'New Trends in Crisis Management Practice and Crisis Management Research: Setting the Agenda', *Journal of Contingencies and Crisis Management,* 9(4): 181–8.

't Hart, P., Rosenthal, U., and Kouzmin, A. (1993) 'Crisis Decision Making: The Centralization Thesis Revisited', *Administration & Society,* 25(1): 12–45.

Hillyard, M.J. (2000) *Public Crisis Management: How and Why Organizations Work Together to Solve Society's Most Threatening Problems,* Lincoln, NE: Writers Club Press.

Howlett, M. (2011) *Designing Public Policies: Principles and Instruments,* New York: Routledge.

Janis, I.L. and Mann, L. (1977) *Decision-Making: A Psychological Analysis of Conflict, Choice and Commitment,* New York: The Free Press.

Jordan, A. and Schout, A. (2006) *The Coordination of the European Union: Exploring the Capacities of Networked Governance*, New York: Oxford University Press.

Lagadec, P. (1993) *Preventing Chaos in a Crisis: Strategies for Prevention, Control and Damage Limitation*, London: McGraw Hill.

Lagadec, P. (2002) 'Crisis Management in France: Trends, Shifts and Perspectives', *Journal of Contingencies and Crisis Management*, 10(4): 159–72.

Lodge, M. and Wegrich, K. (2013) *Executive Politics in Times of Crisis*, Basingstoke: Palgrave.

Miller, A.H. (2001) 'The Los Angeles Riots: A Study in Crisis Paralysis', in U. Rosenthal, A. Boin and L.K. Comfort (eds), *Managing Crises: Threats, Dilemmas, Opportunities*, Springfield, IL: Charles C. Thomas, pp. 49–60.

Moynihan, D.P. (2009) 'The Network Governance of Crisis Response: Case Studies of Incident Command Systems', *Journal of Public Administration Research and Theory* 19(4): 895–915.

Olmeda, J.A. (2008), 'A Reversal of Fortune: Blame Games and Framing Contests after the 3/11 Terrorist Attacks in Madrid', in Boin, A., A. McConnell and P. 't Hart (eds), *Governing after Crisis*, New York: Cambridge University Press, pp. 62–84.

Paul, L. (2005) 'New Levels of Responsiveness: Joining Up Government in Response to the Bali Bombings', *Australian Journal of Public Administration*, 64(2): 31–33.

Perrow, C. (1999) *Normal Accidents: Living with High-Risk Technologies*, New York: Basic Books.

Post, J.M. (2004) *Leaders and Their Followers in a Dangerous World: The Psychology of Political Behaviour*, Ithaca, NY: Cornell University Press.

Preston, J. (2012) *Disaster Education: Race, Equity and Pedagogy*, Rotterdam: Sense Publishers.

Preston, T. (2008) 'Weathering the Politics of Responsibility and Blame: The Bush Administration and its Response to Hurricane Katrina', in Boin, A., A. McConnell and P. 't Hart (eds), *Governing after Crisis*, New York: Cambridge University Press, pp. 33–61.

Rose, J., O'Keefe, P., Jayawickrama, J. and O'Brien, G. (2013) 'The Challenge of Humanitarian Aid: An Overview', *Environmental Hazards*, 12: 74–92.

Rosenthal, U., Boin, R.A. and Comfort, L.K. (2001) 'The Changing World of Crisis and Crisis Management', in U. Rosenthal, R.A. Boin and L.K. Comfort (eds), *Managing Crisis: Threats, Dilemmas, Opportunities*, Springfield, IL: Charles C. Thomas, pp. 5–27.

Shergold, P. (2005) 'Coping with Crisis', *Public Administration Today*, 5(October–December): 43–48.

Stark, A. (2010), 'A New Perspective on Constituency Representation: British Parliamentarians and the "Management" of Crises', *Journal of Legislative Studies*, 16(4): 495–514.

Stark, A. and Taylor, M. (2014) 'Citizen Participation, Community Resilience and Crisis-Management Policy', *Australian Journal of Political Science*, 49(2): 300–315.

Tierney, K., Lindell, M.K. and Perry, R.W. (2001) *Facing the Unexpected: Disaster Preparedness and Response in the United States*, Washington, DC: Joseph Henry Press.

Weick, K.E. (1993) 'The Collapse of Sensemaking in Organizations: The Mann Gulch Disaster', *Administrative Science Quarterly*, 38: 628–52.

Williams, P. (1989) *Crisis Management: Confrontation and Diplomacy in the Nuclear Age*, London: Martin Robertson.

Winerman, L. (2009) 'Crisis Communication', *Nature*, 57: 376–378.

FURTHER READING

The starting point for all students of crisis management should be Boin, A., 't Hart, P., Stern. E. and Sundelius, B. (2005) *The Politics of Crisis Management: Public Leadership Under Pressure*, Cambridge: Cambridge University Press. Its key strength is that it views crisis management as a political activity rather than a technical exercise focused on the resolution of threats. A number of other writings by these authors and other colleagues help flesh out the political nature of crisis management: see Rosenthal, U., Charles, M.T. and 't Hart, P. (eds) (1989) *Coping with Crises: The Management of Disasters, Riots and Terrorism*, Springfield, IL: Charles C.Thomas; Rosenthal, U., Boin, R.A. and Comfort, L.K. (eds) (2001) *Managing Crises: Threats, Dilemmas, Opportunities*, Springfield, IL: Charles C. Thomas. A specifically UK dimension is given in McConnell, A. (2003) 'Overview: Crisis Management, Influences, Responses and Evaluation', *Parliamentary Affairs*, 56(3): 393–409.

Some articles/book chapters are very useful for particular aspects of crisis responses. A seminal work, 't Hart, P. (1993) 'Symbols, Rituals and Power: The Lost Dimension in Crisis Management', *Journal of Contingencies and Crisis Management*, 1(1): 36–50, examines why the 'appearance' of the crisis response matters significantly, including leaders visiting disaster sites. For a ground-breaking analysis of the dangerous tendency to think that the current or next crisis will play out the same way as a previous one, see Brändström, A., Bynander, F. and 't Hart, P. (2004) 'Governing by Looking Back: Historical Analogies and Crisis Management', *Public Administration*, 81(1): 191–210. For the psychology of crisis responses and the effect of stress on decision-makers, see Flin, R. (1996) *Sitting in the Hot Seat: Leaders and Teams for Critical Incident Management*, New York: John Wiley & Sons; Flin, R. and Arbuthnot, K. (eds) (2002) *Incident Command: Tales from the Hot Seat*, Aldershot: Ashgate Publishing; Post, J.M. (1991) 'The Impact of Crisis-Induced Stress on Policy Makers', in A. George (ed.) (1991) *Avoiding War: Problems of Crisis Management*, Boulder, CO: Westview Press, pp. 471–94; Post, J.M. (2004) *Leaders and their Followers in a Dangerous World: The Psychology of Political Behaviour*, Ithaca: Cornell University Press. Overlapping with the psychology of crisis responses is the propensity for groups to behave dysfunctionally in crisis situations. The classic work here is Janis, I.L. (1982) *Groupthink*, 2nd edition, Boston: Houghton Mifflin. For a sympathetic critique and substantial development in this area, see 't Hart, P. (1994) *Groupthink in Government: A Study of Small Groups and Policy Failure*, Boston: Johns Hopkins University Press; and 't Hart, P., Stern, E.K. and Sundelius, B. (eds) (1997) *Beyond Groupthink: Political Group Dynamics and Foreign Policymaking*, Ann Arbor: University of Michigan Press. It is also worth noting that Irving Janis has written several books which deal with the perils of making difficult decisions. Of particular use in terms of understanding crisis behaviour is Janis, I.L. (1989) *Crucial Decisions: Leadership in Policymaking and Crisis Management*, New York: Free Press.

There are many books which deal with communication issues in crisis situations. Some are better than others, although for guides to good practice, it is worthwhile checking out Nudell, M. and Antokol, N. (1988) *The Handbook for Effective Emergency and Crisis Management*, Lexington: Lexington Books; Coombs, W.T. (1999) *Ongoing Crisis Communications: Planning, Managing and Responding*, Thousand Oaks, CA: Sage; Fink, S. (2002) *Effective Crisis Management: Planning for the Inevitable*, Lincoln, NE: iUniverse; and Regester, M. and Larkin, J. (2002) *Risk Issues and Crisis Management: A Casebook of Best Practice*, 2nd edition, London: Kogan Page. A particularly

189

thought-provoking approach to crisis communications is provided in Lagadec, P. (1993) *Preventing Chaos in a Crisis: Strategies for Prevention, Control and Damage Limitation*, Maidenhead: McGraw-Hill. A particularly stimulating approach which focuses on the need for ethical and effective crisis communication to tackle the competing narratives which emerge in crisis situations is found in Millar, D.P. and Heath, R.L. (eds) (2004) *Responding to Crisis: A Rhetorical Approach to Crisis Communication*, Mahwah, NJ: Lawrence Erlbaum Associates. A more conceptual and thought-provoking take on crisis communications can be found in Sellnow, T.L. and Seeger, M.W. (2013) *Theorizing Crisis Communication*, Chichester: John Wiley & Sons.

The most useful starting point for understanding why crisis responses exhibit various response patterns is 't Hart, P., Rosenthal, U. and Kouzmin, A. (1993) 'Crisis Decision Making: The Centralization Thesis Revisited', *Administration & Society*, 25(1): 12–45. As a supplement to this with a particular focus on the strengths and weaknesses of bureau politics, see Rosenthal, U., 't Hart, P. and Kouzmin, A. (1991) 'The Bureau-Politics of Crisis Management', *Public Administration*, 69(2): 211–33. The issue of cross-agency coordination in crisis responses is an increasingly relevant one – especially with moves towards 'joined up' approaches to crisis management. For a perspective on the limitations but also the strengths of cross-institutional responses, see Hillyard, M. J. (2000) *Public Crisis Management: How and Why Organizations Work Together to Solve Society's Most Threatening Problems*, Lincoln NE: Writers Club Press. For a more recent examination of organizational cooperation, see L.M. Svedin (2009) *Organizational Cooperation in Crisis*, Farnham: Ashgate.

Chapter 7

After the crisis

Evaluation, learning and accountability

LEARNING OBJECTIVES

By *the end of this chapter you should:*

- be aware that what happens 'after' the crisis is a significant factor in crisis management;
- be aware that post-crisis stages are characterized by learning and accountability dynamics which often conflict;
- have developed a solid understanding of the problems and processes associated with evaluating crisis management performance;
- have developed a clear understanding of the nature of post-crisis inquiries and the problems associated with learning through inquiries; and
- be aware that the aftermath of each crisis is different and that the institutional, political, economic and social contexts are important in terms of shaping post-crisis outcomes.

KEY POINTS OF THIS CHAPTER

- Evaluations of crisis management policy have to overcome a series of complex methodological problems in order to define successes and failures.
- Efforts to learn after crises often result in small-scale changes because reforms are constrained by institutional legacies and intransigent public policies.
- Crises are socially constructed in the aftermath period through interactions which 'frame' their nature and the performance of key actors and organizations.

- There is a range of outcomes in the post-crisis stage which may be political and policy oriented, and success in one category does not automatically mean success in the other.
- Post-crisis outcomes are shaped by many factors, particularly the nature and salience of the crisis, the timing of the event(s), party politics, the affected policy area and the degree of symbolism attached to the threat.

KEY TERMS

- **Evaluation** – may come in a variety of formats but is generally an investigation into the circumstances surrounding 'what went wrong', and what lessons can be learned.
- **Post-crisis accountability** – processes and issues relating to ensuring that crisis managers (from elected politicians through to public officials) are answerable for their roles/decisions in causing and managing crisis, with the possibility of sanctions being applied where necessary.
- **Post-crisis learning** – processes and issues related to ensuring that policies/institutions and procedures/values are able to adapt or reform after a crisis, in order that mistakes are not repeated and that society is better prepared should a similar crisis arise again.

POST-CRISIS EVALUATION: LEARNING AND ACCOUNTABILITY IN CONTEXT

At this stage in the crisis management cycle, emergency management issues cede to other concerns around policy evaluation, learning and accountability. What were the causes? Could it have been avoided? Is anyone to blame? Could it have been better managed? What lessons can be learned? Such questioning emanates from political executives, political parties, media, ordinary citizens victims and their families, lawyers, and more.

This period might be slower paced than the acute stage in terms of the demands made on public managers but it would be a mistake to describe the aftermath of a crisis as prosaic. In fact, these periods can be very dramatic because efforts to account for what happened can stimulate extreme emotions, prompt radical change and electrify political relationships. For this reason analysts have begun to recognize that this stage of the management cycle is a point in the life of a crisis that can actually be more problematic than the emergency that preceded it (Rosenthal 2003: 132). This is because the shift to recovery issues often means that 'what began as an accident or series of incidents turns into a story about power, competence, leadership and legitimacy (or lack of it)' (Boin et al. 2005: 100).

192

In broad terms, we need to come to grips with two closely entwined dynamics if we wish to understand this stage. These relate to *learning* and *accountability*. In the aftermath of a crisis 'lesson learning' is certainly encouraged, if not demanded. As Wildavsky (1988: 245) notes about the recovery period, 'learning is a golden concept: everybody is for it'. Indeed, the literature on post-event learning is often characterized by an assumption that crises will lead to rational policy evaluations, clear-headed lessons and organizational improvements which will enhance future crisis management efforts. In this sense, post-crisis learning is very much about looking forward in positive ways to a new and safer future (Boin et al. 2008). However, public managers need to ask why it is that public sector organizations continue to repeat the mistakes of the past, despite their engagement in lesson learning processes?

To a large extent, the answer to this question can be found in the concept of accountability or, more accurately, in the political reality of accountability as it plays out in public sector systems. Unlike learning, accountability is very much about looking back so that that an account of what happened can be constructed (Boin et al. 2008). In these accounts, individuals and organizations involved in decision-making need to explain and answer for their actions (explanatory accountability) and they also have to make commitments to change what went wrong (amendatory accountability). This is the essence of accountability; explaining and changing problematic policy pathologies (Pyper 1996).

However, the search for proper accountability can easily become a search for someone or something to (unfairly) blame, a means of self-promotion or an exercise in political manoeuvring through which culpable actors escape censure. In such contexts, clear-headed evaluations are replaced with political machinations which prejudice meaningful change. We must be careful, therefore, not to assume that lessons will be learned from a crisis because in many instances 'the more we know about a crisis, the less likely we are to learn from it. This is the case, because in the politics of blaming, information is tailored to be ammunition . . . data are selected and moulded to construct winning arguments in a battle for political-bureaucratic survival' ('t Hart and Boin 2001: 184).

Central to both accountability and learning is the issue of *evaluation*. If we are to hold decision-makers to account or put in place 'lessons learned' insights, we need to have a clear idea of what success and failure means in crisis management terms. What worked and what did not? This seemingly simple question is made complex by a range of problems which are inherent to any evaluation of policy. The most important of these is the simple fact that one person's policy success is another person's policy failure. Unfortunately, this issue of subjectivity creates a grey area in which political interpretations of success and failure can flourish.

Finally, it is again important to understand that evaluative processes do not exist in a vacuum. They too have to be understood in *context*. This means locating them within (at least) three environments:

- the larger systemic environment in terms of the democratic, public sector and crisis management system relevant to the crisis;
- the historical or chronological environment, which takes into account the timing at which the crisis arrives in terms of the pertinent organizations; and
- the crisis itself in terms of its threat, inconceivability and impact.

Each of these contexts will have an important bearing on the nature of accountability and learning at this stage.

We begin this chapter by tackling the thorny issue of crisis management evaluation in the hope that having a clearer set of prescriptions about 'good' and 'bad' crisis management might curb detrimental post-crisis politics. We then move onto discussing learning and accountability and we conclude by drawing attention to the contextual factors that can influence the quality of both. In each area we wish to show the importance of performing post-crisis functions correctly. Decisions at this stage can have profound effects when the next threat arrives. If there is too much blame, crisis leaders may act as timid followers of procedure next time rather than real decision-makers. If there is insufficient accountability, the credibility of future crisis managers may be damaged by sceptical public opinion. And if no learning takes place at all in these periods, then future crises and crisis management mistakes become inevitable.

THE CHALLENGE OF EVALUATION: WHAT CONSTITUTES A SUCCESSFUL CRISIS RESPONSE?

More often than not crises enter into folklore as high-profile failures of some sort. Levees fail to prevent floods and presidents fail to respond; nuclear meltdowns and space shuttle explosions are said to be caused by failed safety cultures; and global financial crises emerge out of the failures of financial regulation. However, crisis management successes do exist but they are under-reported. In Australia, government responses to asylum crises, terrorist attacks and floods have been defined as successful either in terms of the effectiveness of crisis management policy or the political gains that came with strong leadership (Dyrenfurth 2005; Paul 2005; Arklay 2012). Similarly, in Europe, responses to the HIV-in-the-blood-supply crisis of the 1980s and 1990s have been defined as successful on programmatic and political terms (Albæk 2001). In the United States, the reassuring actions of Tylenol after their stock was poisoned with cyanide has become a classic case study in effective crisis communications (Argenti and Druckenmiller 2004), and in South America community responses to natural disasters have been lauded (Maskrey 1994). The key question when reviewing these cases is what actually constitutes success and failure when it comes to crisis management?

It would be something of an understatement to claim that there are methodological problems associated with this question. McConnell (2011), for example, draws

194

attention to no fewer than seven significant problems in the evaluation of crisis management efforts:

1. *Perceptions* – success and failure cannot be considered indisputable facts but rather the result of subjective perceptions. Facts can tell a story of success or failure but they are always interpreted by evaluators differently depending on their values and aims.

2. *Benchmarks* – there is no definitive set of performance indicators for crisis management although some, such as the SPHERE targets for international humanitarian responses, have gained popularity. Despite this, using one set of benchmarks risks privileging one set of values above others. For example, privileging policy effectiveness targets may overlook the importance of protecting human dignity and democratic rights during a crisis.

3. *Winners and losers* – crisis management can be a zero-sum game, which means that the interests of some have to be compromised so that the crisis is ended. The managing of the threat of the volcanic ash cloud that travelled across Europe in 2008 is a good example. While the grounding of flights across Europe allowed aviation authorities to claim success in terms of safety, thousands of disgruntled tourists stranded around Europe questioned why the decision was taken without solid scientific evidence.

4. *Boundaries of evaluation* – where do we 'draw the line' in terms of evaluation? Political opportunists may either wish to narrow the evaluation process so that it focuses on a blameworthy individual or, conversely, they may seek to broaden out the analysis to examine a whole system or sector as a potential failure. The nature of the evaluation is another politically loaded issue: should a technical inquiry explore managerial issues or should a broader inquiry examine political and social cultures too?

5. *Time* – following on from the above, the question of time is also an evaluative issue. Short-term, medium-term or long-term analyses will lead to different results. For example, consider a crisis such as the 2001 foot and mouth epidemic in the United Kingdom. In this case, many acute-stage failures were evident but in the longer term those failures prompted many substantive improvements in crisis management policy. A short-term analysis would lead to a verdict of failure but a longer-term evaluation would have to consider lesson-learning successes.

6. *Goals* – stable policies have clear goals but in the turmoil of a crisis goals can be fluid, contradictory and contingent on events. And in a context of high uncertainty, information deficits and unintended consequences can mean that defining any goal can be problematic.

7. *Alternatives* – how can we possibly know what would have happened if decision X had not been taken or been taken in a different way? Although some crisis analysts have addressed this question by building alternative scenarios to what actually happened

195

in real crises (Rosenthal and Pijnenberg 1991), we are still some distance from being able to use counterfactuals to evaluate performance. (See Box 7.1.)

Consideration of these issues is absolutely crucial but we do not wish to present an image of the policy evaluation process as an insurmountable task. Public managers can engage in crisis management evaluations. Below we present one pathway through which an evaluation can be tackled, developed by McConnell (2010, 2011). This model instructs evaluators to focus upon *process*, *decisions* and *politics* and its key strength is that it provides clear definitions of crisis management success and failure based on these three areas. Let us begin with the definition of success:

> A crisis management initiative is successful if it follows pre-anticipated and/or relevant processes and involves the taking of decisions which have the effect of minimising loss of life/damage, restoring order and achieving political goals, while attracting universal or near universal support and/no or virtually no opposition.
>
> (McConnell 2011: 68)

And the definition of failure represents something of a negative mirror image of the above:

> A crisis management initiative fails if it follows unanticipated and/or non-relevant processes and involves taking of decisions which have the effect of

BOX 7.1 POTENTIAL BENCHMARKS FOR CRISIS EVALUATION

- Stated objectives of crisis managers
- Benefit to individuals/groups/localities under threat
- Level and speed of improvement
- Adherence to industry standards, e.g. risk management standards, crisis management protocols
- Adherence to appropriate laws
- Adherence to contingency plans
- Comparison with the crisis experience of another jurisdiction
- Level of expert/political/public support for the initiatives
- Benefits outweighing costs
- Degree of innovation adopted
- Preservation or enhancement of moral/ethical principles

Source: Derived from McConnell (2011).

heightening loss of life/damage, acting as a barrier to the restoration of order and damaging political goals, while attracting universal or near universal opposition and/no or virtually no support.

(McConnell 2011: 70)

In both definitions we can see the importance of process, decisions and politics:

- *Process* – there are three aspects to an evaluation of process. The first relates to the following of 'pre-anticipated processes'. This means adherence to the plans, procedures and frameworks created during pre-crisis stages. When crisis managers execute contingency plans perfectly, replicate scenario training in real situations or adhere to a set of established preparedness principles, they might be able to claim some degree of success. The second aspect relates to the phrase 'relevant processes' which is designed to capture the fact that 'sticking' to plans and procedures as *the* route to crisis management success can be problematic. Hence, a second measure of success might be found in the ability of crisis managers to engage in ad hoc attempts to make plans, procedures and policies more relevant by amending them or even abandoning them altogether. What matters in this evaluation is the extent to which a process matches the reality of the crisis. The third aspect of evaluating process relates to the degree of support it attracts. Processes which have little support can rarely be considered successful. For example, a contingency plan which is only supported by a small percentage of a crisis management network will have little effect.

- *Decisions* – these are primarily evaluated in terms of their effects on the crisis response. In general, three categories exist in this aspect of an evaluation: minimizing loss, restoring order and achieving political goals. In this last aspect, decisions can be evaluated like processes in that they should attract support and credibility. However, it is vital to see decisions as analytically distinct from agreed-upon processes. They are distinct because they represent separate interventions often requiring initiative or intuition. For this reason they do not relate to actions which implement pre-prepared processes. For example, the 1999 evacuation of Florida residents in anticipation of Hurricane Floyd proved overly problematic because decision-makers chose to publicize a very vague definition of households at risk. The result was that many thousands were evacuated who did not need to be. Returning to our earlier points, this could be seen as effective or ineffective – a decision which was either 'overkill' or precautionary. The important *analytical* point here, however, is that it has to be evaluated as a contingent decision that was distinct from pre-crisis planning processes.

- *Politics* – as the previous two sections have intimated, political successes are primarily measured in terms of enhancements in political support, credibility and legitimacy. A basic yardstick in this regard can be found in opinion poll 'bounces' for leaders in the wake of their crisis leadership. In the wake of 9/11,

197

for example, approval ratings for George W. Bush rose exponentially. A second way of measuring success is to review the absence of critical voices or public anger, particularly if a crisis has been mismanaged. At a broader level, the ability of a political leader or organization to maintain its policy agenda or maintain its broader ideological or political values in the face of a crisis can also be considered a measure of success. For example, in the face of the global financial crisis, the United Kingdom's Liberal Democrats, operating in a coalition with the Conservative Party, have been forced to compromise a number of their election promises and party values in order to support public sector cuts designed to reduce the government's debt. These actions, widely viewed as compromises of their intrinsic values rather than crisis management measures, have led to public criticism of the party's leaders.

This framework (see Table 7.1) certainly advances the evaluation of crisis management behaviour significantly, not least because it allows an evaluator to plot out degrees of success and failure across a spectrum. Despite their use in everyday language, success and failure are not absolute terms. Crises can simply not be categorized definitively into one box or another. Therefore evaluators need to develop a spectrum upon which their evaluations can be better gauged. In doing so there is a greater chance that meaningful lessons can be learned from a crisis.

This framework, however, is not without its problems, particularly if the focus of analysis is on a public sector organization or political institution rather than a policy (Stark 2011). There is a complexity issue involved as a public sector organization might perform a specific function which spans all three evaluative dimensions simultaneously. Hence one organizational function could be the subject of a complicated and overlapping series of evaluations which could fall victim to hindsight bias. In addressing this issue, Stark (2011) suggests a simple two-stage evaluative process through which an institution's functions are first defined and then linked to the expectations of key actors in a crisis.

This type of evaluation focuses much more on the political reality of this stage of the crisis process and recognizes that specific groups will evaluate the same organization differently, depending on their specific interests. It is therefore an attempt to understand how evaluation works in a subjective political world. The question for an evaluator is: how did an organization frustrate or facilitate these expectations? The answers that emerge represent an evaluation that is more appreciative of politics and the fact that fully objective forms of analysis are an impossible target in a political context (see Box 7.2).

POST-CRISIS POLICY REFORM AND LEARNING

In theory, crises create not only enormous potential for policy reform, but also for learning. The word learning evokes positive images, taking reform beyond mere policy

Table 7.1 Success and failure in crisis management

Processes		
Success	Failure	Types of evidence used to assess
Adherence to processes relevant to resolving crisis in hand, e.g. as specified in contingency plans OR considered 'good practice' in the crisis management field (such as bringing stakeholders and responders together) OR improvised because of their relevance OR bypassing the contingency plan in order to save lives/restore order	Adheres to processes which are not relevant to resolving the crisis in hand, i.e. specified in contingency plans OR considered 'good practice' in the crisis management field OR improvised because of their relevance OR bypassing the contingency plan in order to save lives/order	Inquiry reports, witness testimonies, contingency plans, expert briefings, stakeholder briefings, best practice documents
Utilizing processes which have constitutional and/or stakeholder legitimacy/support	Utilizing processes which do not have constitutional and/or stakeholder legitimacy/support	Inquiry reports, witness testimonies, expert briefings, stakeholder briefings, opinion polls, party statements, media reports and commentary
Attracting universal or near universal support for processes and/no or virtually no opposition	Attracting universal or near universal opposition for processes and/no or virtually no support	Inquiry reports, witness testimonies, stakeholder briefings, opinion polls, party statements, legislative debates, media reports and commentary, internet forums

(Continued)

Table 7.1 *(Continued)*

Decisions

Success	Failure	Types of evidence used to assess
Decisions which help contain or eradicate threats	Decisions which do not contain threats, allowing them to escalate	Inquiry reports, witness testimonies, contingency plans, expert briefings, stakeholder briefings, best practice documents
Decisions which help minimize damage to people, property and any actors or institutions affected by the crisis	Decisions which damage people, property and any actors or institutions affected by the crisis	Inquiry reports, witness testimonies, stakeholder briefings, opinion polls, party statements, media reports and commentary
Decisions which help restore order and stability	Decisions which prevent the restoration of order and stability	Inquiry reports, witness testimonies, stakeholder briefings, expert briefings, opinion polls, party statements, media reports and commentary
Attracting universal or near universal support for decisions and/no or virtually no opposition	Attracting universal or near universal opposition for decisions and/no or virtually no support	Inquiry reports, witness testimonies, stakeholder briefings, opinion polls, party statements, media reports and commentary, legislative debates, internet forums

Politics

Success	Failure	Types of evidence used to assess
Enhancing reputation and/or electoral prospects for leaders' parties and governments	Damaging reputation and/or electoral prospects for leaders' parties and governments	Opinion polls, media reports and commentary, party statements, legislative debates, internet forums
Easing the business of governing by making the issue manageable	Detrimental to the business of governing because the issue is unmanageable	Government briefings, opinion polls, media reports and commentary, party statements, legislative debates, internet forums
Maintaining government's desired policy agendas, either the status quo or policy change	Knocks off course government's desired policy agendas, either through the status quo or policy change	Government briefings, opinion polls, media reports and commentary, party statements, legislative debates
Maintaining government's broad governance agenda and promotion of values, either through conservation or reform	Knocks off course government's broad governance agenda and promotion of values, either through blocking desired conservation or creating an otherwise undesired reform momentum	Government briefings, opinion polls, media reports and commentary, party statements, legislative debates
Attracting universal or near universal support for political implications and/no or virtually no opposition	Attracting universal or near universal opposition for political implications and/no or virtually no support	Inquiry reports, witness testimonies, stakeholder briefings, opinion polls, party statements, legislative debates, media reports and commentary, internet forums

Source: McConnell (2011).

Figure 7.1 *A crisis management success/failure spectrum*

Source: McConnell (2011).

BOX 7.2 MATCHING EXPECTATIONS TO ORGANIZATIONAL OUTPUTS

The process through which this evaluation operates is relatively simple. Certain crisis actors will have specific expectations about how public organizations should operate in relation to their interests. The larger the gap between these expectations and the actual outputs of an organization, the greater the likelihood of accusations of failure. This process therefore requires that research takes place into what a range of actors wants from crisis management responses. Stark (2011) defines three broad categories of crisis actor.

- *Crisis manager expectations* – these are actors 'inside' the machinery of a government-led response who share some common features. Hence front-line responders, local and central bureaucrats, appointed members of an executive, and elected political leaders can all be classified under the term crisis manager. Two features unite this group. Crisis resolution will be their primary objective with a subsidiary goal being to come out of the crisis cleanly, free from association with blame and the threat of reforms.
- *Citizen expectations* – citizens will have different expectations of a crisis response depending on their proximity to the effects of disruption. While crisis managers and citizens will be united by their desire to resolve the crisis, the directly affected are far more likely to want a crisis response that is cognizant of their views. Such expectations can easily conflict with the wishes of crisis managers who may want to be insulated from citizen demands or engage in more authoritarian forms of crisis management.
- *Opportunistic expectations* – numerous actors gravitate towards the politics of a crisis, even if not directly affected or required for the purposes of resolution. These actors are labelled opportunistic here as they are united by their exploitative motivations. Opportunistic actors can include individual or

> groups of elected representatives, journalists, shunned crisis management agencies or even organizations from other governance tiers (e.g. at the local or supranational levels) that have been excluded from a crisis response. Unlike crisis managers and affected citizens, public concessions from opportunistic actors about the need to end the crisis quickly may mask the fact that the escalation, exacerbation or politicization of events may better serve their interests.
>
> Source: Stark (2011).

changes into the language of societal improvement. However, once we try and dissect the meaning of this universal 'cure all', we realize that it is both complex and contested. Some see the term as entirely relative to individual perceptions, while others exhibit varying degrees of positivism, specifying certain conditions for learning to have taken place: the rectification of deficiencies, or the correction of a mismatch between intentions and outcomes.

For our purposes, it is useful to recognize a relative congruence, despite differences in language between a number of approaches which differentiate between alterations and improvements to technical aspects of organizations/policy, and changes in core beliefs. We should be aware here of the distinction between 'shallow' and 'deep' types of learning in analyses which focus upon 'double-loop' and 'single-loop' learning (Argyris and Schön 1996; Argyris 1999). Single-loop learning is the most common after crises. It refers to 'the correction of practices within the existing policy paths and organizational frameworks. It is learning to deal with manifest problems without having to change core beliefs and fundamental rules of the game' (Boin et al. 2005: 121). Many would argue, however, that single-loop reforms deal with symptoms rather than causes and that they entrench rather than reform problems in the status quo. Double-loop learning refers to learning around the larger context within which technical operations occur – cultures, paradigms, the organizational foundations of an institution (Argyris and Schön 1996). Learning here is not simply connected to strategies for effective performance but to the very cultures that define effective performance. However, double-loop learning tends to receive the least attention from public managers because it is costly in time and effort and is unlikely to provide actors with short-term reciprocal forms of 'pay-back' (Korac-Kakabadse et al. 2002).

The shallow and the deep dimensions of learning can also be seen in the similarities shared by a number of typologies of public policy, which differentiate between (1) alterations and improvements to aspects of organizations/policy, and (2) changes in core beliefs and goals (Hall 1993; Sabatier and Jenkins-Smith 1993; Rose and Davies 1994). This congruence between studies has led Boin et al. (2008: 16–17) to typify three broad forms of post-crisis learning and reform:

- *Fine-tuning* – this involves small-scale and incremental 'tweaks' to pre-existing policies. For example, after the *Challenger* disaster, NASA implemented a series of technical single-loop reforms but failed to address its risk philosophy and risk culture in any significant manner (Boin 2008: 250–1).

- *Policy reform* – this involves the reform of policy principles and institutional values. In the aftermath of the 2001 foot and mouth crisis, for example, a slow process of adaptation sought to shift the farming sector away from the principles of intensive farming, which were based around excessive levels of production, to a more sustainable style of farming based upon environmental principles.

- *Paradigm shift* – this is the most significant type of change when the consensus around the values, ideas and goals which underpin a policy sector organization or society are changed. The changes in foreign policy and government structure introduced after 9/11 around the concept of 'homeland security' are arguably one example, although it could equally be argued that these reforms helped solidify a fundamental ideological continuity. Currently, debates about the reforms that have emerged after the global financial crisis suggest that despite the massive shocks caused over recent years, a paradigm shift has not taken place. Post financial crisis, it is 'business as usual' for many (see Box 7.3).

Keeping in mind the spectrum of reform responses outlined above, we can say that post-event periods tend to be characterized by fine-tuning and limited policy reforms rather than substantive paradigm shifts. One of the major reasons for this relates to the strength of pre-existing institutions, policies and ideas. A wealth of literature exists that argues and illustrates that the past profoundly shapes the future in terms of public management. Public policy is said to be largely 'path dependent' in these accounts, which means that previous decisions create what are known as 'self-reinforcing mechanisms' (Pierson 2005; Streeck and Thelen 2005; Kay 2005). If change is to be engineered after a crisis, these mechanisms have to be 'loosened'. Severe crises that bring trauma, drama and future uncertainty can provide the necessary shock to shake policies out of their normal trajectories but this is not always the case. Reinforcing mechanisms can be strong and immutable and they come in many forms: well-established policy frameworks can generate inertia if they are institutionalized within an organization for a long period of time; stakeholders who benefit from policy outcomes can be intransigent, encouraging the status quo and resisting change; and the politics surrounding a policy may benefit political elites and powerful interests who may seek to keep reform off the agenda. The crucial point to be made for crisis situations is twofold: (1) past decisions can restrict large-scale change even after a crisis has exposed them as problematic; (2) the extent of change will depend on the nature of the crisis in relation to the strength of the self-reinforcing mechanisms that are resistant to change. However, not all organizations are the same. Some agencies seem to exhibit an ability to break free from the past in order to promote learning and change. For present purposes, it seems useful to get a brief sense of two broad 'ideal' types of institution at opposite ends of the spectrum.

204

BOX 7.3 WAS THE 'CREDIT CRUNCH' REALLY A CRISIS?

There can be no doubt that the events which have come to be labelled respectively as the 'credit crunch' and the 'global financial crisis' were catastrophic. The narrative alone is dazzling: banks liquidated, nationalized and merged; governments defaulting on debt and being downgraded on credit ratings; and anti-capitalism protests and international financial institutions fighting over the sovereignty of nations. How could these events not be considered anything but a monumental crisis?

One rather controversial argument, presented by Professor Colin Hay, suggests that we should not use the term 'crisis' in this context, because policy-makers have failed to reform the 'boom and bust' economic system that led to the credit crunch in the first place. Hay defines crises 'as moments of decisive intervention' which are characterized by the inevitability of reform. This allows him to make his case that these events were not a crisis because no meaningful intervention has been found to reform the status quo. However, Hay's concern is not to downplay the catastrophes that occurred between 2007 and 2012. Instead, his real claim is that deepseated crisis tendencies remain in the economic system, yet no substantive reform agendas have been put on the table to fix them.

While we might disagree with Hay's limited definition of a crisis, it is difficult to disagree with the argument that the kind of large-scale reform needed to prevent a reoccurrence of the credit crunch has not taken place. As house prices slowly rise again, investment bankers return to trading deals and governments seek to animate private markets by reducing public sector 'waste', we might ask: what have we learned from this crisis and what has really changed? If the answer is 'not much' then maybe Hay is right to question whether we can use the term global financial *crisis*.

Source: Hay (2011).

The most conducive to reform would be high-reliability organizations (HROs), such as air traffic control systems and firefighting bodies, where matters of safety are of paramount importance because they are at the heart of what the organization is set up to do (Weick and Sutcliffe 2001). Their systems and cultures are ingrained with an understanding of the need to anticipate errors, make systemic adaptations, learn in the event of failure and engage in deeper 'deuterolearning', i.e. learning how to learn (Argyris and Schön 1996). Therefore, they have the capacities to 'puzzle' (work out what went wrong and what is needed to fix it) as well as the capacities to 'power' (bring about the requisite change) (Boin et al. 2005). Some non-HRO, risk regulators in particular (Hood et al. 2003), will tend in principle towards high-reliability values. However, most departments of state, public sector functional agencies and so on may not give such a high priority to safety (although rhetorically they may do). Nevertheless, they may possess some characteristics which assist learning and reform. This would include leadership willingness to use a combination of persuasion and muscle in order to bring about change. There would also be a critical mass of financial resources, technology and staffing devoted to 'puzzling' and 'powering'. Such institutions might also have previous experiences of crises, which indicate the dangers of not learning lessons.

At the opposite end of the spectrum, there is a broad institutional type with limited institutional capacity for learning and reform. Typical public sector type organizations would tilt more towards this model. Issues to do with disaster readiness, safety, crisis management and risk management have to compete against core and powerful goals of organizations which are established to deal with other matters. Such institutions would tend to lack extensive experience of crises but are nevertheless vulnerable to their effects in the future. This vulnerability may play out in 'threat rigidity' (denial of risks and refusal to engage in adaptive behaviour) or through forms of institutional leadership that focus more on insulating the organization from costly learning and reform dynamics. Of course, each institution needs to be considered on a case-by-case basis, and it is very probable that the vast bulk of institutions will be positioned somewhere between the two poles – but lean more towards the non-HRO element.

ACCOUNTABILITY AND BLAME GAMES

A second reason for the abundance of fine-tuning reform and the absence of larger paradigm shifts post-crisis can be found in the nature of public accountability. Generally speaking, the dynamics of accountability operate on two broad levels. First, accountability is discussed outside formal governmental processes in the realms of the media and popular debate. It would be inconceivable, in the age of social media, for a crisis to be devoid of such scrutiny. Second, there is the more formal area of official inquiries and investigations. As indicated in Box 7.4, inquiries come in a variety of forms.

In principle, crisis investigations are meant to get to the heart of 'what went wrong' and 'what should be done'. Information is gathered, evidence is heard, witnesses are spoken to, experts are consulted, reports are written and recommendations are produced. The outcome is intended to be an impartial, convincing and authoritative 'solving' of the questions, uncertainties and debates surrounding the crisis. Policy-makers then consider the recommendations, weigh up other factors such as finance and possible conflicts of interest with other policies, and then take appropriate action. If followed, this process would almost certainly lead to double-loop forms of learning and reform but we know that such ideals translate less easily into practice.

BOX 7.4 FORMS OF POST-CRISIS/DISASTER INQUIRY

■ *'Blue Ribbon' inquiries, Presidential Commissions and Royal Commissions* – executive initiated (in whole or in part) and wide-ranging in their investigation of an event or events of national or sub-national significance (e.g. 2002–4 National Commission on Terrorist Attacks upon the United States; 2010–11 National Commission on the BP Deepwater Horizon Oil Spill and Offshore Drilling; 2011–12 New Zealand Canterbury Earthquakes Royal Commission; 2013–14 Australian Royal Commission into Institutional Responses to Child Sexual Abuse).

■ *Executive Statutory inquiries* – where ministers and/or legislatures use specific statutory powers to set up an inquiry, although establishing an inquiry is still discretionary (e.g. 2003–5 Special Commission of Inquiry into the Waterfall Rail Crash, New South Wales, Australia, under the Special Commission of Inquiry Act 1983; 2011–12 UK Leveson Inquiry into the Culture, Practice and Ethics of the Press, under the Inquiries Act 2005).

■ *Executive ad hoc inquiries* – where establishing an inquiry is discretionary and without recourse to specific legislation (e.g. 1997–2000 Phillips Inquiry into BSE in the United Kingdom; 2001–2 Lessons Learned inquiry into foot and mouth in the United Kingdom; 2006 Tasmanian State Government inquiry into the Beaconsfield mining disaster).

■ *Legislative inquiries* – initiated at the discretion of legislatures as a whole or a specific committee within the legislature, or occasionally an informal coalition of legislative members (e.g. 1999–2000 Belgian Parliamentary inquiry into the dioxin contamination of foodstuffs; 1997–8 UK House of Commons Defence Select Committee into the Chinook helicopter crash; 2010–11 Inquiry of the Canadian Parliamentary Coalition to Combat Antisemitism).

■ *Internal departmental/agency inquiry* – where the initiative comes from the specific organization responsible for the relevant policy area (e.g. 1998–2001 UK Department of Health 'Bristol Babies' inquiry in the cardiac services and the death of young children undergoing complex heart surgery; 2012–13 New Zealand Ministry of Innovation, Business and Employment Independent Investigation into the role of officials in the Pike River tragedy.

■ *Accident board inquiry* – where the inquiry is conducted by a body which is charged solely with the purpose of accident investigation (e.g. 2002–4 Bahamas Maritime Authority inquiry in the sinking of the Prestige oil tanker off the coast of Spain; 2003 Space Shuttle Columbia Accident Investigation Board; 2014 UK Marine Accident Investigation Branch Investigation Report into the Eshcol accident.

One of the first factors that can compromise an accountability process can be seen in the format and remit of a post-crisis inquiry. Accountability mechanisms come in a variety of formats but the vast majority are at the discretion of political executives who have considerable freedom to shape the nature of the investigative process. Inquiries may have a number of limitations (actual and/or perceived) in terms of learning. They include:

- a struggle to be established at all because of resistance from political executives and/or the authorities requiring investigation;
- chairperson/members appointed with predisposed views that may produce a bias in the inquiry process and outcomes;
- restriction of the committee terms of reference;
- witnesses unwilling/unable to appear;
- political interference in the investigative process;
- lack of resources (time, personnel or finance) to complete a thorough investigation;
- bi-partisan membership of parliamentary/legislative inquiries can lead to accusations of political bias in the investigation and outcomes; and
- the closed nature of some inquiries may lead to accusations of 'cover up'.

A second issue that can compromise accountability processes arises out of the socially constructed nature of crises. All crises and disasters are, to some extent, social constructs. They are a mixture of objective events and the perceptions of those events that are held by groups of actors. Depending on the specific crisis, events can be a complex interaction of technological, institutional, political, economic and geophysical elements. And in turn these objective elements of a crisis are then perceived and understood by different groups depending on their values. A simple example of a crisis being socially constructed can be seen in evaluations of wars and theatres of conflict. Once they are resolved the 'winners' get to define which side was 'right' and 'wrong', which side committed atrocities and which side acted ethically. These are social constructions – widely disseminated views about what has occurred which become conventional wisdom.

As a consequence, crisis inquiries and their outcomes are subject to a variety of different interpretations and are fought over by different interests. Following on from our previous chapter we use the term 'framing' as a shorthand label for these contests, which can occur on a number of levels. In some inquiries, the conflict can be around the nature of the knowledge being generated. Inquiries tend to look to 'science' and the 'law' as the benchmarks against which to judge the actions of crisis managers (Snider 2004). In reality, however, science and the law are just as contested as the social sciences, which is one reason why we often see political protests about inquiry findings, despite their 'scientific' impartiality. The most common contests, however, are not about the scientific nature of inquiries. They are instead fights for survival; to avoid blame and frame the culpability of others. Actors will use a variety of strategies to argue their case and apportion blame. At the level of ideas, they may attempt to frame post-crisis debates in particular ways. This is particularly evident in the burgeoning literature on the 'blame game' (Hood 2002; Brändström and Kuipers 2003). Actors may seek to frame a crisis in terms of:

- *Severity* – the extent or otherwise to which core values have been violated. For example, playing down a crisis involves framing events as 'disturbances' or 'incidents'. The implication is that those responsible are not responsible for significant failings.
- *Causes* – whether the crisis is 'stand-alone' or something which is embedded in a deeper system-wide or policy failure. For example, a set of circumstances portrayed as isolated and ad hoc implies that 'blame' lies with particular decision-maker/operator failures.
- *Responsibility* – whether blame is concentrated with a single actor or is dispersed among many actors. For instance, the levying of blame at one individual means that an individual has the propensity to be made a scapegoat.

Framing contests are exacerbated by various decisions. In the (common) event of multiple inquiries – typically making different and sometimes conflicting recommendations – framing contrasts can run wild as there is no definitive account of events. Paradoxically, therefore, the existence of several inquiries can impede 'learning' because it allows competing interests to coalesce and champion the particular investigation which suits their views/interpretation. In the aftermath of the 1989 Exxon Valdez oil spill, for example, the disaster was the subject of over fifteen different investigations. A second factor here is that the growth throughout the Western world of agencies/quangos/non-departmental bodies which are at arm's length of government generally makes it easier for political elites to pass responsibility on to more localized chief executives/departmental heads. For instance, during the Scottish exams crisis of 2000, Scottish Executive ministers successfully 'passed the buck' to the quasi-independent Scottish Qualifications Authority (Clarence 2002). Similarly, the Blair government was highly effective in avoiding the backlash from the crisis of funding surrounding London's Millennium Dome by deflecting responsibility onto the Millennium Commission and the New Millennium Experience Company (Gray 2003).

If we examine accountability mechanisms as political processes rather than a means of learning, we can see a number of different outcomes. The outcomes may be so 'explosive' that they prove difficult for crisis managers to survive, or they may be 'damp squibs', allowing those in positions of formal political or administrative power to continue with little or no challenge to their authority. However, despite such intense pressures for due accountability for 'what went wrong', outcomes do not normally involve the career slaughter of those in positions of authority. There are broadly three types of outcomes (Boin et al. 2009):

- *Hero* – a crisis may bolster leadership fortunes because the threat is perceived to be well handled, such as in the cases of Mayor Rudolph Giuliani after 9/11 and Queensland Premier Anna Bligh after the Queensland floods. A variant on this theme is where mistakes are made, but leaders accept responsibility and enhance their credibility and legitimacy on the part of a sufficient coalition of popular, media, stakeholder and party political opinion.

- *Villain* – a crisis may be instrumental in a downturn in career fortunes or maybe even a complete downfall. This latter fate befell Spanish Prime Minster José Maria Aznar after the Madrid bombings, Belgian Prime Minister Jean-Luc Dehaene after the dioxin scandal, and Icelandic Prime Minister Geir Haarde after the global financial crisis.

- *Escapologist* – a crisis makes only marginal difference or no difference at all, blending into and being overtaken by newer issues considered to be of greater political significance. A case in point is what happened to Australian Prime Minister John Howard. In particular, during his second and third terms of office, he managed to survive with little or no electoral damage from a series of crises related to his government's policies on detention centres, immigration and refugees.

We can also return to the three types of learning and reform we set out previously in the chapter and draw out the political outcomes in relation to each type. At one extreme, inquiries may be little more than political fixes, designed to protect key interests and those benefiting from the current policy regime. The outcome of such events is likely to be very modest fine-tuning or ideally no change whatsoever. Some inquires have been the subject of considerable flak in this vein: the congressional and White House investigations into the Katrina crisis response represent one such example. On the congressional side, the decision not to investigate the president's actions (taken by a Republican Congress in relation to a Republican president) led to the withdrawal of every Democrat member of the committee. Unsurprisingly, this investigation and the one performed by the White House both allowed the president to escape censure for his failures in crisis leadership (Preston 2008). A further type has the symbolism of change – a form of palliative – but little or nothing changes in terms of policy/practices. The collapse of Jerusalem's Versailles banquet hall in Israel in 2001 during a wedding party (captured on video and widely distributed throughout news networks) produced virtually no change to building regulations or their monitoring in a society where the policy agenda is dominated by security issues (Schwartz and McConnell 2008). Another is instrumental adaptation, where recommendations are taken on board by policy-makers in a pragmatic way (reluctantly or because they genuinely recognize that something needs to change in order to reduce vulnerabilities for the future). The final and most progressive format is where inquiries act as genuine driving forces for innovative policy change. The O'Connor Report into the Walkerton water contamination crisis in Ontario, for example, was highly influential in reforming the 'hands-off' approach to water regulation that had been characteristic of Ontario's neoliberal government (Snider 2004).

210

FACTORS INFLUENCING THE CRISIS AFTERMATH

A key theme throughout our previous chapters has been that crisis management actions need to be seen as part of a larger social, political and policy-oriented universe. We make this argument so that we can discuss the larger factors that affect crisis behaviour. Therefore, we need now to ask: what are the contextual issues that are relevant to evaluation, learning and accountability? Five issues seem particularly pertinent.

The nature of the crisis

The intrinsic nature of each particular crisis may have the potential to destroy the fortunes of crisis decision-makers or assist in their salvation. And the type of crisis will have a significant bearing on the ability of reformers to learn and implement change.

All things being equal, what we might call a classic crisis (unexpected, sudden, severe damage) is the type of crisis most liable to have a detrimental impact on the fortunes of senior decision-makers via accountability dynamics. Why didn't they see it coming? Why weren't they better prepared? Were they culpable? Many careers have foundered amidst the drama and turmoil of the unexpected – especially when there is significant loss of life, damage to property, or damage to key interests. One example is Michael Brown, the head of the US Federal Emergency Management Agency, who resigned amid the widespread perception (and pressure from the Bush administration) that his agency had failed to be properly prepared for, and been unable to show capability in coping with, the devastation that was wreaked by Hurricane Katrina. By contrast, slow-burning crises such as climate change are less liable to make or break political/bureaucratic fortunes. There are no unforeseen, dramatic focusing events (sudden loss of life, damage to property and so on) to concentrate the minds of the general public, media, stakeholder and political opinion. There may be warnings of cataclysmic focusing events in the future (such as floods as a consequence of global warming) but this is rarely sufficient to prompt a dramatic change in the fortunes of senior figures.

If we turn to learning dynamics with the same comparison, we can also claim that an unexpected crisis is more liable to act as a catalyst for policy change than the crisis of the slow-burning variety such as climate change. The shock of the unexpected can make policy-makers stumble into reform promises which shape the agenda for debate and rapidly attract support from policy entrepreneurs/stakeholders and public opinion. It then becomes hard to undo this commitment, even if it were feasible. In the United Kingdom, for example, Margaret Thatcher responded to a local property tax crisis by committing the government to abolishing a 400-year-old tax, despite British history being littered with failed attempts to find a suitable alternative. This set in motion a policy process that would lead to the ill-fated poll tax (McConnell 1995). By contrast, the threats posed by creeping crises are less inclined to produce reform. Longer-term issues have to compete for 'policy space' against short-term policy-making based to a large extent on electoral cycles, stakeholder power, political fixes, sudden crises and

211

so on. Policy reform in the face of creeping crises is of course possible, and change through incremental steps is a key feature of modern societies. However, policy entrepreneurs regularly seek to portray creeping crises in much more focused terms because they realize that such moves are more liable to be effective. This is the reason why advocates of significant adaptation in the face of climate change are always searching for hard-hitting statistics and potentially shocking stories. They need to 'manufacture' the conditions that are created naturally by sudden crises so that citizens and policy-makers have a sympathetic ear to their concerns.

Another issue in this area relates to the scope and depth of the crisis. In large-scale crises involving national trauma, such as the Breivik shootings in Norway, there is less inclination to 'play politics'. Solidarity and recovery are the order of the day. These events can be contrasted with policy disasters and fiascos, where the crisis is more about a scandal than a national trauma. In these instances, opportunities exist to use accountability mechanisms for political purposes. We also need to consider the extent to which a crisis has a detrimental effect on powerful interests. Political scientists have much debated the relative powers of citizens, special interests and bureaucrats. Such debates aside, we detect a simple tendency. The more powerful the interests affected by the crisis, the more likely it is that their view will prevail over less powerful interests in the post-crisis period. One example is the power of the US food and drink industries in effectively blocking long-term plans by the World Health Organization to learn from the ongoing obesity crisis through enhanced public education campaigns in relation to diet, health and physical activity. The opposite also applies. Many crises and disasters in particular have left devastating impacts on vulnerable peoples and groups, but little happens after the crises because these groups are not in the position to exert influence on longer-term policy reforms (Wisner et al. 2004). In recent years, however, the voices of some survivors and families of victims have been strengthened through well-articulated campaigns, the use of websites, and effective interaction with a media that is increasingly interested in the newsworthiness of post-crisis battles against officialdom. The 2001 Walkerton water contamination crisis is a good example of such influence – citizens were represented by the Canadian Environmental Law Association, which had a considerable influence over the recommendations of the official inquiry – the O'Connor Report. Family groups were also influential in pressurising the Bush administration to opt for an 'independent' and broad-ranging 9/11 Commission (as opposed to a congressional inquiry). However, such campaigns are not guaranteed to be successful. The families of the 7/7 London bombings in London, for example, failed to obtain a public inquiry into the events.

Timing

The timing of a crisis is crucial. In policy terms, John Kingdon (2003: 1) neatly captured the importance of timing when he wrote simply of 'an idea whose time has come'. We might say something similar about the fortunes of crisis decision-makers. The timing

212

may be so significant that it destroys careers, or helps provide good fortune for those leaders who would otherwise be exposed to the winds of societal change. For example, it may happen in the wake of other similar crises and so there is a predisposed momentum for leadership change. In effect, the rhetoric is that of 'one crisis too many'. For example, UK Home Office failures surrounding foreign prisoners being released from jail (rather than considered for deportation) escalated over 2005 and 2006 to the point that Home Secretary Charles Clarke was sacked. Alternatively, crisis may hit at a crucial point in the electoral cycle – notably after an election when a new leader is enjoying a 'honeymoon' period – and so the momentum for change is blunted. There is no scientific formula that would allow us to calculate optimum times, because other factors come into play such as luck. Yet electoral fortunes are certainly important. If a governing party is weak (and growing weaker) in terms of popular support, a crisis may cause further damage to the fortunes of party leaders, because the crisis raises further and serious questions about their capacities to govern. At the time of the SARS outbreak in Hong Kong in 2003, the administration was already weak and the target of large-scale demonstrations. Its crisis response was also subject to heavy criticism in an inquiry by the Hong Kong Legislative Council. This led to the resignation of Health Minister Yeoh Eng-kiong – a move which many within the government hoped would ease public discontent. By contrast, if a crisis hits when a party is buoyed by strong popular support, party leaders are liable to have a fairly high degree of inherited support/sympathy for their crisis response

Party politics

In the Western world, members of political executives are almost exclusively members of political parties. In the case of prime minsters, presidents, chancellors and others at the apex of government hierarchies, they are also party leaders – operating in a variety of constitutional contexts. This gives rise to a number of factors that may strengthen and/or weaken the position of crisis decision-makers in the aftermath of crises.

Internal party politics can be a critical factor in shaping whether or not a political leader will survive. If a leader's position is precarious, the arrival of a crisis will often provide party critics with the opportunity to challenge his/her leadership credentials. The European sovereign debt crisis and subsequent pressures for austerity measures across many nations, saw an end to the career of Irish Taoiseach Brian Cowen in 2011, when he lost support from with the coalition government headed by his party Fianna Fáil. Correspondingly, a leader with strong internal party support is less liable to come under attack as a consequence of crisis – even if many within the party have reservations about the handling of the crisis. For many years until his eventual resignation in 2011, Italian Prime Minister Silvio Berlusconi remained a largely popular figure within Forza Italia and latterly the People of Freedom Party, surviving innumerable sex and corruption scandals

There is also the relationship between government and opposition to consider. If a government does not have the support of the main opposition party or parties on a particular crisis issue, this opposition helps contribute to any broad coalition seeking to damage the government and its leaders. Correspondingly, when government has opposition support on a crisis issue, the fortunes of government figures are more liable to be strong and secure. This is particularly (but not exclusively) the case in major threats to national security, where bipartisan support is common.

There are also a number of party political factors which can help promote reform and learning. First, a leader with strong support in his/her party is generally well placed to command the political legitimacy needed to proceed with reform (if so desired). Second, a leader whose party has strong popular support in elections/opinion polls is better able claim a broad representative mandate for reforms. Third, and crucially, policy change is facilitated when government has a strong working majority in the legislature – this is almost certain in parliamentary systems but much less so in semi-presidential and presidential systems. If political elites can garner the requisite number of votes, they have enormous practical power to introduce new legislation, even though others may disagree. An example of all three conditions is John Major succeeding Margaret Thatcher and placing abolition of the disastrous poll tax at the top of his leadership campaign and his agenda (Butler et al. 1994). The Conservative Party rallied round its new leader, there was overwhelming public support for abolishing the poll tax and the Conservatives had a comfortable majority in the House of Commons.

The opposite also applies. Reforms may never get off the ground (or may flounder if they do) for many reasons. While a leader with precarious support in his/her party may try and seize on post-crisis reform as a last-ditch attempt to galvanize support, weak leaders are more liable to defend the status quo after a crisis. To do otherwise is high risk, with the possibility of a further slide in support. This tendency towards the status quo is heightened further if a majority in the legislature is small and weak (especially in parliamentary systems) or non-existent (especially in semi-presidential and presidential systems). The most powerful barrier to post-crisis policy reform is the conservative-minded leader with strong party and popular support – particularly (but not exclusively) in parliamentary systems.

Some policy sectors are riskier than others

Policies cover a wide range of spheres such as health, education, criminal justice, national security, transport, tourism and the economy. As a consequence, there is variance in the actors, institutions, stakeholders and policy instruments operating in each sphere. When any particular policy area is hit by 'crisis' and the threats typically associated with it, the impact on those leaders who are responsible/accountable for these policy areas may vary. Potentially, there are many aspects of 'policy' that are relevant to post-crisis situations. For example, the fortunes of some actors may be helped because dealing with crisis is a fairly routine part of his/her portfolio (e.g.

national security and home affairs). In such cases, post-crisis scrutiny and attacks on performance may be so regularized (they come with the job) that criticism needs to reach higher levels to be capable of doing real damage to political fortunes. However, there is one particular aspect of 'policy' that, we would suggest, is particularly important in influencing political fortunes in the wake of a crisis. We can most usefully outline this by drawing on the distinction between policy communities and issue networks.

The key factor here is the degree of consensus within the particular policy community/issue network. Rhodes and Marsh (1992) differentiate between issue networks (where there is a large number of participants, holding widely disparate views) and policy communities (where there is a much smaller number of participants who operate on the basis of a broadly shared consensus). Our contention is that as we move towards the issue network end of the spectrum where we find high fragmentation in numbers and political views, leaders in post-crisis situations are more liable to find themselves surrounded by those who call for their resignation. The contaminated blood scandal in France is a case in point (Steffen 2001). Health Minister Edmund Hervé was an eventual casualty of a crisis that escalated because a fragmented network of tension-ridden agencies and associations did not rally behind the government's explanations of its role. The opposite also applies. The greater the degree of consensus in a policy community, the less likely it is for leaders to see their fortunes slide, because there is a consensus-based community to rally round. The Swedish experience of contaminated blood stands in stark contrast to that of the French (Albæk 2001). One reason why there were no political/administrative casualties as a consequence of the Swedish crisis is that there was already a high degree of corporatist-style consensus in this area of health policy, and this continued into the inquiry which was representative of virtually all major interests.

Overall, our simple point is that 'policy' matters. It is a further piece in the jigsaw which helps us explain the conditions which, to varying degrees, render crisis decision-makers vulnerable to a slide in their careers after a crisis.

Crisis symbolism

Finally, there is the symbolic potential of the crisis. This refers to the capacity of the crisis to transcend the immediate circumstances on the ground. More specifically, some crises can 'hit a nerve' and expose wider social vulnerabilities and fears. This in turn can raise deep questions about fitness for office or fitness to govern, and may assist demands for a change of leaders or change of regime. One example is the 2005 riots in France which hit many cities including Paris, Dijon and Strasbourg. These raised deeper questions not only about racism and immigration in France, but also the government's hardline attitude to perpetrators. The riots led to intense pressure for the resignation of Interior Minister Nicolas Sarkozy. Correspondingly, the symbolic potential of some crises may be much weaker, localized and confined to a fairly narrow area of policy competence. Examples include coastal erosion in Southwest Washington and a shortage of social workers in Scotland. Such crises are less liable to end careers or spread to other key political/administrative decision-makers in government.

CONCLUSION

What we often observe in the post-crisis period are three intertwined ideals – clear evaluation, democratic accountability and reflexive learning and reform – that are compromised by the realities of policy and politics. Evaluation is compromised by the subjectivity that is inherent in any definition of success or failure. Accountability is compromised when framing and blaming dynamics obfuscate explanations of what occurred. And learning and reform can be compromised by the intransigence of policies, institutions and actors which cannot be shaken from their path dependencies. There is no doubt that we need to hold leaders and agencies to account in the wake of a crisis. Victims demand answers, communities need to air grievances and democratic principles require that those who exercise authority explain themselves to a national audience. However, we need carefully to consider the effects that are created when we pursue accountability because it is the process of blaming that injects the political into attempts to evaluate, learn and change to prevent future crises.

DISCUSSION QUESTIONS

1. Evaluate a crisis response of your choosing. Was it a success or a failure in your eyes? How did you come to this conclusion and might it be possible for others to disagree?
2. Examine the summary findings of a post-crisis inquiry. Would you describe the recommendations as examples of an attempt at fine-tuning, policy reform or paradigm shifting?
3. Do you believe that accountability gets in the way of learning? If so, should we really hold people and organizations to account post-crisis?
4. How can we make sure that public sector organizations reform effectively in the aftermath of a crisis?

REFERENCES

Albæk, E. (2001) 'Protecting the Swedish Blood Supply Against HIV: Crisis Management Without Scandal', in M. Bovens, P. 't Hart and B.G. Peters (eds), *Success and Failure in Public Governance*, Cheltenham: Edward Elgar.

Argenti, P. and Druckenmiller, B. (2004) 'Reputation and the Corporate Brand', *Corporate Reputation Review*, 6(4): 368–74.

Argyris, C. (1999) *On Organizational Learning*, 2nd edition, Oxford: Blackwell.

Argyris, C. and Schön, D.A. (1996) *Organizational Learning II*, Reading: Addison-Wesley.

Arklay, T.M (2012) 'Queensland's State Disaster Management Group: An All Agency Response to Unprecedented Natural Disaster', *Journal of Emergency Management*, 27(3): 9–19.

Boin, A. (2008) 'Learning from Crisis: NASA and the *Challenger* Disaster', in Boin, A., A. McConnell and P. 't Hart (eds), *Governing after Crisis*, New York: Cambridge University Press, pp. 232–54.

Boin, A., 't Hart, P. and McConnell, A. (2009) 'Towards a Theory of Crisis Exploitation: Political and Policy Impacts of Framing Contests and Blame Games', *Journal of European Public Policy*, 16(1): 81–106.

Boin, A., McConnell, A. and 't Hart P. (eds) (2008) *Governing after Crisis*. Cambridge: Cambridge University Press.

Boin, A., 't Hart, P., Stern, E. and Sundelius, B. (2005) *The Politics of Crisis Management: Public Leadership Under Pressure*, Cambridge: Cambridge University Press.

Brändström, A. and Kuipers, S. (2003) 'From "Normal Incidents" to Political Crises: Understanding the Selective Politicization of Policy Failures', *Government and Opposition*, 38(3): 279–305.

Butler, D., Adonis, A. and Travers, T. (1994) *Failure in British Government: The Politics of the Poll Tax*, Oxford: Oxford University Press.

Clarence, E. (2002) 'Ministerial Accountability and the Scottish Qualifications Agency', *Public Administration*, 80(4): 791–803.

Dyrenfurth, N. (2005) 'The Language of Australian Citizenship', *Australian Journal of Political Science*, 40(1): 87–109.

Gray, C. (2003) 'The Millennium Dome: "Falling From Grace"', *Parliamentary Affairs*, 56(3): 441–55.

Hall, P. (1993) 'Policy Paradigms, Social Learning and the State: The Case of Economic Policy Making in Britain', *Comparative Politics*, 25(3): 275–96.

't Hart, P. and Boin, A. (2001) 'Between Crisis and Normalcy: The Long Shadow of Post-Crisis Politics', in U. Rosenthal, A. Boin and L.K. Comfort (eds), *Managing Crises: Threats, Dilemmas, Opportunities*, Springfield, IL: Charles C. Thomas, pp. 28–46.

Hay, C. (2011) 'Pathology without Crisis? The Strange Demise of the Anglo-Liberal Growth Model', *Government and Opposition*, 46 (1): 1–31.

Hood, C. (2002) 'The Risk Game and the Blame Game', *Government and Opposition*, 37(1): 15–37.

Hood, C., Rothstein, H. and Baldwin, R. (2003) *The Government of Risk: Understanding Risk Regulation Regimes*, Oxford: Oxford University Press.

Kay, A. (2005) 'A Critique of the Use of Path Dependency in Policy Studies', *Public Administration*, 83(3): 553–71.

Kingdon, J. (2003) *Agendas, Alternatives and Public Policies*, 2nd edition, New York: Longman.

Korac-Kakabadse, N., Kouzmin, A. and Kakabadse, A. (2002) 'Revisiting Crises from a Resource-Distribution Perspective: Learning for Local Government?', *Local Governance*, 28(1): 35–61.

McConnell, A. (1995), State Policy Formation and the Origins of the Poll Tax, Dartmouth: Aldershot.

McConnell, A. (2010) *Understanding Policy Success: Rethinking Public Policy*, Basingstoke: Palgrave Macmillan.

McConnell, A. (2011) 'Success? Failure? Something In-Between? A Framework for Evaluating Crisis Management', *Policy and Society*, 30(2): 63–76.

Maskrey, A. (1994) 'Disaster Mitigation as a Crisis of Paradigms: Reconstructing after the Alto Mayo Earthquake', in A. Varley (ed.), *Disasters, Development and Environment*, New York: John Wiley & Sons.

Paul, L. (2005) 'New Levels of Responsiveness – Joining Up Government in Response to the Bali Bombings', *Australian Journal of Public Administration*, 64(2): 31–33.

Pierson, P. (2005) *Politics in Time: History, Institutions, and Social Analysis*, Princeton, NJ: Princeton University Press.

Preston, T. (2008) 'Weathering the Politics of Responsibility and Blame: The Bush Administration and its Response to Hurricane Katrina', in Boin, A., A. McConnell and P. 't Hart (eds), *Governing after Crisis*, Cambridge: Cambridge University Press, pp. 33–61.

Pyper, R. (ed.) (1996) *Aspects of Accountability in the British System of Government*, Wirral: Tudor.

Rhodes, R. and Marsh, D. (eds) (1992) *Policy Networks in British Government*, Oxford: Clarendon Press.

Rose, R. and Davies, P.L. (1994) *Inheritance in Public Policy: Change without Choice in Britain*, New Haven, CT: Yale University Press.

Rosenthal, U. (2003) 'September 11: Public Administration and the Study of Crises and Crisis Management', *Administration and Society*, 35: 129–43.

Rosenthal, U. and Pijnenberg, B. (1991) *Crisis Management and Decision Making: Simulation Oriented Scenarios*, Dordecht: Kluwer.

Sabatier, P.A. and Jenkins-Smith, H. (eds) (1993) *Policy Change and Learning: An Advocacy Coalition Approach*, Boulder, CO: Westview Press.

Schwartz, R. and McConnell, A. (2008) 'The Walkerton Water Tragedy and the Jerusalem Banquet Hall Collapse: Regulatory Failure and Policy Change', in Boin, A., A. McConnell and P. 't Hart (eds), *Governing after Crisis*, Cambridge: Cambridge University Press, pp. 208–31.

Snider, L. (2004) 'Resisting Neo-Liberalism: The Poisoned Water Disaster in Walkerton Ontario', *Socio and Legal Studies*, 13(2): 265–89.

Stark, A. (2011) 'Legislatures: Help or Hindrance in Achieving Successful Crisis Management?' *Policy and Society*, 30(2): 115–27.

Steffen, M. (2001) 'Crisis Governance in France: The End of Social Corporatism?', in M. Bovens, P. 't Hart and B.G. Peters (eds), *Success and Failure in Public Governance*, Cheltenham: Edward Elgar, pp. 470–88.

Streeck, W. and Thelen, K. (eds) (2005) *Beyond Continuity: Institutional Change in Advanced Political Economies*, New York: Oxford University Press.

Weick, K.E. and Sutcliffe, K. (2001) *Managing the Unexpected: Assuring High Performance in an Age of Complexity*, San Francisco: Jossey-Bass.

Wildavsky, A. (1988) *Searching for Safety*, New Brunswick, NJ: Transaction.

Wisner, B., Blaikie, P., Cannon, T., and Davis, I. (2004) *At Risk: Natural Hazards, People's Vulnerability and Disasters*, London: Routledge.

FURTHER READING

The aftermath of crises/disasters is the most understudied of all the phases of crisis management. For the potential of crises to bring about change, see Birkland, T.A. (1997), *After*

Disaster: Agenda Setting, Public Policy, and Focusing Events, Washington DC: Georgetown University Press. Much can be gained by exploring some of the public literature on policy change and learning. We particularly recommend the (now) classic work Sabatier, P.A. and Jenkins-Smith, H.C. (eds) (1993) *Policy Change and Learning: An Advocacy Coalition Approach*, Boulder, CO: Westview Press. A more organizational perspective on learning comes from Argyris, C. and Schön, D. (1996) *Organizational Learning II*, Reading, MA: Addison-Wesley. A managerially focused approach which is highly recommended for its specific focus on disasters is Toft, B. and Reynolds, S. (2005) *Learning from Disasters: A Management Approach*, 3rd edition, Leicester: Perpetuity Press. It is particularly useful in examining the connections and potential for learning across many apparently disparate disasters. Boin et al. (2005) *The Politics of Crisis Management: Public Leadership Under Pressure*, Cambridge: Cambridge University Press, provides an astute overview of the post-crisis tension between the need to consolidate and the need to reform. Boin et al. (2007) also provide the first book devoted to post-crisis inquiries, accountability and learning. It is entitled *Crisis and After: Case Studies in the Politics of Investigation, Accountability and Learning.* It includes case studies on the aftermath of 9/11, the Madrid bombings, the boxing day tsunami, Space Shuttles Challenger and Columbia, and Hurricane Katrina.

The recovery period for disasters is not covered in this chapter, but readers would be advised to acquaint themselves with some of this literature. A useful starting point is Schneider, S.K. (2011) *Dealing with Disaster: Public Management in Crisis Situations*, 2nd edition, Armonk, NY: M.E. Sharpe. Its particular strength is in focusing on how the debate ensuing in the aftermath of disasters is linked to our expectations before the disaster. An excellent overview of some of the issues to be addressed and the problems that are likely to ensue in the recovery period is provided by Emergency Management Australia in their (2002) document *Recovery*, which is part of a larger series on various aspects of disaster management. It can be accessed at <http://www.ema.gov.au/> by following the link to the Australian Emergency Manuals Series. Urban areas, where there is a concentration of population, economic activity, social problems and intense politics, are often the site of modern disasters. For an excellent introduction to the symbolic and structural aspects of recovery, see Vale, L.J. and Campanella, T.J. (eds) (2005) *The Resilient City: How Modern Cities Recover from Disaster*, New York: Oxford University Press. See also the practitioner-oriented Phillips, B.D. (2009) *Disaster Recovery*, Boca Raton, FL: CRC Press.

Chapter 8

Risk and crisis management in a global world

LEARNING OBJECTIVES

By the end of this chapter you should:

- be aware of the main reasons why managing domestic risk and crisis management is increasingly becoming an international phenomenon;
- have an understanding of a range of emerging global risks, classified as 'growing', 'interval' and 'speculative', that are a reflection of globalization and modernity;
- understand the key issues in the practice of international humanitarian crisis management;
- show cognizance of the fact that an increasingly important crisis activity for governments is how to rescue its citizens caught up in international disasters/ conflicts; and
- understand the challenges presented by 'transboundary' crises and the issues surrounding responses to these threats on the global stage.

KEY POINTS OF THIS CHAPTER

- The complexity and interconnectedness of modern societies mean that risks and crises will frequently cross borders and organizational boundaries.
- Emerging risks can be defined but they are difficult to quantify and forecast with precision.
- A range of risks currently exist which are well documented, difficult to quantify concisely and likely to grow in importance in the future. These relate to climate change, demographics, energy security and development economics.

- Government agencies continue to prioritize the risk of a global influenza pandemic while private insurers are prioritizing a range of technological risks that could have significant effects on public sector liability cover.
- Humanitarian crisis management efforts have advanced considerably since the 1990s through the concept of Disaster Risk Reduction but problems still remain. Crucial concerns relate to the strengthening of the crisis management capacities of domestic governments, the lack of citizen participation in risk reduction and the need to use more indigenous knowledge in risk reduction.
- Domestic governments must begin to design and institutionalize risk and crisis management processes that can respond to 'remote' and 'transboundary' crisis issues.

KEY TERMS

- **Emerging risks** – potential new threats that could result in severe consequences that are difficult to quantify.
- **Interval risks** – risk which appear periodically and frequently. We know that such risks will occur but we cannot predict their arrival or magnitude.
- **Speculative risks** – primarily technological risks which may or may not develop into meaningful problems.
- **Disaster risk reduction** – a global concept promoted by the United Nations Hyogo Framework which aims to increase the capacity of developing nations to cope with disaster.
- **Remote crisis management** – public authorities in one country attempting to manage a crisis from afar when its citizens are caught up in disaster/conflict in another country.
- **Transboundary crisis management** – preparing, responding and recovering from crises which move across and change throughout functional and geographical spaces.

THE PARADOX OF GLOBALIZATION

There should be no doubt that the globalization of risk and crisis management has brought about some benefit for both. International codes of conduct, standards and mechanisms for exchanging information, for example, all facilitate enhanced performance on the global stage for private insurers and raise the aggregate standards of the risk management industry generally. And, as Legrand and McConnell (2012: xv) note, 'emergency management is progressively becoming imbued with international synergies in the form of international non-governmental organizations, emergency laws, common protocols and shared understandings . . . Such coordination is commonly translated into benefits such as the provision of aid, equipment, personnel, expertise and more.'

However, the forces of globalization also present problems. The 'wiring' which connects nations together is becoming increasingly complex and layered, which means that risks and crises can travel fast and impact widely through, for example, financial systems, migration patterns and shared data sources. Moreover, as we progress into a brave new world of technological progress, complex and unquantifiable risks appear like mirages on the edge of our horizon. We are aware that some potential problems may exist – in the electromagnetic fields generated by our phones, in the chemicals within our household products or the masses of data we surround ourselves with – but they are intangible, indistinct and exist in an unpredictable future. They may either be inaccurate predictions of a grim future (like the so-called millennium bug) or accurate forecasts of chronic problems that will have to be dealt with by risk and crisis managers (like asbestos in building infrastructures).

This suggests that the forces of globalization are both a blessing and a curse for the crisis and risk manager. On the one hand, they open up innovative and exciting new avenues to deal with collective problems but on the other they also open up a 'Pandora's box' of new risks and pathways for risk escalation. As a consequence of this paradox it is difficult to determine who is reacting to what and there is something of the 'chicken and the egg' to narratives about the global governance of risk and crises. Are public agencies reacting to new global risks or is the creation of global governance channels actually a cause of some of these new global risks? Regardless, what we can say for sure is that each dynamic is self-reinforcing. As risks and crises become more global so too do the responses to them. What this means is that there is an inevitability to the globalization of risk and crisis management. As a consequence, every risk and crisis manager should have the capacity to view their everyday duties as one part of a larger international context.

This chapter is designed to aid this understanding. First, it provides those concerned with risk with a broad, and somewhat cautious, forecast of a range of emerging global issues that are likely to be of concern over the coming years. We then discuss three types of global crisis management: humanitarian aid, remote crisis management and transboundary crisis management.

EMERGING GLOBAL RISKS

In this section, we discuss a range of emerging global risks. Emerging risks have been simply defined as 'newly developing or changing risks that are difficult to quantify and could have a major impact on society and the insurance industry' (Swiss Re 2013: 5). Such risks are certainly difficult to quantify and therefore difficult to predict through normal actuarial capabilities. When we factor in the international component – the need

BOX 8.1 CORE ATTRIBUTES OF EMERGING RISKS

- *Identification* – their existence is undisputed; however, they cannot be proven in a clear and comprehensive manner (e.g. climate change is now largely undisputed, but the actual extent of the potential harm is still open to debate).
- *Describability* – they can be described, but not necessarily in a conclusive manner (e.g. cyber risks may be described in terms of what has been experienced in the past, but future manifestations of such a risk may be almost impossible to relate).
- *Causality* between the source of risk and resultant losses – in many cases a causal relationship cannot be conclusively proven (examples include cancers 'caused' by EMF, proximity to nuclear power stations or use of mobile phones).
- *Assessability in monetary terms* – the scope of consequences can only be assessed imprecisely (a new form of terrorist attack, e.g. biological or radiological, could result in few or numerous human casualties and/or minimal or catastrophic property damage, making estimates of loss extremely difficult).

Source: Adapted from Swiss Re (2003: 19).

to identify emerging risks pertinent to many nations – this predictive task becomes somewhat Herculean (see Box 8.1).

When a problematic event is viewed with hindsight, ignored warnings that signalled an emerging risk are always quite clear and we wonder why we never sensed them. However, when we try to forecast emerging risks ourselves we learn just how difficult prediction can be. At least four factors provide evidence for Smil's (2008: 2) assertion that the only reliable forecast is our inability to produce reliable forecasts! First, cataclysmic events that have caused significant ruptures across the globe have been largely unforeseen. For example, if we turn the clocks back a handful of years and search through predictions about future disasters and crises (including our own) we can find no forecasts about a global financial crisis caused by the banking industry. Second, predictions about potential calamities have not come to pass. Here we might recall how expectations of a global blackout caused by failed computing technology on the first day of the millennium caused a costly fiasco in public and private sectors around the world (Quarantelli et al. 2007: 29).

Long-term forecasting can also be jaundiced by preconceived views and values about social, political and technological issues and how they contribute to humankind's progress or demise. Population forecasts, for example, are a regular feature in bleak Malthusian narratives about global inequality and resource depletion. There should be no doubt that demographic changes, particularly in relation to human migration and displacement, present significant global risks. Yet we need to be careful because, as Smil

(2008: 3) shows in relation to UN statistics, population growth forecasts are often grossly inaccurate. Comparing 1991 predictions with the 2004 reality, for example, shows how the UN over-anticipated growth by some 600 million people (roughly the equivalent of the entire population of Latin America). Similar issues relate to predictions about energy resources. In this area the optimists bravely predict a soon-to-be-realized move away from fossil fuels to renewable energy while the pessimists predict new cold wars as nations increasingly guard finite resources of gas, oil and coal. Neither forecast appears particularly accurate given that fossil fuel consumption still dominates industrial use and the fossil fuel export business continues to boom (Smil 2008).

Finally, forecasts about emerging global risks are often characterized by speculative predictions, which, while certainly possible and undeniably exciting, are perhaps best left to the writers of fiction. These speculative threats can be placed on a scale. At one end are the large-scale history-changing (or ending) events which are possible but statistically unlikely to occur over the next half a century: the large asteroid, the massive volcanic eruption and the tectonic shift that creates multiple, simultaneous tsunamis are all examples. At the other end of the scale we can find much speculation around risks which owe more to Hollywood movies and internet conspiracy theorists than they do to hard science. In this area, we can locate fears about artificial intelligence, human cloning and secret societies comprised of global capitalists. Such speculation only serves to muddy the waters when more meaningful forecasts are made. Below we try to cut a path through these problems by defining emerging global risks in a rather cautious manner; that is, by only including: (1) risks that we already know about, which are likely to increase in global importance in the future; (2) risks that we know arrive at fairly regular intervals and that are likely to appear in the near future; (3) speculative risks that have been recognized by the insurance industry as potential problems.

GROWING RISKS

A range of risks exists which is well-documented, difficult to quantify concisely and likely to grow in importance. Out of these risks, anthropogenic global warming is the most commonly recognized. There is a consensus in the scientific community about the reality of global climate change, the increase in CO_2 emissions and the depletion of the ozone layer. Although there are some natural explanations for climate change, such as solar and volcanic activity, most scientists agree that the gases emitted by burning coal and other fossil fuels contribute to the 'greenhouse effect'. Of course, sceptical dissenting voices still exist about whether climate change is being caused by humankind but these remain an ever-decreasing (though still vocal) minority. Despite this minority, PSOs around the world now have to factor climate change into their preparations for risk and crisis management. In terms of the latter, this means quite simply preparing for adverse weather conditions and their effects. For some, like the United Kingdom, this means an increased concern with coastal flooding and storms as evidenced in the

2013–14 floods. For others, like France during the 2003 heatwave or Spain and Portugal during the 2012 drought, the concern is lack of rainfall, water restrictions, forest fires and crop failure. Some particularly unlucky countries, like Australia, vacillate between both extremes as long droughts are punctuated by devastating floods.

From a risk perspective, in the short term, consideration has to be given to the location, construction and protection of buildings and other structures. What was once safe ground may now be floodplain, and what was once verdant land may now be subject to drought. This means that joining up land-use planning, planning legislation and risk management is absolutely essential if we are to adapt to the risks of climate change. Likewise, PSOs should review both their own vulnerability, and the level of demand for their services which may be generated should adverse circumstances arise. In the short to medium term more legislation may be passed to force businesses and domestic users to reduce their energy consumption and minimize waste, and these measures too can have consequences for the continuity of public sector business.

Both crisis and risk management, however, are capable only of managing the symptoms of climate change. If we believe that the greenhouse effect is being caused by human action, then the only way to combat the problem is to reduce carbon emissions in absolute terms. However, the collective nature of the problem means that a collective action solution is required across many governments and this is one reason why successive international agreements about carbon reductions have largely failed to bring about change.

Closely linked to the issue of climate change is the issue of energy security, which is increasingly attracting attention from crisis and risk analysts. Guaranteeing energy security means ensuring the long-term sustainability of energy at an affordable cost and it is far from easy. In the European Union, for example, over 80 per cent of oil and over 50 per cent of gas is imported and this means that countries are vulnerable to fluctuating costs, the demands of energy suppliers and potential competition for supplies from elsewhere. The most severe outcome may be that imports are cut off by supplying countries, leading to blackouts and energy shortfalls. Indeed, this is exactly what has happened in a number of eastern European countries (see Box 8.2). For insurers, prolonged blackouts mean property losses, business interruption and liability claims of various kinds. In the European Union, this emerging risk is being taken very seriously, particularly because of the increasing economic power of China, which is now building more pipelines to Russian gas so that it does not have to rely on overseas energy shipments. For the EU, this competition over finite Russian gas resources means the creation of policies that pursue renewable energy, increase the efficiency of existing European oil resources and create infrastructure to enhance imports of energy are all absolutely crucial forms of global risk management.

Population growth is another long-term trend that is set to continue and that is recognized as a risk inducer. Although growth forecasts are problematic, we do know beyond doubt that the world's population is increasing. Thomas Robert Malthus, the eighteenth-century cleric, claimed that population growth was the largest danger to

BOX 8.2 ENERGY SECURITY IN EUROPE

The countries of the European Union rely heavily on gas from Russia, channelled through eastern European pipelines. However, over the past decade this energy supply has become increasingly unstable as the Russian government uses its control of gas as a foreign policy weapon, terrorists disrupt the flow of gas through pipes and eastern European countries engage in disputes with Moscow over the price of gas and infrastructure maintenance. Past failures provide an indication of future risks. In 2006, the supply of gas was cut off from Ukraine due to a dispute over prices. The same year, terrorists blew up two pipelines connecting Russia and Georgia, halting the flow of energy into that country, and in Lithuania a number of pipelines stopped shipping gas because of concerns with the ownership and safety of infrastructure. In 2008–9, familiar problems resurfaced again in the Ukrainian–Russian relationship, leading to a reduction in the gas supplied to Ukraine, which severely affected several European countries. The combination of political tension, technical issues and security concerns means that pricing and supply are far from stable and the political disintegration of Ukraine in 2014 will only exacerbate the energy supply risks for European states. The pivotal position of Ukraine in terms of energy security is one reason why the European Union and Moscow are prepared to engage in a stand-off, with each questioning the legitimacy of the other's foreign policy. As that conflict deepens, the fragility of the energy supply increases, making energy insecurity one of the most pressing risks on the agenda of European governments.

humankind. According to Malthus, if left unchecked, population growth would lead to a doomsday scenario in which the world's finite resources would be stripped bare. This view encouraged Malthus to view deadly social ills, such as poverty, disease and squalor as an acceptable price to pay for the control of population size. Thankfully, Malthus's theory and his ideas have been largely rejected today but this does not mean that population growth is not an issue. The challenge today, however, relates more to the way in which population growth enhances the inequitable distribution of resources. As more people populate developing nations in particular, new vulnerabilities materialize as people search for land and resources that are unclaimed (Smith and Petley 2009: 337). Inevitably, this leads them to settle in hazardous, disaster-prone areas which are not cultivated. Conversely, we now know that over half of the world's population lives in urban centres and that the UN has predicted that over two billion of the population will live in slum dwellings by 2030 (UNFPA 2007) (see Box 8.3). The hazards and risks that these families face are a damning indictment of 'progress' in the twenty-first century.

BOX 8.3 RISKS IN THE MEGACITY

The megacity can be seen as the ultimate manifestation of a globalized world. Defined as cities with over ten million inhabitants, the twenty-four megacities of the world, which hold over 4 per cent of the world's population, represent global migration hubs, centres of rural to urban movement and dense spaces in which socio-technical systems overlap in complex ways. In the words of one insurer, megacities can be seen as highly problematic manifestations of humankind's development because 'an organism with more than ten million living cells gradually risks being suffocated by the problems it has itself created – like traffic, environmental damage and crime. This is especially true where growth is too rapid and unorganic, as is the case in most megacities in emerging and developing countries' (Swiss Re 2004: 1). Indeed, the list of risks that a megacity's inhabitant could be exposed to is seemingly endless. Below we provide a quick synopsis of some that are unique to these habitats:

- *Natural catastrophes mediated through micro communities* – imagine a natural disaster in a city such as Tokyo with its thirty-five million inhabitants, twenty-three municipalities and 2,000 plus km² area. The impact of the event is likely to be cascaded in a different manner in each locality meaning that disaster management (and pre-crisis preparedness) measures will have to be adapted to each environment within a megacity.
- *Infrastructure and technological risks* – issues of sewage, soil and groundwater health, failing infrastructure, refuse and infectious disease are pertinent to megacities. Pollution, however, is a particular problem. In Kuala Lumpur, half of the city's air pollution is dust and soot; in Bangkok 1,400 deaths a year are attributed to dust alone; and in China the rate of lung cancer in cities is six times that found in rural areas.
- *Terrorist attacks* – there is little point in a terrorist attack unless it causes disruption en masse. This naturally points those willing to commit atrocities towards megacities. Hence we have seen sarin gas releases in the Tokyo underground, bomb explosions in the London transport system and of course 9/11 in New York.
- *Settlement problems* – cities grow fast and public services cannot keep pace. In developing nations this means cities within cities and districts, like the favelas of Brazil, which develop their own laws, customs and standards of living. For the inhabitants, this means the institutionalization of squalor and slum life and for the city as a whole this socio-economic disparity is the order of the day. One need only walk through a major thoroughfare or large train

station in Delhi or Bombay to see such disparities. These inequalities also operate globally. A resident in the poorest area of Chicago, for example, has a better standard of living than 80 per cent of megacity inhabitants in developing nations.

Sources: Munich Re (2004); Kötter (2004).

Closely linked to this is the issue of development or, more precisely, of certain types of development. Hazards may be natural or man-made, but they merely animate the vulnerabilities that we have created in our communities. Many of these vulnerabilities are created as nations seek (and are encouraged) to develop and modernize in certain ways. Here we need to confront the collective resource dilemmas, dependency relationships and lack of regulation of capital and technology that can emerge as a nation 'develops'. These can be error-inducing problems that incubate risks.

Thus while many may look at the increasing GDP of a developing nation and think that the fortunes of its population are improving, the reality may well be that below the economic headline, people are increasingly being exposed to new risks. These can come in many forms. Economic growth in Southeast Asia is correlated with increased sex trafficking and sex tourism, for example (McMichael 2012: 165). In Uganda, disaster management has been used as a rationale to relocate farmers and villagers away from their land and into urban areas so that their land can be sold to more profitable industry (Jenkins et al. 2013). In Qatar, more than five hundred Indian migrant workers have been killed since 2012 on building projects for the forthcoming soccer World Cup, and in Shanghai, the fast pace of industrialization relies upon highly vulnerable, socially excluded city dwellers for cheap labour (Smith and Petley 2009). These examples show us that global and national modernization presents significant risks, which are unevenly distributed amongst vulnerable groups.

Worth noting here is a final trend which can be labelled the 'changing world order'. By this we mean the seemingly inexorable rise of a number of national economies and the decline of others over recent decades. At the forefront of this trend is the rise of China. Once a sleeping giant restrained by Maoist ideology, China's ascent as a superpower is made all the more apparent by the relative debt burden being shared by the United States and Western Europe in the wake of the global financial crisis and the decline of the Japanese economy since the 1990s. A second issue to consider here is the strengthening of the so-called BRIC economies, which include China alongside Brazil, Russia and India. As predictions of their increased industrial growth continue, the political map of powerful nations is being redrawn. What all of this means is of course difficult to forecast, but we do know that the BRIC economies will continue to grow. If anything, this growth should be taken as a sign that the world's economic system will become even more global and more interdependent. National economic systems, even in strong countries, will have to be seen as one small part of a larger economic fabric of the future which will reflect many different political, ideological and cultural views.

INTERVAL RISKS

Interval risks relate to those sudden crises which appear and disappear with some regularity, although the timing of their appearance is impossible to predict. Here we can include the typical natural catastrophe – cyclone, flood, earthquake. However, in this category we can observe two particular risks that are important for the discussion of global and transboundary crisis management which features below.

The first major interval risk is an influenza pandemic of serious proportions. Every year influenza epidemics travel around the countries of the world. However, pandemics occur when new strains emerge that human immune systems cannot fend off. In 1918 an influenza pandemic, which became known as the Spanish flu, swept around the globe killing an estimated fifty million people (Johnson and Mueller 2002). In 1957 and 1968, two more pandemics materialized, killing around three million people, and in 2009 a new strain of H1N1 influenza moved around the globe. Estimates of the death toll caused by the 'swine flu' pandemic range between 230,000 and 285,000. Although the death toll has reduced at each pandemic since 1918, there is a case to be made that the strains since then have been somewhat mild in comparison. Indeed, pessimistic forecasts based on a 1918-style virus sweeping around the enlarged population of the world today have claimed that as many as seven million people could die (Stöhr and Esveld 2004). For this reason the UK Civil Contingencies Risk Register places an influenza pandemic as the highest priority risk, stressing that the swine flu episode of 2009 is not necessarily indicative of the severity of future pandemics. Grim predictions about pandemics are often made alongside narratives of globalization, which emphasize how global interconnectedness will hasten the spread of infection. Such was the story in relation to SARS and avian flu in the middle of the previous decade. Both crises highlighted how disease has no respect for the sovereign borders of the nation state.

The second interval risk worth commenting on here is the nuclear threat, which has materialized on several occasions over the past century. Several scenarios can be included here. The first is the accidental meltdown caused by malfunction, such as that seen in Three Mile Island (1979) and Chernobyl (1986). The second is the meltdown caused by natural catastrophe, such as that witnessed in Fukushima in 2011. The third is the still present threat of a nuclear weapon detonation. A regular fear during the Cold War, this risk is now relegated to a concern with 'rogue' states such as Iran and North Korea and, even more unlikely, terrorist activity. Regardless of the trigger or mechanism causing the threat, we can see that each scenario is truly transboundary. Whether it is a radioactive plume that travels across borders (as was the case after Chernobyl), an earthquake translating into plant malfunction (Fukushima) or an intentionally detonated nuclear device, the effects will be truly global in nature.

229

SPECULATIVE RISKS

The speculative risks documented here are on the radar of the largest insurance providers as potential problems which cannot be quantified easily at this time. Looking across the high-risk predictions of Swiss Re (2013), for example, provides an indication of a range of speculative risks, including:

- *Nanotechnology* – involves the use of particles at the molecular level to improve cosmetics, household products and electronics. The danger of nanotechnology is not necessarily acute – we would know by now if it were immediately deadly – but there may be longer-term chronic problems which will only become apparent over time (like the problem of asbestos fibres)

- *Prolonged power blackouts* – these would have a devastating effect on society due to our complete reliance on electricity. Potential causes here relate to adverse weather conditions, space weather conditions, terrorist disruptions (all rather unlikely) and ageing infrastructure and technology when combined with growing usage demands (much more likely).

- *Endocrine disrupting chemicals (EDC)* – these are chemicals that affect the hormone systems of humans causing cancer, birth defects and problems during pregnancy. Evidence of a relationship between these chemicals – found in many everyday products such as plastic bottles, cans, detergents and even food – and problematic reproductive processes has already been found. If a relationship is established beyond doubt, it will have a massive impact on the risk management practices of every organization, particularly the liability rates of those directly involved with EDCs.

- *Big data* – this problem is constituted by huge amounts of data that can no longer be controlled by traditional data management techniques. There are problems of veracity caused by big data because social media (which churns up masses of information) is not always accurate. This can cause issues of liability if it is relied upon for decision-making. Problems also relate to intellectual property rights and data protection/information security issues. As the 2013 National Security Agency scandal showed, big data can be used by government organizations in ways that are unethical and prejudice human rights. Big data, if mistreated, can create severe issues of liability for the PSO.

- *Electromagnetic fields* – a long-running debate exists about the extent to which mobile phones and broadcast antenna may be detrimental to human health. According to Swiss Re (2013: 11), anxiety over electromagnetic fields has risen despite the inconclusive evidence on both sides of the argument. Given their ubiquitous nature and centrality to modern communications, any conclusive evidence about carcinogenic health risks emanating through mobile technology would have a massive impact on every industry.

Whether global risks are slowly growing along a continuous and predictable pattern, spiking periodically to cause discontinuity and acute shock or sitting uneasily on the horizon as a potential threat, they all share two common features. First, they are all a reflection of modernity. By this we mean they are a consequence of the systems, increasingly global in nature, which human beings have built around themselves for various purposes. Our phones, our electricity, our cities and our economies all present risks. And even natural catastrophes, which are surely the oldest of all risks, are now defined by the impact they have on human and ecological systems. Second, in an increasingly interconnected world, these risks are potentially shared by everyone and are certainly capable of moving quickly and changing shape as they exploit the connected avenues of modern society. This context of global emerging risks means that when things do go wrong there is a need for global crisis management.

In the next section we discuss three types of global crisis management. The first type is the most well-known – humanitarian aid.

HUMANITARIAN CRISIS MANAGEMENT

Humanitarian aid is what comes to mind when most think of global crisis responses. Indeed, there is now a massive constellation of international actors who work on preventing, responding to and recovering from natural catastrophes around the world. These agencies can be found in traditional government departments, such as the Department for International Development (DfID) in the United Kingdom or the Agency of International Development in the United States (USAID). All government organizations work in partnership with a range of international non-governmental organizations that perform humanitarian forms of disaster management. These include the Red Cross and Red Crescent, Oxfam and Médecins Sans Frontières. The public sector and voluntary agencies are complemented by international policy actors, such as the United Nations and the European Union. In the UN, the two principal offices are UNOCHA (coordination of humanitarian aid) and UNISDR (the coordination of disaster risk reduction), and in the EU the role is occupied by DG ECHO (Directorate General Humanitarian Office). These international actors, alongside the domestic public sector agencies, provide direct services 'in the field' and also fund and coordinate non-government activities that promote disaster management globally.

Although international humanitarian aid responses to disasters have been commonplace throughout the twentieth and twenty-first centuries, the 1990s represents a real watershed moment as the United Nations declared that decade as the International Decade for Natural Disaster Risk Reduction. A chain of events followed on from this which ultimately led to the creation in 2005 of what has become known as the Hyogo Framework. In essence, the framework is a series of agreed-upon principles which promote effective disaster management under the headline of disaster risk reduction (DRR). It has been the responsibility of UNISDR to promote these principles on the global stage and to encourage the implementation of best practice in disaster management terms, particularly in the most vulnerable nations.

However, the UNISDR can be seen as more of an advocator for best practice than an enforcer or regulator of policy. With a comparatively meagre budget in UN terms and very little authority on the world stage, UNISDR was initially criticized because of its inability to make meaningful strides vis-à-vis the reduction of vulnerability (Hannigan 2012). Nevertheless, the Hyogo Framework does still constitute the most meaningful attempt at a collective solution to the problem of global vulnerability. Moreover, as a series of symbolic principles it is important, not least because it recognizes and publishes the link between climate change and vulnerability to disaster and the link between development, vulnerability and disaster. As such, it is at the forefront of an international process which promotes disaster risk reduction in ways that are sympathetic (to some extent) with the concerns of development scholars. The Hyogo Framework is due to be replaced in 2015. The hope must be that its replacement not only updates and refreshes these principles but also provides the UNISDR with the means to tenaciously to promote disaster management across the next decade.

The Hyogo Framework has five priorities for action. Through these we can also discuss some of the most pressing issues facing international humanitarian crisis management:

■ *Priority 1 – ensuring that disaster risk reduction is a national and local priority with a strong basis for implementation.* This entails developing institutional and legislative frameworks (within national governments) for DRR at the national and the local level. These platforms should be well resourced and capable of facilitating community participation in disaster management. Thus the UNISDR has two key challenges in this regard: how can it encourage national governments that lack resources to prioritize disaster management? And, if national platforms for disaster management are created, how can they be encouraged to devolve power and resources to citizens so that they can respond to the crises they face? As we already know from our discussion of community resilience, citizen participation is beginning to be seen as the key to enhancing crisis management efficacy in the twenty-first century. This is especially true in terms of disaster risk reduction in countries that have weak or corrupt governments, minimal resources or multicultural populations with different needs. Box 8.4, for example, provides an excellent example of what can be achieved by giving power to those affected by disaster.

■ *Priority 2 – identifying, assessing and monitoring risks and enhancing early warning.* Although primarily oriented towards enhancing the technical dimensions of early warning systems, this priority gives us an insight into another requirement for international crisis management, which is the need to translate scientific knowledge for affected communities. For example, how might a remote indigenous island community interpret the science and findings of the International Panel on Climate Change? Without some cultural translation of the risk science, the findings are meaningless to this community. Indeed, a long-standing criticism of the Hyogo Framework and the process that led up to it was that the social sciences and the people affected by crises were deprioritized in favour of the hard sciences (Handmer 1995). In other words, seismologists, engineers and hydrologists had more voice in the creation of DRR policies than the people that would be impacted by the crises themselves. This is a key issue for early warning systems. It is one thing to determine that a disaster is about to strike but it is quite another to have communities aware and responding to that threat in an adequate manner.

- *Priority 3 — using knowledge, innovation and education to build a culture of safety and resilience at all levels.* In the Hyogo Framework, education is seen as the key to building 'cultures of resilience'. However, there are a number of significant challenges to be overcome if we are to facilitate meaningful disaster management outcomes through education (i.e. purposive local action that reduces vulnerability and responds to threats). At least three problems have already been identified within what is an embryonic field of study: (1) for meaningful education to occur, and consequentially for vulnerability to reduce through action, multiple types of learning are required for multiple audiences. How we educate schoolchildren and how we educate local elders in a community will be completely different; (2) indigenous knowledge, which often has a real capacity to reduce risk, has to be interleaved with more scientific knowledge bases; (3) there is a danger of unintentionally communicating problematic narratives and discourses through disaster management education. These last two points reflect a growing space in disaster management literature which indicates that local, indigenous knowledge must be harnessed if policy is to be effective. Local practices, customs and lived experience can be an essential source of information in terms of risk, vulnerability and approaching disaster. Efforts are now being made to build policy models for risk management that incorporate grassroots knowledge of this nature into risk reduction efforts (see, for example, Mercer et al. 2010).

- *Priority 4 — reducing underlying risk factors.* This objective represents something of a 'black box' containing many different policy priorities from land use planning to social protection measures. Social protection measures represent an interesting policy solution and have proved popular but not without controversy. Social protection schemes provide cash transfers often in exchange for services from citizens affected by disaster. Thus the villagers who can no longer farm might receive wages for working on the rebuilding of local infrastructure, or the flood-affected citizen might receive a direct cash payment rather than an aid parcel. On one level, social protection is viewed as a step forward as it is seen to be empowering the victim. Rather than receiving aid, with its connotations of charity, they receive a lump sum of money which can provide them with consumer sovereignty while reducing the stigma attached to aid by linking the payment to some form of work. From another perspective, social protection is viewed as turning those affected by disaster either into welfare claimants or, more controversially still, into low-paid workers. In many ways, this tension cuts to the heart of the issue in terms of international humanitarian aid. Are western forms of crisis management helping or hindering non-western cultures? Are we simply replicating bigger pathological problems of economic development via disaster management? Or are these solutions genuinely needed and wanted in developing nations?

■ *Priority 5 – strengthening preparedness.* At the heart of this priority is the need for preparedness frameworks and contingency plans of the sort discussed in Chapter 5. Given what we know about the difficulties of creating, implementing and refreshing preparedness measures, the question for the UNISDR is: are these mechanisms the most effective measures for public sectors which may be under-resourced and lacking in crisis management expertise? Moreover, contingency plans and preparedness measures are very much templates for western forms of disaster management. Are these suitable for every culture? Might it be better, ultimately, to build preparedness from the bottom up? Such questions need to be tackled in the development of the next framework document.

All too often humanitarian forms of crisis management are bound up with a western view of the powerful, sophisticated developed nation providing a 'hand-up' to the impoverished developing community who cannot help themselves when catastrophe strikes (Bankoff 2001). However, contemporary studies of humanitarian crisis management and development teach us to look beyond this caricature. In fact, more careful analyses allows us to make the case that: (1) many of the vulnerabilities that exist in developing nations are caused by processes of development that are encouraged by the developed nations and their institutions (such as the World Bank) and many of the crisis responses engaged by developed states are far from helpful (see, for example, Middleton and O'Keefe 1994; Wisner et al. 2004; Rose et al. 2013). Nevertheless, positive stories do exist of humanitarian aid efforts which do not patronize victims or replicate western templates of the good life.

REMOTE CRISIS MANAGEMENT

A second form of global crisis management activity that has been especially high profile in recent years arises in situations when public authorities in one country need to intervene in order to protect/rescue their citizens who are caught up in an overseas crisis/ disaster. The Asian Boxing Day tsunami of 2004 generated a mass of such activities, especially from some countries with a substantial number of nationals in the region (Sweden had about 30,000). Hurricane Katrina prompted similar reactions. Even though the numbers in New Orleans were often small, the political significance for each country was potentially considerable. Governments needed to be seen to be doing something to locate and perhaps rescue their citizens – innocent victims of the worst US natural disaster in recent times. The following year, in 2006, the swift and

BOX 8.4 INTERNATIONAL AID WORKING WELL

In their excellent book, *Post-Disaster Reconstruction: Lessons from Aceh*, Mathew Clarke, Ismet Fanany and Sue Kenny provide an insight into the problems and potential successes of international aid. Focusing on the recovery from the 2004 earthquake and tsunami in Aceh, Indonesia, the authors initially provide a sceptical account of international humanitarian aid relief in the area. They document a sense of humiliation and marginalization amongst the tsunami-affected communities as international humanitarian organizations vied for publicity in the region, established projects that they could 'market' to international audiences and applied their own western policy templates which did not elicit local participation.

However, the case of Lampuuk, a coastal village in Aceh which was severely affected by the tsunami, is a success story. In this region, survivors created what has been described as a model for cooperation in terms of international disaster recovery practice. Bankrolled by the Red Crescent, a group of survivors created the Lampuuk Recovery Center (LRC), which became a forum through which the local community controlled the rebuilding efforts of international organizations. This example of citizen participation and power in terms of disaster recovery is rare. Indeed, such was the power of the LRC that it was able to reject offers of housing from certain international agencies when they were not right for the community, cancel the contracts of builders when problems arose, and ensure that local victims had significant influence over the design and build of their new community. This example of direct citizen participation supported by a powerful non-governmental organization is far removed from the typical process of humanitarian aid. All too often a one-size-fits-all solution is delivered to victims without consultation. This often results in quick-fix housing and unsustainable forms of recovery, which allow the aid organization to claim success while local communities continue to struggle.

Source: Clarke et al. (2010).

intense escalation of conflict between Israel and Lebanon generated similar pressures for states to make arrangements to remove their citizens to safety. Some 100,000 individuals from over one hundred countries throughout the world were trapped in Southern Lebanon.

Remote crisis management (Schwarz and McConnell 2009) or consular emergencies (Tindall and 't Hart 2011) present difficult challenges for officials and political elites alike. High expectations from media and citizens that leaders should 'know what is going on' are coupled with expectations that action will be swift and effective. However, the country/region affected by crisis is liable to be in turmoil – perhaps even conflict-ridden. In all likelihood it will be struggling to engage in recovery and rescue efforts, as well as trying to make sense of rapidly unfolding events. In such situations, and from the perspective of 'remote' countries, existing communication channels (through foreign embassies, diplomatic postings and local offices) may well be broken. Public authorities may have very little information beyond that available through international news networks such as CNN, the BBC and Sky news. In such contexts, demands for swift action can be immensely challenging. For example, when the Asian tsunami hit on Boxing Day 2004, the Australian Government quickly convened its Interdepartmental Emergency Taskforce (IDETF). When it met on the morning of 27 December, the estimated death toll was 11,000–12,000 (the actual number was in excess of 200,000), with an initial estimate of 14,000–15,000 Australians in the areas – later scaled down to about 1,600. In actual fact, later figures would reveal that just over twenty Australians lost their lives in the disaster (Shergold 2005).

The information gap aside, there are many difficult logistical issues involved in organizing airlifts, sending medical, forensic and criminal experts and more. Indeed, even obtaining internal financial authority to incur such expenditures can be difficult (as public servants in Australia found out in relation to the 2002 Bali bombing – see Paul 2005). Perhaps the most crucial issue is obtaining a rapid 'joined up' response. For Australia, Bali was one such challenge, as was its response to the Asian tsunami. The latter required cooperation and coordination between at least eleven different agencies, ranging from the Department of Foreign Affairs and Trade (taking the lead and establishing hotlines, using its diplomatic links and providing support to families) to the Australian Federal Police (victim identification) and the Department of Defence (logistics of transporting engineering and medical materials and experts). Sweden's broad response to the tsunami was similar. A detailed summary of its reactions and activities is provided in Box 8.5.

For political elites, their crisis management challenges are especially those of the symbolic variety. If there is considerable criticism of the response, how should they react? Acceptance of responsibility for delays can be the dignified thing to do and can in fact diffuse criticism (as happened in Norway and Finland after the Asian tsunami, see Brändström et al. 2008). Alternatively, 'passing the buck' or blame strategies may have some impact in diluting criticism, but they can be risky approaches when societies expect leaders to exercise leadership. Attributing causal factors to unpredictable acts of nature or 'bolts from the blue' may not provide much of a defence from critics (as George W. Bush found out with Hurricane Katrina). Furthermore, virtually every internationally high-profile crisis or disaster generates swift hindsight speculation and rationalizing from the citizens, experts and (especially) the media. The very fact that a bad event did happen can often lead to suggestions of an 'accident waiting to happen', 'disaster in the making' or 'inevitable crisis'. The logic of such arguments is that the existence of advance warning signs means that we should have had workable plans in place. Of course as students of crisis management we know that it is all too easy to

BOX 8.5 SUMMARY OF ACTION BY THE SWEDISH MINISTRY FOR FOREIGN AFFAIRS AFTER THE 2004 BOXING DAY TSUNAMI DISASTER

1. *Action in Thailand* – Sweden's Ambassador to Thailand Jonas Hafström and staff travelled to Phuket on 26 December and set up a temporary embassy office in the premises of the honorary consulate at Pearl Village Hotel. The Swedish Embassy in Bangkok was given staff reinforcements to cope with the assistance work. Some seventy-five ministry officials were sent to Thailand in relays to relieve staff on the spot.

2. *Evacuation* – it is estimated that more than 20,000 Swedes were in Thailand when the natural disaster occurred. In the space of a few days some 14,000 of them had left the country on charter flights, scheduled flights or one of the seventeen flights organized by the Ministry for Foreign Affairs. The airlift ended on 4 January. An additional air transport for remaining Swedes was arranged by the ministry and arrived at Arlanda Stockholm Airport on 8 January.

3. *Medical transport* – a total of sixteen air ambulance flights were provided to bring injured Swedes from Thailand to Sweden. These flights were initiated by the Ministry for Foreign Affairs in cooperation with Germany, Iceland, Norway and other countries.

4. *Medical care provided* – starting on 28 December groups of Swedish medical staff were flown down to the areas affected. The Swedish Rescue Services Agency, SOS Alarm and the county councils sent a total of 200 doctors, nurses, psychologists and other rescue service personnel. Preparations were made to send additional medical personnel if necessary. Medical equipment was transported on a number of occasions.

5. *Identification work* – on 27 December, the Ministry for Foreign Affairs decided in consultation with the National Criminal Investigation Department and the National Board of Forensic Medicine to send an identification team to Thailand. This team was supplemented as needs became clear. The identification commission had thirty-two people on the spot in Phuket, working with identification teams from twenty-two other countries. The Swedish team was supplemented with two additional forensic assistants. The National Criminal Investigation Department also had a team on the spot to continue looking for deceased persons.

6. *Home transport of the deceased* – the Government appointed Johan Hederstedt, formerly Supreme Commander of the Swedish Armed Forces to be responsible on the spot in Phuket for ensuring that deceased Swedes who have been

identified were brought home in dignified a manner. The National Police Board was responsible for coordination of home transports and for reception of the deceased on arrival in Sweden.

7. *Other action* – on 28 December, the Ministry for Foreign Affairs sent SMS messages to all Swedish mobile phones in Thailand, Sri Lanka and India appealing to Swedes to get in touch with relatives, the local embassy or the ministry. Another SMS message was sent to Swedes in Thailand urging them to book places on evacuation flights, and a message was sent with the telephone number of a helpline provided by BRIS (Swedish Society for the Protection of Children's Rights in the Community) for traumatized children and parents. In early January a notice was placed in the national newspapers in Thailand. In this notice the royal family, the government and the people of Sweden expressed their gratitude to Thailand for the exceptional support and assistance given to Swedes affected by the disaster. Minister for Foreign Affairs Laila Freivalds left on 28 December on a two-day visit to the area affected by the disaster. The prime minister visited Thailand on 18–19 January along with his colleagues from Norway and Finland.

Source: Adapted from Swedish Ministry for Foreign Affairs Press Release <http://www.regeringen.se/sb/d/5166/nocache/true/a/37821/dictionary/true>.

construct after-the-fact rationalizations, but the real world of politics does in fact exhibit a powerful and strong tendency to do just this. Contingency planning to deal with crises in other countries (and being held to account when there are none) is precisely the sort of expectation that rests on the shoulders of political elites. When Swedish Prime Minister Persson blamed his officials for the widely perceived slow response to its citizens caught up in the Asian tsunami, his government's popularity and his status as 'father of the nation' suffered substantial damage (Brändström et al. 2008).

Routinely, crises and disasters prompt a combination of centralized and decentralized responses (see Chapters 5 and 6). Operational matters are dealt with primarily by local operators and officials; elites may get involved in some (such as approving aid and granting authority for others to act), but their challenges tend to be more strategic and symbolic. Managing crises from afar stretches the relationship between centralization and decentralization and poses a significant challenge for decision-makers. Not only is there significant geographical space between many aspects of both, but local operational matters need to be conducted in another country with its own institutions, laws, elected government, sovereign powers, cultures and media – many of these are liable to be in a state of flux. Remote crisis management is accompanied by high expectations but has exceptional logistical and strategic-symbolic difficulties.

238

TRANSBOUNDARY CRISIS MANAGEMENT

Public authorities in each individual country can no longer plan for, resolve and recover from crises/disasters within a hermetically sealed national environment. Domestic crisis management is increasingly an international activity involving engagement with a wide range of global interests. Crises can change shape and travel widely at great speeds. Chapter 1 introduced the so-called transboundary crisis, which is a threat 'characterized by the potential to cross *geographic* and *functional* boundaries, jumping from one system to another' (Boin and Rhinard 2008: 4, original emphasis). Moreover, as these 'jumps' occur, crises can change shape, morphing from one threat type to another.

The challenges presented by these crises are severe. First, they require institutional crisis management policies which cross borders, organizational fiefdoms and disciplinary boundaries. As a crisis of this nature moves and changes rapidly, decisions over who is responsible for its resolution and who takes the lead in crisis management terms become difficult. Second, they are difficult to 'sense' and 'frame'. As they emerge from complex interactions we may not be able to define them easily in the first instance, and as they change they may escape initial interpretations. Third, we know that these crises spread through the connections we build but we have no idea how temporarily to disconnect these pathways (Boin and Rhinard 2008: 7). In some cases, disconnection may be straightforward. Imposing an import and export ban on a country with a virulent animal disease, for example, might be one way of severing connections. How might we achieve this, however, if the crisis is spreading through information technology channels or the interconnected energy pipelines of Europe?

The challenges posed by transboundary crises are clearly severe but we are beginning to understand what is required from the international community to meet them. We suggest a five-point agenda for developing capacity to respond to transboundary threats.

1. *The ideational component of risk and crisis management policy needs to be developed.* Public managers need to challenge pre-existing ideas about risks, crises and their resolution. If your organization is likely to face a transboundary crisis then its risk and crisis policies need to be as contemporary as the threats it will face. This means appreciating the dynamics of crisis escalation and change in terms of globalization, interconnectedness and modern complexity. Patrick Lagadec (2009), for example, advocates that public managers need radically to change the way they think about threats so that a new cosmology of risks and crises can be accommodated. If a public sector organization is well prepared for a domestic risk that is anticipated to be relatively static then it will not necessarily be ready for the arrival of a highly dynamic international crisis. The challenge for the public manager, therefore, is to think in transboundary terms so that policy preparations are rooted in transboundary ideas.

2. *Incentives need to be found to overcome collective action issues.* Nations, sectors and agencies need to work together to get ahead of these crises. However, as Rhinard

(2009) stresses in relation to the European Union's efforts to meet transboundary threats, security and safety are public goods. Everyone benefits from increases. If, for example, twenty-five of the EU's twenty-eight countries cooperate and improve the system's ability to respond to these crises, then the two 'free-riding' nations will still benefit from an aggregate improvement in security. This is a classic collective action dilemma and it applies to all efforts to prepare collectively for crises. How can we encourage everyone to sink costs into preparedness when the benefits can be enjoyed for free? Overcoming collective action dilemmas requires incentives and in the EU this usually means the threat of sanctions through the European Court of Justice for non-compliance with legislation. However, crisis management is a sensitive policy area. Nations do not readily give away their sovereignty in this policy space (see Ekengren et al. 2006), and as a consequence what little legislation exists in the EU is about institution building rather than coercing real collective action. In the absence of legal or monetary incentives, the only remaining stimulus is the threat or memory of disruptive crises.

3. *Enhance the adaptive quality of policy measures.* Meeting transboundary crises requires the ability to adapt quickly. Crisis managers need somehow to keep pace with events as they change and this means that crisis responses need to be customized in ways that will allow them to adapt rapidly to threats as they move (Ansell et al. 2010). This is no easy task and, in reality, we do not yet have enough knowledge about transboundary crises to present concrete solutions for crisis managers; at the moment, the best thing that public organizations can do to prepare to 'keep up' with a transboundary crisis is to develop their understanding of their crisis management network and their network management skills. If a network has the right scale and a diverse range of actors then the possibility exists for it to escalate and change character in response to transboundary threats.

4. *Enhance sense-making capacities.* This would seem quite obvious but studies have shown that the perceptions of policy-makers – how they perceive the time they have at their disposal to make decisions and their degree of surprise about the nature of events – are crucially important variables affecting decision-making in these crises (Hermann and Dayton 2009). What we need to do, therefore, is work on sense-making processes so that they can reduce the surprise element associated with transboundary crises and also 'track' changes in events so that policy-makers can keep pace cognitively. The Rapid Reflection Force mechanism mentioned in Chapter 6 might be one method of approaching this challenge.

5. *Develop resilience in society.* An emerging theme over previous chapters has been that citizens can take responsibility for crisis management actions and that resilience against threats can be developed 'out there' beyond government capacities. Increasing the ability of non-governmental actors to deal with crises means that fast-moving threats can be challenged and resisted by different socie-

tal actors as they move through sectors and organizations. This is something of an ideal because the reality will always be that some (probably many) sections of society that have not experienced a crisis before will be unprepared and unable to respond to a transboundary threat. Nevertheless, we can see the potential for societal resilience. We see it in the 'emergent' citizen groups that respond voluntarily to crises, we see it in the resistance of communities to chronic droughts, famines and plagues, and we see it in the global solidarity of humankind when distant others try to help disaster victims on the other side of the planet. This solidarity and strength suggests the potential of social resilience.

CONCLUSION

In terms of risk, the world is becoming a smaller place. German sociologist Ulrich Beck (1999) writes of a 'world risk society' in which the forces of modernization have turned in on themselves, not just at the national level but also at the global level. The interconnectedness of our IT and communication systems, changes in our global climate, mass migration and the demands made on our increasingly small reserves of water, fossil fuels and food require better understanding of current and emerging future risks. Global changes can have local impact and affect both the demand for and the types of services offered by public sector organizations. If, as Schwartz (2003) argues, nothing that will happen in the future is really a 'surprise', then we need better strategies for identifying, evaluating and treating risk today, in order to reduce the likelihood of further nasty surprises in future.

From the perspective of crisis management, we see that many crises/disasters require varying degrees of international cooperation and can affect citizens not only in their own home countries but also when they are many thousands of miles away from home. Learning to cope with crises remotely has presented new and difficult challenges for governments and other agencies. Risks and crises are no respecters of national boundaries and can spill over borders, affecting numerous countries at the same time. The need to interact with agencies and institutions in other nations, and to share learning, is obviously vital if future threats and crises are to be effectively managed.

DISCUSSION QUESTIONS

1. Choose a public sector organization you are familiar with. Can you forecast the emerging risks that might affect it over the next ten, twenty or fifty years?
2. In relation to the above, what difficulties did you encounter when making your forecasts?

3. What are the main implications of the increasing internationalization of crisis management and to what extent do you think these trends will continue?
4. Can you map out a range of transboundary threats that might impact on a public sector organization? How would you prepare to address such threats?

REFERENCES

Ansell, C., Boin, A. and Keller, A (2010). 'Managing Transboundary Crises: Identifying the Building Blocks of an Effective Response System', *Journal of Contingencies and Crisis Management*, 18(4): 195–207.

Bankoff, G. (2001) 'Rendering the World Unsafe: "Vulnerability" as Western Discourse', *Disasters*, 25(1): 19–35.

Beck, U. (1999) *World Risk Society*, Cambridge: Polity Press.

Boin, A. and Rhinard, M. (2008) 'Managing Transboundary Crises: What Role for the European Union?' *International Studies Review*, 10(1): 1–26.

Brändström, A., Kuipers, S. and Daléus, P. (2008) 'The Politics of Tsunami Responses: Comparing Patterns of Blame Management in Scandinavia', in Boin, A., A. McConnell and P. 't Hart (eds), *Governing after Crisis*, Cambridge: Cambridge University Press, pp. 114–47.

Clarke M., Fanany, I. and Kenny, S. (2010) *Post-Disaster Reconstruction: Lessons from Aceh*, Abingdon: Earthscan.

Ekengren, M., Matzén, N., Rhinard, M. and Svantessan, M. (2006) 'Solidarity or Sovereignty? EU Cooperation in Civil Protection', *European Integration*, 28(5): 457–76.

Handmer, J. (1995) 'A Safer World for the 21st Century? The 1994 Yokohama World Conference on Natural Disaster Reduction', *Journal of Contingencies and Crisis Management*, 3(1): 35–7.

Hannigan, J.A. (2012) *Disasters Without Borders: The International Politics of Natural Disasters*, Cambridge: Polity Press.

Hermann, M.G. and Dayton B.W. (2009). 'Transboundary Crises through the Eyes of Policymakers: Sense Making and Crisis Management', *Journal of Contingencies and Crisis Management*, 17(4): 233–41.

Jenkins, D.H., Harris, A., Tair, A.A., Thomas, H., Okotel, R., Kinuthia, J., Moford, L. and Quince, M. (2013) 'Community-Based Resilience Building: Normative Meets Narrative in Mbale', *Environmental Hazards*, 12: 47–59.

Johnson, N.P. and Mueller, J. (2002). 'Updating the Accounts: Global Mortality of the 1918–1920 "Spanish Flu" Influenza Pandemic', *Bulletin of the History of Medicine*, 76(1): 105–115.

Kötter, T. (2004), 'Risks and Opportunities of Urbanisation and Megacities', Proceedings of FIG Working Week 2004 in Athens, FIG, Copenhagen.

Lagadec, P. (2009) 'A New Cosmology of Risks and Crises: Time for a Radical Shift in Paradigm and Practice', *Review of Policy Research*, 26(4): 473–86.

Legrand, T. and McConnell, A. (eds) (2012) *Emergency Policy*, Farnham: Ashgate.

McMichael, P. (2012) *Development and Social Change: A Global Perspective*, Thousand Oaks, CA: Sage.

Mercer, J., Kelman, I., Taranis, L. and Suchet-Pearson, S. (2010) 'Framework for Integrating Indigenous and Scientific Knowledge for Disaster Risk Reduction', *Disasters*, 34(1): 214–39.

Middleton, N. and O'Keefe, P. (1998). *Disaster and Development: The Politics of Humanitarian Aid*, London: Pluto Press.

Munich Re (2004) 'Megacities – Megarisks. Trends and Challenges for Insurance and Risk Management'. Available at: <http://www.preventionweb.net/files/646_10363.pdf> (accessed 18 May 2014).

Quarantelli, E.L., Lagadec, P. and Boin, A. (2007) 'A Heuristic Approach to Future Disasters and Crises: New, Old, and In-Between Types', in H. Rodríguez, E.L. Quarantelli and R.R. Dynes (eds), *Handbook of Disaster Research*, New York: Springer, pp. 14–41.

Rhinard, M. (2009), 'European Cooperation on Future Crises: Toward a Public Good?', *Review of Policy Research*, 26(4): 439–55.

Rose, J., O'Keefe, P., Jayawickrama, J. and O'Brien, G. (2013) 'The Challenge of Humanitarian Aid: An Overview', *Environmental Hazards*, 12(1): 74–92.

Schwartz, P. (2003) *Inevitable Surprises: A Survival Guide for the 21st Century*, London: Free Press.

Schwarz, Y. and McConnell, A. (2009), 'Remote Crisis Management: Australia's 2006 Rescue of Citizens Trapped in Lebanon', *Australian Journal of International Affairs*, 63(2): 235–50.

Smil, V. (2008) *Global Catastrophes and Trends: The Next 50 Years*, Cambridge, MA: MIT Press.

Smith, K. and Petley, D.N. (2009) *Environmental Hazards: Assessing Risk and Reducing Disaster*, New York: Routledge.

Stöhr, K. and Esveld, M. (2004) 'Will Vaccines be Available for the Next Influenza Pandemic?' *Science*, 306: 2195–2196.

Swiss Re (2003) *Emerging Risks: a Challenge for Liability Underwriters*. Available at: <http://media.swissre.com/documents/emerging_risks_a_challenge_en.pdf> (accessed 11 June 2014).

Swiss Re (2013) *Swiss Re SONAR Emerging Risk Insights*. Available at: <http://media.swissre.com/documents/SONAR_+Emerging_risk_insights_from_Swiss_Re.pdf> (accessed 11 June 2014).

Tindall, K. and 't Hart, P. (2011) 'Evaluating Government Performance During Consular Emergencies: Toward an Analytical Framework', *Policy & Society*, 30(2): 137–49.

United Nations Population Fund [UNFPA] (2007) *State of World Population*, New York: UN Population Fund.

Wisner, B., Blaikie, P., Cannon T., and Davis, I. (2004) *At Risk: Natural Hazards, People's Vulnerability and Disasters*, New York: Routledge.

FURTHER READING

Risk management

Schwartz, P. (2003) *Inevitable Surprises: A Survival Guide for the 21st Century*, London: Free Press.
Written by one of the world leaders in scenario planning, this book challenges readers to view 'surprises' as largely inevitable if the factors underlying them are carefully examined. Schwartz looks ahead to some of the next big surprises (e.g. arising from ageing populations, migration and technological change) and surmises that although we can do nothing about the past, we can try to do something about the future. Neither denial nor defensiveness is viewed as a useful response. Instead, Schwartz advocates a range of strategies that will better prepare society for dealing with future threats.

Issues of emerging risk are addressed in the OECD report into *Emerging Systemic Risk in the 21st Century: An Agenda for Action.* Available at: http://www.oecd.org/governance/risk/37944611.pdf (accessed 4 August 2014). Swiss Re, leading insurer, offers its insights into emerging risks in Swiss Re (2013) *Swiss Re SONAR Emerging Risk Insights.* Available at: <http://media.swissre.com/documents/SONAR_+Emerging_risk_insights_from_Swiss_Re.pdf> (accessed 4 August 2014).

Crisis management

Most literature on crisis management in a global world approaches the topic from the angles of development studies, international security, international relations, political economy and disaster sociology. For students of public administration and management, the most useful sources to get a sense of the principles and practices of crises/disasters that have an international dimension are the websites of relevant national and international institutions. For example, see the International Federation of Red Cross and Red Crescent Societies <http://www.ifrc.org> for information on the extent of worldwide humanitarian aid efforts and cooperation with governments. The EU's Civil Protection news and policies can be found at <http://ec.europa.eu/echo/civil_protection/civil/>. Details of the World Health Organization's role in crises and emergencies can be found at <http://www.who.int/hac/crises/en/>. One of the best national sites with extensive information about crisis/disaster/emergency management practices is Emergency Management Australia <http://www.ema.gov.au/>.

Conclusion

The previous edition of this book concluded by discussing the fact that risk and crisis management practices existed as distinct concerns, largely unconnected to each other despite their many commonalities. We can see very few reasons to change our focus in this new edition, as practitioners and academics in both communities still remain divided. The professional distinctions, institutional environments, academic silos and terminological distinctions that we identified as barriers to convergence seven years ago still largely remain. However, the clear blue water that exists between these two disciplines seems even more illogical today because of the pace at which our societies produce interconnected problems. Surely, in the face of globalizing tendencies which homogenize and join up pathologies, there is now an even greater need to consider the synthesis of crisis and risk management knowledge. As a consequence, we need to reiterate our argument again that *the divisions between risk and crisis management knowledge are a problem for any public sector organization that needs to address contemporary threats.* If public authorities want to enhance their capacity to anticipate and cope with risks and crises then a greater synergy is needed between the fields of risk and crisis management.

If this holistic approach to risk and crisis is to be achieved, then it has to be incentivized. Readers will recall that in Chapter 2 we provided a list of justifications for engaging in the practice of risk management. We wish to use this conclusion in a similar manner by providing two justifications for synthesizing the analysis of risk and crisis issues.

What can crisis management analysts learn from their risk counterparts? The first justification is that a greater amalgamation between these two disciplines will enhance the way in which each understand issues of globalization and the need for collective action. As we move into the century, the means through which collective action can be created in the first instance and then maintained as crisis responses adapt represents the biggest challenge for those interested in the institutional design of crisis management policy. We believe, for example, that crisis management practitioners could benefit enormously from analyses of global risk management standards because it could lead to a better understanding of the ways in which crisis management doctrine might be diffused internationally. The benefits of evaluating ISO31000 from a crisis management point of view, for example, are twofold. First, in terms of process, there are considerable gains to be made in understanding how a standard which does not have to be adopted comes to be implemented across so many G8, G20 and BRIC economies. There are lessons here for the United Nations and the European Union, in particular, as they attempt to promote international forms of disaster management cooperation. Second, we can also see an important debate about the outcomes produced by international standards as risk management experts question whether or not standardization is beneficial in a context of high uncertainty. That debate is one example of a risk discourse that is particularly apposite for crisis analysts because it reflects their own concerns about the tensions between rigid procedure and the need to customize crisis responses to unique circumstances.

What can risk managers learn from crisis management studies? The second justification relates to issues about power, symbolism, meaning making and politics. Risk management today is a highly sophisticated technical endeavour but it is one that often ignores the way in which political and public perceptions play a role in the creation and management of threats. When we see new risks being defined by the media or crises being fashioned into existence by politicians, we are bearing witness to the power of language in terms of risk and crisis creation. When we see technical contingency plans and risk prevention strategies being undermined because of a lack of legitimacy amongst stakeholders, or clinical policy evaluations failing because of political opinion post-crisis, what we are actually recognizing is the simple fact that the 'success' and 'failure' of managerial strategies often depends upon politics. It is therefore crucial for us to understand that technical success exists in one realm and political and social evaluations of that success exist in quite another. In this regard, risk management analysts, particularly those concerned with reputation, credibility, blame avoidance and risk communication, could certainly benefit from the politico-symbolic research which has been undertaken by crisis analysts. What this shows is that crisis management thinking can open up new analytical environments through which the nature of risk can be explored.

These are of course only two justifications for greater convergence. There are many more that, among other things, emerge from shared concerns about forecasting in uncertainty, similar environmental drivers, the need to create and utilize planning documents, and the concept of resilience. The shared interest in resilience, suggests a potentially fruitful strategy through which we might begin to bridge the gap between risk and crisis management. The United Kingdom's Civil Contingencies Secretariat is proof that cutting-edge risk management can cohabitate a single organizational space with cutting-edge crisis management. It is the concept of resilience that allows this synergy because it is integrative and elastic in nature. It may well be, therefore, that this is one concept which can facilitate meaningful integration in other areas. Over the coming years, it might be wise for us all to think about the ways in which our combined knowledge can make us more resilient to global risks and crises.

Managing risk in public service organizations

A case study

THE AUSTRALIAN QUARANTINE AND INSPECTION SERVICE, NORTHERN AUSTRALIA[1]

The Australian Quarantine and Inspection Service (AQIS) is part of the Australian Government Department of Agriculture, Fisheries and Forestry (DAFF). AQIS provides quarantine inspection for international passengers, cargo, mail, animals and plants and their products arriving in Australia, and inspection and certification for a range of agricultural products exported from Australia. Quarantine controls managed by AQIS at Australia's borders aim to minimize the risk of exotic pests and diseases entering Australia, to protect agricultural industries (exports worth AU$32 billion annually to the economy) and Australia's unique environment.

The Northern Australia Quarantine Strategy (NAQS) is an AQIS programme and was established to minimize the risk to Australia from exotic pests and diseases that could enter Australia from countries to its north. NAQS does this by:

- identifying and evaluating quarantine risks facing northern Australia;
- providing early detection and warning of new pests through scientific surveys and monitoring, border activities and public awareness; and
- undertaking surveillance and capacity-building activities in Indonesia, Papua New Guinea and East Timor, in collaboration with the relevant authorities, to strengthen regional quarantine integrity.

The strategy helps underpin Australia's ability to maintain and expand its export markets, protect plants and animals, and promptly identify any new pests, weeds or diseases that breach Australia's borders.

---

1 This case study is adapted from the winning entry in the 'Innovative Initiative' category of the *Comcover Awards for Excellence in Risk Management 2005* and is reproduced with the permission of AQIS.

247

Risk management framework

NAQS has developed and implemented a risk management framework that identifies quarantine risks in northern Australia and prioritizes surveillance activities to mitigate the risks accordingly. The framework is derived from methodologies used to assess the likelihood of the introduction of pests and diseases associated with the international trade in agricultural products (in line with methodologies described by the World Trade Organization and Australian Standard 4360:2004). The primary focus of the framework is to identify pests and diseases likely to enter Australia and to ensure that surveillance activities are appropriately undertaken in response to quarantine threats. The framework is capable of adapting to new and emerging pest and disease threats and forms the basis of the pre-border, border and post-border activities of the NAQS programme.

The framework is implemented through the subdivision of northern Australia between Cairns and Broome into more than thirty zones. Zones are ranked according to the estimated vulnerability to exotic pest and disease incursion. Surveillance for exotic pests and diseases is undertaken in each of the zones at a frequency determined by the risk management process. Factors considered in the risk assessments include habitat differences between zones, the diversity of pests and diseases likely to enter Australia and the different possible pathways for the migration of pests and diseases to Australia. The outcomes of the risk assessment process are applied in strategic and business planning, management decisions, and administrative resources and activities.

NAQS encourages a risk management culture through participation in risk review processes by scientific staff, external experts and key stakeholder groups. Risk assessments are also constantly updated when new or emerging pest and disease threats become apparent. In planning the activities of the NAQS scientific programme, the scientists conduct risk assessments for each of the NAQS zones and design survey and monitoring activities based on the assessments.

The surveillance strategy developed through the assessment of risks and the allocation of resources provides the maximum possible level of protection for Australia from exotic pests and diseases. The activities of the scientific programme then guide the public awareness and extension activities of NAQS to ensure that the correct areas are targeted to increase the chance of early detection of pests and diseases.

Risk management implementation

Specific risk management strategies are implemented at the pre-border, border and post-border stages of the quarantine continuum to address the identified risks.

1. *Pre-border activities* – NAQS conducts offshore quarantine surveys as part of pre-border risk mitigation activities, screening for a range of exotic pests and diseases that are of joint concern to Australia and neighbouring countries. For example, the highly pathogenic avian influenza (HPAI) outbreaks in the region led to an

248

adjustment of targeted surveillance work to provide additional focus on extra screening of birds that may exhibit the disease. Surveillance activities undertaken in East Timor, Indonesia and Papua New Guinea indicate that the pests and disease status of these countries is significantly different from Australia, which further provides Australian agricultural industries and authorities with details of emerging threats and diseases. In addition to overseas survey work, NAQS allocates resources to conduct ongoing pre-border assistance and capacity building in neighbouring countries via activities such as training and technical support. These activities help strengthen the neighbouring countries' capacity to diagnose and respond to pest and diseases, complement domestic surveillance activity undertaken by NAQS and strengthen regional quarantine integrity to further mitigate quarantine risks to Australia.

2. *Measures at the border* – NAQS border inspection staff in the Torres Strait screen flights, vessels, passengers and cargo from the quarantine zones established in the Torres Strait to prevent the introduction into Australia of pests and diseases from Papua New Guinea and eastern Indonesia. The Torres Strait is of particular strategic importance to Australian quarantine, both due to location and the movement of traditional vessels between the two countries under the Torres Strait Treaty. NAQS staff on all inhabited islands in the Torres Strait Protected Zone, on Thursday Island, Cape York, and in Cairns undertake this screening. These border surveillance arrangements resulted in the interception of numerous examples of quarantine risk material, including live animals, banana planting material and fresh meat products in 2004–5. As a further example of the implementation of the risk management process, NAQS staff responded quickly to the increased threat posed by HPAI by alerting quarantine inspectors on the Torres Strait islands, adding additional inspectors, increasing the hours when officers are on duty, and instigating night patrols in addition to diurnal vessel inspections. Targeted communication activities to inform locals of the heightened risk were also held in the region as part of the 'Top Watch' communication campaign.

3. *Post-border measures* – the risk management framework and derived strategies form the basis of NAQS surveillance activities undertaken in northern Australia between Cairns and Broome. Domestic scientific surveillance activity is comprised of surveys (field-based sampling) and monitoring (trapping systems for specific pests). The division of the area into more than thirty zones and the surveillance undertaken in each of the zones is dictated by the implementation of the risk assessment process. As an example of the adaptive nature of the risk assessment methodology, the emergence of HPAI in the regions, and subsequent risk assessment modification, has led NAQS veterinarians to undertake additional testing of domestic and wild birds, both onshore and offshore at key locations. This work increases knowledge of the types of bird flu virus present in birds migrating from Siberia to Australia via East Asia, helping authorities to better manage the bird and human health implications of HPAI. Further examples include the strategic placement of fruit fly and

249

screw-worm fly traps in northern Australia at locations identified as most at risk of incursion.

Non-insurance risk transfer

The risk analysis and response strategies focus on key points along the continuum of quarantine. Under this risk management approach, Australia's quarantine framework uses a nationally coordinated system of surveillance, inspection and control including pre-border (overseas) risk mitigation activities, intervention at the border (airports and seaports) and post-border measures to prevent the establishment and spread of pests, diseases and other threats. Pre-border and border risk management measures aim to reduce the likelihood of outbreaks occurring in Australia, while post-border risk management measures are directed at reducing the consequences of any emergencies which result from a pest or disease entering Australia.

The very significant potential economic, ecological and social consequences of many of these risks create an environment in which non-insurance risk transfer measures are even more important than usual. NAQS and AQIS strategies to manage these non-insurable risks focus on ensuring that the responsibility for such risks is allocated to, and accepted by, those parties best able to control them.

In many cases, the broad scope of the risks means several different parties will jointly be responsible for developing and implementing risk mitigation strategies. This risk transfer is primarily undertaken through joint emergency contingency planning, consultative response arrangements (including clear national agreements on sharing of decision-making, operational responsibilities and cost-sharing) and effective participation in international policy-setting forums.

Insurance risk transfer

The AQIS Risk Management Framework links the management of AQIS risks to the treatment strategies for these risks. A fundamental treatment strategy outlined in the Framework is transferring the consequences of these risks to outside parties, namely insurance agencies.

AQIS has a keen appreciation of the risk environment in which it operates. As a result of a number of major diseases reported in other countries in recent times, such as SARS and HPAI, human health remains a risk to AQIS and has been identified as a major priority in business plans for the organization in 2005/6. Insurable risk is first mitigated to the extent possible. For example, regular travel to remote locations in eastern Indonesia, East Timor and Papua New Guinea exposes staff to a range of disease risks such as malaria, Japanese encephalitis and dengue fever. Officers are funded to seek professional advice and service relating to medical risks of travel to remote on-shore and off-shore areas. Service includes appropriate vaccinations, antimicrobials and prevention of insect bites.

250

Business continuity planning

AQIS has a well-developed and structured approach to business planning that addresses many of the preliminary requirements considered necessary for business continuity planning. All AQIS regions have in place individual Business Continuity plans. There is also an overarching document that outlines the AQIS Business Continuity Planning framework.

In designing and implementing risk management responses to quarantine where the risks are mostly external to the department, it is imperative that effective emergency planning is the foundation of any effective response strategy.

AQIS works closely with industry, stakeholders and other border agencies to ensure it is able effectively to maintain Australia's quarantine integrity. This allows AQIS to continue to deliver its public sector obligation to provide services in times of adverse circumstances, its duty of care to its people and its stakeholder/client expectations. As an organization, AQIS continues to take the lead in the Australian public service in business planning and risk management.

A further example of AQIS' Business Continuity Planning is the organization's participation in Exercise Minotaur 2002 (a simulated foot and mouth disease outbreak), Exercise Jigsaw 2005 (a simulated outbreak of avian influenza) and an in-house exercise to prepare for the national Exercise Eleusis 2005 (a simulated outbreak of avian influenza) involving industry, national and local government and government agencies.

Communication

Public awareness activities undertaken by NAQS complement the scientific risk assessment of both target lists and zone risk ratings. Target lists are used to focus the production of public awareness material towards pests and diseases of most concern, and the distribution of public awareness material is further guided by risk assessments of individual NAQS zones.

Training and awareness

NAQS officers take part in rigorous exercises to prepare them for their work in often rugged and remote regions and difficult conditions. Safety is of the utmost concern to NAQS, and precautions and training are in place to minimize the risks to staff working in hazardous environments. Detailed security plans are developed and approved prior to all overseas field activities. Specialist training is provided for those who regularly work in helicopters, are involved in the safe and humane shooting of feral animals and/or use four-wheel drive vehicles.

Other risks faced by NAQS officers include becoming stranded in the bush; driving long distances over rough terrain; sunburn; dehydration; encountering crocodiles and snakes and buffalo. Training, precautionary measures and safety equipment are in place to equip staff to deal with these risks. Commonwealth and state legislation requires all work to meet occupational health and safety (OH&S) requirements. AQIS has OH&S committees in place which meet regularly to discuss issues and ensure safety of staff.

Resources

Resources are allocated on the basis of assessed risk to achieve a balance of off-shore, border, post-border, operational, scientific and public awareness activities for optimal efficiency. The time NAQS invests in public awareness is repaid tenfold when the public assists by reporting strange pests, animal diseases or suspect vessels. This is consistent with the Australian government's commitment to engendering a shared responsibility for quarantine between AQIS and the communities it serves.

Monitoring and review

The risk assessment framework used to manage quarantine risks is subject to constant review when new pests and disease risks become apparent. Further to this, comprehensive reviews of both the methodology and the assessments are undertaken periodically. Examples of the responsive adaptation of the risk management framework are the changes put in place following the incursion of classical swine fever into the Indonesian province of Papua on the island of New Guinea and the emerging threat posed by avian influenza in 2005.

Significant risks to the programme's effectiveness are monitored and reviewed on an ongoing basis to meet the changing environment in which NAQS operates. New travel advice information on safety and security of staff whilst overseas is just one factor that is constantly monitored. NAQS ensures any changes are fully evaluated to assess their impact, and if required programme activities are adjusted to meet the new circumstances.

Measurement and performance

AQIS' performance is regularly measured by ongoing monitoring, evaluation and reporting of intervention levels and effectiveness at the border. This is based on a framework developed by the Australian National Audit Office.

The AQIS business planning framework provides a mechanism for NAQS to evaluate performance against business plan objectives. Formal business plan reviews are conducted by the AQIS executive on a biannual basis and the status of key risks is evaluated and reviewed. In a NAQS context, performance of the risk management framework is measured by the early detection and probability of successful eradication of pests and diseases that have arrived in Australia. As a consequence, NAQS detected numerous pests and diseases including the papaya fruit fly, prickly croton and Siam weed, which have since seen eradication and control programmes undertaken to limit the spread and impact of these pests.

Agricultural exports are worth AU$32 billion annually to the economy. In a recent study the Productivity Commission estimates a foot and mouth disease breakout in Australia would cost the economy AU$9 billion, with Queensland likely to bear the brunt of this with losses to tourism and beef industries. The potential impact of many of the target list diseases can be measured in billions of dollars. It is well documented that early detection of pests and diseases can significantly reduce costs associated with control and eradication, or can mean the difference between eradication, or the establishment of a new pest, weed or disease.

The impact of the risk management strategies undertaken by NAQS can be measured in terms of greater protection for Australian agricultural industries, environment and human health from threats that are present in countries to the immediate north.

QUESTIONS

1. What were the key aspects relating to NAQS' implementation of the quarantine risk management framework?
2. What is the significance of risk management culture within an organization?
3. What is the difference between insurance transfer and non-insurance transfer?
4. How can an organization ensure good communication both internally and externally, with its key stakeholder groups?
5. What might other public service organizations learn from this case study?

Crisis management

A personal account by Ed van Thijn, former Mayor of Amsterdam

FATAL FLIGHT LY-1862 (THE BIJLMER DISASTER)[1]

On the evening of Sunday 4 October 1992 at 6.37pm, an El Al freight plane (Boeing 747) came down on two ten-storey apartment buildings in Amsterdam South-East, a densely populated district. I was watching a soccer match on TV and couldn't believe my ears when my spokeswoman called me to tell me that there was a serious rumour that a plane had crashed. I clung to the word 'rumour' and continued watching, but a few minutes later the head of the security department called and asked me to come immediately to the crisis centre in City Hall. I had to put aside my deep inner feeling to go to the disaster area and went directly to the crisis centre, many miles away from the fatal area. But according to the Disaster Law, I had to be there, as mayor and the person with prime responsibility for the rescue operation. I was the first who arrived but in half an hour (one hour after the crash) the entire team of leading officials (the chiefs of the fire brigade and the police) were present and stayed together for over more than two weeks.

In the meantime all operational teams were in full action. The initial stages were hugely chaotic but after three hours the fire was mastered, the area was cleared of spectators and journalists, and a step-by-step rescue operation was proceeding. A big indoor sports hall was made available for survivors.

In the crisis centre we tried to make an estimate of the size of the disaster. We learned that eighty apartments had been burned out, and that 150 adjacent apartments had to be evacuated. We were seriously handicapped by the fact that a large number of illegal immigrants were living in that area, and that therefore the official registers were not really reliable.

---

1 For a detailed account and analysis of this disaster, see U. Rosenthal, P. 't Hart, M. van Duin, Boin, A., M. Kroon, M. Otten and W. Overdijk (1994) *Complexity in Urban Crisis Management: Amsterdam's Response to the Bijlmer Air Disaster*, London: James & James.

We opened several special telephone numbers and after a couple of hours 600 people were reported missing, a number that had increased to 1,588 by the following day. In the meantime the media had only one urgent question: the estimated number of casualties. On Monday morning I decided to come out with a provisional estimate of at least 250 victims.

It took more than thirty-six hours before we were able to start the salvage operation (a very frustrating experience) because of the danger of collapse. First of all, a number of surrounding apartments had to be dismantled. When the salvage operation finally began bit by bit (there was a huge pile of debris in the middle of the two damaged apartment blocks) it proceeded in an irritatingly slow manner. Each time human remains were found, the entire operation stopped so that the identification experts could start their work. In the crisis centre we calculated that, should the pace continue to be this slow, the operation could last for many weeks. My personal guess was that such an extended period would be unacceptable for at least three reasons: (1) the danger to public health; (2) fatigue of the rescue workers; and (3) the terrible need for certainty and mourning among the diverse group of relatives (most victims came from all over the world including Surinam, the Dutch Antilles, Ghana and Somalia). I took an extremely hard decision: to accelerate the salvation operation by using heavy equipment and to move the identification process to a hangar at Schiphol Airport, taking the risk that at the end of the process some of the victims could not be identified. I made this decision on Friday night (9 October) at 6.00pm. The entire job needed to be finished. Two days later, on Sunday 11 October, a huge mourning ceremony was due to take place.

In the meantime an enormous police operation had started. Within seventy-two hours, fifty detectives found out what the real number of missing persons actually was. They linked thirty-six different registers and delivered the names of the people living in the eighty apartments – of which only forty were demolished by the crash. The others burned out while the inhabitants were able to escape. They reduced the list of missing persons from 1,588 to 110 by tracing most of the people personally – even abroad. At the end of the week, forty-three victims were reported. All of them were identified.

The complication of the many illegal residents was solved by offering them a residence permit as long as they could provide proof that they were residing in the disaster area. Many thousands applied but only 110 of them were accepted.

One innovation was the way we in which we managed the flow of information. From the beginning we 'centralized' contact with the media, starting up a cycle of press conferences twice a day: one at 6.30am and the other at 5.30pm. The timing allowed us to be included in the major Dutch newscasts. This meant that we had to organize our daily internal briefings one hour before. So we had busy nights during the entire two weeks. All the press conferences were chaired by me.

On Sunday 11 October, one week after the aeroplane came down, two impressive mourning ceremonies took place. In the morning there was a silent procession in which

20,000 participated. In the afternoon a huge memorial service was held in a large conference centre, attended by 15,000 people. Tribute was paid to the great diversity of cultures and religions of the victims.

Looking back at those hectic days I think that my staff did an excellent job. Of course, there were many complaints even many years later, although we developed – from the beginning and on the advice of experts – a comprehensive plan for after-care. We wanted to behave as a caring government throughout. But after the crisis centre was closed down, it was soon back to bureaucracy as usual. In the crisis centre, working conditions were optimal – borne out by a number of evaluation reports. The decision-making process was clear and transparent (the mayor was in command), there was a common sense of urgency and a sense of direction, a team spirit was predominant and, above all, the discipline of time pressure (with Friday night at 6.00pm as a deadline) worked remarkably well. All those conditions are absent under normal circumstances. Is there a lesson here for city governments?

Ed van Thijn, former Mayor of Amsterdam, 1983–94

Index